THINKING

Units of Study

THROUGH

in Reading and Writing Workshops 4–12

GENRE

HEATHER LATTIMER

Stenhouse Publishers

Portland, Maine

Stenhouse Publishers
www.stenhouse.com

Credits
Pages 22–23: Excerpt from *An American Childhood* by Annie Dillard. Copyright © 1987 by Annie Dillard. Reprinted by permission of HarperCollins Publishers, Inc.
Pages 29–30: Excerpt from "Everything Will Be Okay" by James Howe. Reprinted with permission of the author.
Pages 67–69: Excerpt from "Death of an Innocent: How Christopher McCandless Lost His Way in the Wilds," copyright © 1993 by Jon Krakauer. Reprinted by permission of the author.
Pages 113–115: "In a Peaceful Frame of Mind" reprinted by permission of International Creative Management, Inc. Copyright © 2001 by Anna Quindlen. First appeared in *Newsweek,* February 4, 2002.
Pages 156–157: "The Flowers" from *In Love & Trouble: Stories of Black Women,* copyright © 1973 by Alice Walker. Reprinted by permission of Harcourt, Inc.
Pages 199–200: Excerpt from "Snow" in *The Rose and the Beast,* copyright © 2000 by Francesca Lia Block. Used by permission of HarperCollins Publishers, Inc.
Pages 242–243: Introduction by Tobias Wolff to "Cathedral" by Raymond Carver, in *You've Got to Read This: Contemporary American Writers Introduce Stories That Held Them in Awe,* edited by Ron Hansen and Jim Shepard, copyright © 1994, HarperCollins. Introduction reprinted by permission of the author.

Library of Congress Cataloging-in-Publication Data
Lattimer, Heather, 1971–
       Thinking through genre : units of study in reading and writing workshops 4–12 / Heather Lattimer.
           p. cm.
       Includes bibliographical references (p.) and index.
       ISBN 1-57110-352-X (alk. paper)
           1. Language arts (Elementary) 2. Language arts (Secondary) 3. Literary form. I. Title.
LB1576.L365 2003
428'.0071—dc21   2002042828

Cover photograph by Amy DeVooqd/Artville/Getty Images

Manufactured in the United States of America on acid-free paper
09 08 07 06 05 04 9 8 7 6 5 4 3

To Joe
for believing

CONTENTS

Workshop on Reviews—Response to Literature

Workshop on Essays—Response to Literature

Workshop on Reviews—Response to Literature

I'd never written a foreword before. For a while, I floundered around with it, trying to figure out the nature of the task. Finally, I got up and went to my bookshelves and pulled down a few books with forewords. I read them, with questions in mind: What kind of thing is this? How does it go? When it seems to work, what are the smaller elements making it work? These questions helped me find a length, a structure (or range of structures), a voice, and a relationship to other texts (especially the rest of the book). A sense of genre helped me get started, helped me know how to go forward through the sections of a text, and helped me craft an ending. It let me organize my energy, my attention, and the content of my thoughts.

Genre seems to be a psychological necessity for starting to write or read. A writer has to think, What kind of turn in the great conversation of humanity is this? You can't just write "writing"; you've got to be writing *something*—whether it's a thank-you note or a novel or a journal entry. And until you know what kind of thing you're making, you're going to be silent. As soon as you begin to write, you have already made some kind of decision about what this "piece of writing" is. And, then, what is a "piece" of writing? You could write a letter to a former lover, tear it up, and scatter the pieces to the wind. One of these scraps could come into the hands of another person a few days later, and they would be holding a "piece of writing." But it wouldn't be a text, would it? A text has to have more integrity than that, and more of a whole shape. And we can hold a text in our hands and ask, What is this an example of? One of the answers to that question is the name of a genre.

If we did pick up a stray piece of writing in the street, one of the first things we would do is try to figure out what it was. We would examine the boundaries of the text—its beginning and ending and margins. We'd flip it over to see if there was anything on the back. Before the beginning—before reading the first word—

we have already assessed the genre. We may occasionally fail to figure out what this thing is from such scanning, and in that case, we're going to begin reading it with the question, What have I got here? still in our minds. Once we have determined the nature of this text as a whole, that sense of genre helps us to eliminate possibilities, to constrain the likelihood of what will happen on this page. If we have figured out that this is a poem, we'll be expecting the language to do different things than if it were a set of mechanical instructions. We'll read it differently. Genre is a first frame for a reader's predicting, and in marking this text off from others, it eliminates potential distractions and so makes our reading easier. Attention to genre in reading instruction, then, enables conversations about the totality of a text's structure—the first decision in its design.

Like many aspects of technique in language (letter/sound relationships, sentence structure, text organization) teaching about genres is made more powerful by allowing students to become insiders in the world of that genre. People become insiders in craft when they have to construct the sort of thing they are learning about. The strongest way to teach about poetic devices or features of a fairy tale or the craft of fictional stories is to have students writing them. It gives usability to those aspects of language that are usually supposed to be invisible when we read. The metacognition in attending to features of text, which Heather Lattimer supports in this book, makes sense when the students are going to be making texts in these genres. If the study were focused more on ideas, social action, or building human relationships over stories, then that kind of technical attention might not come up as often. But if students are going to become craftspersons themselves, then they need to attend to how these things are made.

But the making of texts does not occur in isolation. Writers use old cultural tools that were built for particular jobs and relationships. Writing itself is such a tool, as are all the components of the writing system from the alphabet to words to sentences to genres to discourses. Many genres, such as poetry, are older than recorded history. Of course, histories (the wide range of kinds of text that are supposed to refer to past doings and happenings) are genres, too. Memoir is one kind of historical text, and the witness account, the story of "this happened to me," is ancient, even if the ways of talking about "who I am" in contemporary memoirs seem modern. The shapes of these genres, the ways we're used to them going, is a product of all that history of other people's using them (Bakhtin 1986). So even when I'm writing my memoir and saying something that surely no one else has ever said, something that may be unique to me as an individual, I'm nevertheless using a tool that bears the handprints of countless other people's use of it. Teaching genre studies isn't a matter of pressing on cookie-cutters; it's an invitation to reinvent within a tradition.

In the world we live in today, genres are proliferating like snowflakes in a blizzard. New print technologies such as e-mail, on-line chat, and the World Wide

Web, desktop publishing and digital video, interactive role-playing games and real-time simulations, have exploded the number of genres available to writers. That number will continue to grow, too, as these genres and new hybrids develop alongside shifts in technology. We cannot prepare students for all the genres that will be of use in their literate lives. It is laughable at this point to talk about "the genres they need to know," since those genres, very likely, have not been invented yet. What we can anticipate is that they will need to have ways of learning genres, and that, ultimately, is the goal of genre studies. We are handing over to them a flexibility with form and habits of inquiring that allow them to move into new communities and make themselves competent to interact with text there. They need to know how to figure out what forms of text "count" there, research the features of those forms, gather the kinds of data that will feed their writing, plan texts, compose them, revise toward an image of "quality," make text presentable for these people, and get it out to them. They need to know how, as readers, to look at the shape and structure of a new kind of text and fit it with (or contrast it to) other kinds of texts they have known. The effort here isn't to bank up the necessary genres the way one packs a suitcase, in anticipation of exactly what will be needed. Instead, students learn how to learn about a text form.

There are many genres that you won't find in this book. You won't find recipes, county ordinances, or love notes. That's because those genres belong to special social circumstances that cannot be true of all students who happen to be in a class at the same time. Therefore, they're not good curriculum, since they would force most of the class to fake what could just as easily be real relationships with readers. You also won't find petitions, flyers, and pamphlets advocating positions on social issues. That's because, with those genres, the need for a social issue requires that the class take purpose as the organizing principle of curriculum, not genre per se. Heather's work here is on form, structure, shape, elements of craft, leaving the nature of the content mostly up to the writers.

Literature gets the focus here. And we should consider why that is. Others (Christie 1989; Cope and Kalantzis 1993) have taught genre with an eye toward making explicit the features of the genres that are privileged in society, such as, for example, scientific reports. Considered from that perspective, could one argue that Heather has chosen exactly the wrong genres to give emphasis in this book? I don't think so.

If we have students write a scientific report, such as that authored by a scientist who has invented a solution to a problem in her field, we put the students in a *simulation* of a social situation. They can *pretend* to have found something out with their lab experiment, but in actual fact, no one needs to hear from them and no one will learn from what they have done. Even if it were set up so that their classmates would learn from what they'd done (that is, their classmates had not done the same thing but rather had worked on a different aspect of the problem), writing would not need to be a part of the transaction. Why not just tell them orally what they found out? The text itself would not be situated in a free set of human relationships that called it forth.

By contrast, artistic genres, like the ones in this book, create social relations that are most like those between an author and reader outside of school. If a nine-year-old student writes a poem, it is just as much a poem as that by any other living poet. And no living poet would argue with that point. Sure, it may turn out to be a bad poem, but that's not the point. It will be read by readers who hold the same relationship to the text as the relationship readers have to the poet laureate of the United States. Readers entertain poems the way museum goers entertain paintings as they walk up to them. And the relationship between reader and writer does not consist in special asymmetries of knowledge or experience, the way relationships do between readers and journalists, scientists, encyclopedia writers, or authors of business reports. So a child who writes a memoir or short story or feature article or editorial bears *authority*, has as much legitimacy as a speaker as anyone else would writing any of those genres. When teacher, child, and readers all understand that, the identity position of the child writer is much more full of decision-making, negotiating, strategizing, than that of someone who is simply doing what she has been told. And the likelihood is increased of being able to use this knowledge in other situations in which the writer has to make real writerly decisions.

The meaning of *authenticity* is in this relationship between reader and writer. The word has, for many people, a residue of "coming from the central and true soul or self." But that is not the issue here; this is all about relationship. The reader has reason to think she is being addressed in the writer's words, not listening in as the writer talks to someone else. The writer is speaking to a real other person, not pretending to speak to someone else as a demonstration of having learned how to do so. This direct communicative loop is categorically different from writing as it's usually been done in school (Edelsky 1992).

When they write in this way, students have an experience of being writers, not merely students. They are making things other writers they know about have made. They have actually seen things like this in their literate lives, in and out of school. They have been on the other side of this desk, having been readers of other writers' attempts at making just this same sort of text. In so doing, they already have experience at co-composing texts with the writers they have read, since reading involves nothing less (Rosenblatt 1978). The identity of "being a writer" isn't just self-esteem pablum the teacher spouts; it's substantially real, and the kids know it.

This book differs from most written about this subject. Lattimer is intensely committed to bringing reading and writing together in genre studies. Most of us who have written about genre studies have not made as much as she has of the ways one might teach important things about reading in the context of a genre study. Her attention to standards and the language and values contained in conversations of the New Standards Project and the Institute for Learning will be helpful for the teachers in schools who are dedicated to those projects or in states and districts that have been influenced by them (and they are many). She has provided enough detail that both new teachers and experienced teachers who are new to this kind of teaching can lean hard on this book and get the support they need. Teachers who are experienced with genre studies are given enough detail of others' teaching that they can compare it with their own practice and perhaps outgrow themselves.

Because this book is so specific, it will be of special importance that teachers do what writers do—take these genres and make them new, live these lessons out in real relationships with students such that classroom communities transform them in ways Heather Lattimer and the other wonderful teachers of whom she writes would never have imagined. Books about teaching are themselves a special genre, and we have to learn to read them with eyes that can see craft and then compose our own new teaching. Having thought through the process with a master teacher, having taught in her footsteps for a while, having tried on her strategies and resources, the necessary invitation is to invent, to compose, to rush headlong into what is not and cannot be finished.

Randy Bomer

ACKNOWLEDGMENTS

Two years ago, during my maternity leave, I came up with a crazy plan. . . . I decided to write a book. The intervening time has been wild and wonderful. I feel remarkably fortunate to have had the opportunity to try this grand experiment. I have learned a tremendous amount and had the privilege of working with some amazing people.

Among the people to whom I owe a debt of gratitude—

Teachers who allowed me to share their classrooms and their lives in print—Donna Bates, Ila Dawson, Cheryl Hibbeln, Jessica Lawrence, Nina Podhorsky, Jennifer Roberts, and Carolyn Sommer-Inglesias—and their students. I am grateful for your wisdom and admire your strength.

Teachers who shared wonderful insights and provided outstanding models that radically changed my thinking—Steven Ford, Christina Hall, Linda Hoffman, David Honda, Tammy McDaniel, Eva Martinez, Scott Milanovich, Stacy North, Sue Letzkus Page, Wendy Porter, and Liz Roselman.

Administrators who made the research and writing possible—Carol Barry, Chris Hargrave, Rick Novak, Sally Oppy, Wendy Ranck-Buhr, Bobbi Samilson, Cheryl Seelos, and the Literacy Department, San Diego City Schools.

Friends, colleagues, and mentors who offered wisdom and encouragement—Larry Cuban, Dave Downey, Jennifer Green, Sandy Helmantoler, Barbara Livermon, Mary Louise Martin, Jenny Mayher, and Judy Swanson.

Editors who took a chance on a novice writer and saw the project through to completion with patience and humor—Alice Cheyer, Martha Drury, Tom Seavey, Philippa Stratton, and especially Bill Varner.

A friend who read every page and provided insightful feedback—Jennifer Roberts.

And my family—Mom, Dad, Joe, Andy, and Matthew—who supplied inspiration, encouragement, and enduring love.

To all of you . . . Thank you!

CHAPTER 1

Teaching Genre in the Classroom

Coming to Genre Studies: A Reflection

It was February. On the surface, my classroom appeared to be functioning beautifully. Students were all engaged in their independent reading books, they each had a writer's notebook filled with reflections and ideas, and the environment of the class was comfortable and supportive. But still, I worried. I worried that José, now on his fifth Gary Paulsen novel, kept setting aside nonfiction books. How could I help him get the necessary skills to read and enjoy nonfiction? I worried that Mara, full of great insights about Yolen's *The Devil's Arithmetic,* would be unable to share those insights once she got to high school. When could I teach her to write the requisite analytical paper and really make it her own? And I worried that few of the students were being pushed enough in their writing. I simply didn't have enough hours in the day to get around to conferring with each student about their individual needs.

As a teacher, it had taken me a long time to learn to build a literacy workshop in my classroom. I had initially found the whole concept of a student-centered workshop foreign and intimidating. But once I committed myself to the idea, it was wonderful. I loved working more closely with students. I loved their enthusiasm for the work and their increased engagement in class. At the beginning of the year and through most of the fall, the work to build a workshop together was fulfilling and rewarding. But after the students returned from winter holidays, the fun began to wear off.

By this time, students were reading and writing such diverse materials and were at such diverse places in their learning processes that it was nearly impossible to find a common focus. A mini-lesson about nonfiction text features might help José, but it would hardly be relevant to Mara, who really needed some models of authentic literary analysis. More of the instruction began to take place in conferences, but even these could be a struggle. Now that students were in diverse places in their learning, assessing and trying to meet individual needs took more time, and as the time in conferences grew, the frequency with which I saw students diminished. Frustrated by my inability to be in thirty places at once, I spent evenings and weekends searching for the perfect model texts for individual students, writing long responses in their journals, reviewing my conference notes time and again, and making lists to remind myself of all the things that I wanted to be sure to accomplish the next day. This was exhausting. I was wearing myself out, and still I worried that I wasn't pushing students far enough.

About this time, I happened into a colleague's room where the class was studying poetry together as a genre. When Steve Ford had discussed his plans during an English department meeting, I was skeptical. But looking around the room that day, I realized that this was not the traditional "read a sonnet and analyze the rhyme scheme" type of poetry study that I remembered from my own days in school. This was a poetry *workshop.* The students were all focused on reading and writing in the same genre, poetry, but the principles of a student-centered workshop—time, ownership, response, and community (Hansen 1987)—were still there. Students did not resent the limitations imposed by a genre study; they flourished thanks to clear models and expectations and the opportunity to work together to build an understanding. Whereas I had been the only "expert" in my classroom, here the whole room was filled with experts, each able to bring knowledge about poetry to the table, and each able to help his or her peers.

And so began my conversion to teaching through genre. Since then I have been fortunate to be able to experiment with genre studies in my own classroom, observe experts, and share struggles and successes with colleagues. Although I have learned that there are limitations to the application of genre studies in the classroom, I have also learned that there are enormous possibilities. Working with students in a genre study extends the benefits of the literacy workshop, maintaining student ownership and engagement while simultaneously demanding high levels of rigor and building important attitudes of inquiry and reflection.

Defining Genre

At its most rudimentary level, the idea of genre is essentially the idea of a category or type. We all encounter multiple genres every day, and not just in the world of print. There are different genres of movies and television shows, different genres of food and clothing, and different genres of talk. Because we are so familiar with the various types of movie, food, clothing, or talk, we move between them seamlessly, often not even realizing that we have made adjustments in our expectations or behavior. For example, when the phone rings, I pick up and say "hello" in a generally neutral tone, but that tone is adjusted immediately, depending upon who is on the other end of the line. If it is a friend, I relax, use a softer tone of voice, and am not afraid to let the sounds of my life (children playing in the background, dishes clinking as I prepare dinner) intrude on the line. If it is a business call, I find a quiet place, use a professional tone, and think more carefully about the words that I choose. If it is a telemarketer, I am curt, using short responses that reveal little information and allow me to get off the phone as quickly as possible.

Proficient readers and writers make the same kinds of adjustments when picking up a text or sitting down to write. In *Time for Meaning* (1995), Bomer explains the role of genre in literacy as follows:

> Every piece of writing, every text we read, comes to us both as a text—the piece it is—and as a *kind* of text—an instance of genre. And what kind of thing it is puts some limits as to what we expect to find there. Genre, an oft-overlooked cueing system in reading, constrains our prediction, and lays down a track for our reading.

As I have explored the concept of genre in the literacy classroom, and as I have watched my own son learn to read, I have become very aware of these "oft-overlooked cueing systems." I now notice the differences in my process when I pick up the front page of a newspaper, immerse myself in a novel, snuggle up to read a bedtime fairy tale, reference a cookbook, look at real estate listings, or read the school bulletin. I approach each with a different set of expectations, questions, and needs.

Writers similarly view the world through the lens of their particular genre. Donald Murray (1982) explains,

> Most writers view the world as a fiction writer, a reporter, a poet, or a historian. The writer sees experience as a plot or a lyric poem or a news story or a chronicle. The writer uses such literary traditions to understand life.

The process and structure that an author uses to describe events or ideas change dramatically, depending on the writer's purpose and the genre that he or she chooses to use. The process and structure that are used when making a grocery list, for example, are distinctly different from the process and structure that are used to write plans for a substitute, which are distinctly different from the process and structure that are used for writing a student's college recommendation letter, and so on.

In order to become competent, literate members of society, students must be able to navigate multiple genres. They need to know how to confidently read, write, and discuss narrative, informational, persuasive, and analytical texts. Because these forms of text are unique and require unique strategies for reading and writing, it is not safe to assume that students who are competent with one genre will automatically master another. Students need to learn about particular genres through implicit experience and explicit instruction.

Studying Genre in the English or Language Arts Classroom

In the classroom, a genre study is an inquiry into a text form. For a period of four to eight weeks, the class reads exemplary texts in the genre and writes original pieces representative of the genre. The goal of the inquiry is to develop habits of reading and writing that enable students to master the genre itself. A genre study is not about reading a particular text; individual texts are read and discussed for the purpose of developing strategies of comprehension appropriate for the genre. Nor is a genre study about writing a single story or article; individual pieces are written so that students will know and be able to use processes and structures inherent to the genre.

Developing habits of mind is a challenge. It requires that teachers inquire alongside students, coaching rather than instructing. Instead of telling students how to develop a character, I model my own process. Instead of telling students the purpose of an editorial, I pose the question, provide sample texts, and facilitate class deliberation. It can be painful to watch and wait as students come to their own understanding. But it is essential. Students need to *inhabit* the genre if they are to master it (Calkins 1994). They need to explore texts, reflect on their learning, and experiment in their writing. As a class, students need to consider, What makes this genre unique? What do we need to know and be able to do in order to be successful readers of this genre? How can we best interact with this text and what can we take away from it? What language and structures do successful writers of this genre use, and how can that inform our own writing? What processes are appropriate for gathering ideas, drafting, editing, and publishing our work in this genre?

What happens when the answers they come up with are wrong? That's when it's necessary to find a counterexample, model a different approach, or pose a different question. But the amazing thing is how frequently their answers are correct. When given the opportunity and provided with appropriate resources, students very often develop insights into reading and writing in the genre that go beyond expectations. Of course, finding resources and providing opportunities takes time. I invariably find myself rephrasing a single question over and over when planning a lesson, searching for just the right words that will spark appropriate understanding. Crafting a single inquiry-based mini-lesson (designed to last only fifteen to twenty minutes) can take much longer than organizing a period-long literature lecture. But when I see the light go on in students' eyes as they discover a truth about reading or writing, then I know it was worth the time. At the end of a study I want students to leave owning their knowledge. I want them to love the literature that was studied and be able to confidently engage with that genre in the future. Giving students the freedom to interact with text and coaching them toward a deeper understanding through an inquiry-based approach is the best way that I have found to achieve these goals.

Additionally, an inquiry-based approach helps students learn how to learn. During the course of a year I may teach only three or four genres. Over the course of their lives, students will encounter many more. It would be nearly impossible to prepare each student for all the potential text forms that they might encounter over the next fifty, sixty, or seventy years. However, by teaching students to engage in an inquiry-based approach to genre, I hope to prepare them to navigate their own way through unfamiliar text forms in the future. Bomer (1995) explains how this goal works in his classroom:

> Helping students learn how to learn about different genres of writing empowers them to find a way of writing that counts in the different communities they will move through in their lives. I don't teach poetry so that kids will remember all about writing poems and be able to do it forever. I want them to develop habits of mind related to learning a genre, so that they can learn in whatever genres they need.

To work toward this goal, I occasionally step outside the discussion of genre to discuss learning process. Debriefing sessions that begin with What worked today? What didn't? Why? are consistently some of the most powerful learning opportunities that I have experienced in the classroom, for both teacher and students. Thinking about their process helps students monitor their own learning. Listening to their thinking helps me adjust classroom instruction, pacing, and structures to better support student learning.

Building on a Literacy Workshop Foundation

The study of any genre must build upon a strong literacy workshop foundation. Many outstanding authors like Graves (1983), Calkins (1994; 2001), Atwell (1998), Hansen (1987), Allen (1995), Allen and Gonzalez (1998), and Bomer (1995) have written about reading and writing workshops. This text assumes a working knowledge of the concepts behind literacy workshops. Teachers who are unfamiliar with them should consult these texts and work to establish such workshops in their classrooms before beginning a study of genre.

Although the details of a genre study will look somewhat different from those of a strictly defined literacy workshop, the underlying principles remain the same—time, ownership, response, and community (Hansen 1987). Students should have time to read and write daily. Students should have ownership over the books that they read and the pieces that they write; this ownership comes through the opportunity to choose their materials and their topics. Students should read and write authentic texts and be allowed to respond to those texts in authentic ways. And the classroom itself must be a community of learners.

Some advocates of literacy workshop are concerned that bringing any constricting form of genre into the classroom will damage the foundation of the workshop itself. "How can students truly have ownership of material," they ask, "if I limit the type of reading and writing in which they might engage?"

Yet, in recent years, increasing numbers of literacy researchers—Lucy Calkins, Randy Bomer, Nancie Atwell, John Gardner, and Don Murray among them—have acknowledged the importance of focused studies around genre in the classroom. Such studies help teachers better manage the focus and depth of instruction in reading and writing workshops. More important, they provide a powerful opportunity for student learning. Lucy Calkins (1994) explains,

> We regard genre studies as fundamental enough to shape our curriculum around them. We find that when an entire class inquires into a genre, it is life giving. It opens doors and leaves a lot of room for variety and choice, while also allowing the classroom community to inquire deeply into something together.

Although I firmly support and encourage the use of genre studies in the classroom, I understand and respect the concerns of those who hesitate to embrace whole-class studies. Indeed, I believe they bring an important discussion to the table, for we need to ensure that the pendulum does not swing back to a prescribed reading curriculum with genre studies simply replacing the basal anthology as the course requirement. Genre studies need to be implemented for authentic reasons and in an authentic manner. They must build upon and retain the core values of the literacy workshop.

A careful balance needs to be maintained between the genre-specific expectations established by the teacher and the ownership of the work by the students. For example, while the teacher might establish that everyone will write an editorial using the structure of an argumentative essay, it is essential that the students themselves choose the topic of the editorial and the position that they will argue. The teacher chooses the structure, but the students own the content. Similarly, time must be carefully balanced between the time in which we all work together to learn new concepts in teacher-directed activities and the more substantial time during which students independently apply these concepts to their own work.

During the study, it can occasionally be frustrating for the teacher to maintain this balance. It is often tempting to set aside the students' ownership of the workshop and revert to the traditional role of teacher as provider of expert knowledge. After all, if the students all just wrote on the same editorial topic, then we could provide them with lots of facts and arguments that would make their work seem stronger. But that strength would be illusory—the students would not own the work in this situation and consequently they would not own the learning. While, with help, they might produce great editorials this time around, they would be unlikely to be able to apply an improved understanding of the genre to their next editorial. Though it takes longer, and can be challenging, it is essential that the principles of the literacy workshop undergird all our work through the planning and teaching of a genre study if we are to create meaningful learning in the classroom.

Selecting Genres for Study in the Classroom

Choosing which genre to "inhabit" with students requires thoughtful consideration. Genre studies must be selected based on what we observe in the students' learning (both their strengths and their weaknesses), what we know about the genres themselves, and what we are required to teach by our states, districts, or schools. Of these criteria, the most important come from the students themselves. Observation of student behaviors, both academic and social/emotional, provides teachers with clues as to what would be the most effective genres to study. Many adolescents, for example, are very self-involved. This interest in themselves and their own lives provides a wonderful entry point for studying memoir, a genre that not only requires careful introspection but that also boosts students' ability to meaningfully interact with narrative texts.

Of course, standards are the rule of the day in most districts, and as professionals we would be negligent not to consider these standards when choosing what to teach. Fortunately, most of the English and Language Arts standards that I have reviewed, and certainly those in California where I work, are relatively broad, allowing teachers a great deal of flexibility while, quite appropriately, demanding that we expose students to a range of text formats, including narrative text, non-fiction information text, persuasive text, response to literature, and (in some cases) poetry or traditional tales. This requirement actually lends itself quite nicely to genre studies, allowing classroom teachers to shape the requisite instruction in nonfiction information text, for example, into an effective and authentic "feature article" study. Possible connections between state standards requirements and the genre studies included in this book are shown in the following list:

Standards Requirement	Genre Study
Personal narrative	Memoir (Chapter 2)
Fictional narrative	Short story (Chapter 5)
	Fairy tale (Chapter 6)
Information text	Feature article (Chapter 3)
Persuasive text	Editorial (Chapter 4)
Response to literature	Response to literature (Chapter 7)

So what are the genres that should be studied? The reality is that there is no specific list of "best" genres. This can be frustrating because there are times when all of us are overwhelmed by the complexities of teaching and secretly wish that someone would just tell us what to do. Yet, most teachers are independent thinkers; we crave the opportunity to creatively shape our classrooms in response both to our own expertise and to what we see as the needs of our students. Tailoring our genre selection to our own classrooms allows us to do just that.

The six sample genres included in this book—memoir, feature article, editorial, short story, fairy tale, and response to literature—are among my favorite to teach, but this list is by no means exhaustive. Poetry and biography are also very popular and appropriate (for great ideas on how to teach poetry see *A Note Slipped Under the Door* by Flynn and McPhillips). Test-taking genre studies have become popular of late, largely in response to Lucy Calkins's excellent book *A Teacher's Guide to Standardized Reading Tests: Knowledge Is Power*. While all the work done during the year, including the work done in genre studies, should help prepare students for the types of material encountered on standardized tests, the realities of high-stakes testing and the formatting of the tests demands that students be prepared specifically for the types of questions that they will encounter on these tests. As such, a two- to three-week test-taking genre study can be appropriate prior to testing season.

I would caution against choosing genre studies that are too broadly or too narrowly defined. To simply study "nonfiction" as a genre, for example, creates a situation that quickly becomes unwieldy. There are so many different types of nonfiction—information text, feature article, report, editorial, biography, reference text, memoir, autobiography, instruction manual—that choosing "nonfiction" would make it difficult to take students to the depth of understanding expected as part of a genre study. At the other extreme, undertaking a study with a genre that is defined too narrowly is also problematic. Historical fiction and science fiction, for example, can be wonderful genres to read and study with small groups of students, but to engage an entire class in such a specialized study would be a challenge. These specialized genres require a level of background knowledge and interest that makes reading, and especially writing, within the genre quite difficult for many students.

An additional consideration when choosing a genre is the authenticity of reading and writing within that genre. Do adult readers and writers regularly interact with texts in this genre in a meaningful way? Do authors write and publish original work in the genre? Do readers purchase, read, and discuss texts in the genre? If the answer to these questions is no, then teachers should very carefully consider the appropriateness of teaching the genre in the classroom. I would tend to discourage studies of diary writing, for example. Certainly, some adults do keep diaries, but few are ever intended to be published. This is a private form of writing, often used for cathartic purposes; it is not read or discussed publicly.

A final word of caution: genre studies should not become a replacement for the literacy workshop. While students can and should engage in studies of particular genres over the course of a year in English class, there are other important elements to the literacy workshop that do not necessarily fall within the scope of a genre study. At the start of the year, it is essential that significant time be set aside to simply engage students in reading and to build a classroom community. This is especially true for students who are reluctant readers; for these students, getting into a "just right" book is absolutely crucial (see Allen 1995; Allen and Gonzalez 1998). Additionally, teaching classroom routines, developing writer's notebooks (see Fletcher 1993; 1996), introducing reading strategies (see Keene and Zimmerman 1997), and teaching students how to engage in authentic discussions about text are all valuable pieces of a literacy workshop foundation. This foundation must be laid down before work in a genre study begins. This initial work allows students to explore literature broadly, to experiment with ideas and styles that are of interest to them, and to become a part of a literate classroom community—all necessary elements that students will build on in later genre studies. For teachers, this time enables us to get to know our students, to learn of their interests and abilities so that we might shape future genre study work appropriately. Establishing a literacy workshop may take anywhere from a few weeks to several months, depending on the needs of the students.

Like a matched set of bookends, the opportunity for literacy exploration at the start of the year should be paired with a similar opportunity at the end. Once students have mastered the ability to shape their reading and writing within several genres, allow them time and space to experiment further. During a four- to eight-week period of multigenre exploration, students and teachers should work together to set independent learning goals that build on individual strengths and shore up weaknesses. Students may want to experiment further with a previously studied genre, reading more challenging texts, writing about new material, or reworking earlier writing. They may choose to combine genres, exploring a topic in greater depth and responding to that topic with a multigenre paper (see Romano 2000). Or students may decide to follow the investigative approach used in genre studies to explore a new genre independently or as part of a small group. Allowing time in the classroom for students to pursue these choices empowers them to build upon the knowledge gained during studies of specific genres and to define for themselves who they are and who they want to become as readers and writers.

Finally, during that middle part of the year, whole-class novels, studies of themes (see Calkins 2001), reading comprehension strategy studies (see Keene and Zimmerman 1997), or research studies (see Harvey 1998) may be interspersed with studies of particular genres. There is no one right answer. As teachers, we must make choices, and as long as those choices respond to the needs of students, there are many correct answers. A few possibilities for yearlong progressions are shown in Table 1.1.

There is no one right way to plan or teach a genre study. The processes outlined here are the approaches that I have found most helpful teaching genre in my own classroom and working with colleagues in their classrooms. They are included here in the hope that others might find similar processes useful, and because they describe the approach used in subsequent chapters to prepare for and teach studies of specific genres.

Planning a Unit of Study

Once I've selected a genre for study in the classroom, the next step in my planning process is to immerse myself in the genre. Reading, reflecting on, and analyzing outstanding adult-level texts in the genre provides me with an essential reference point. With so many competing claims on our time and resources, it is easy to get lost in the "tyranny of the urgent" (Hummel 1999). Everything from administrative directives to the latest, greatest staff development conference to student relationship crises constantly vie for our attention. By immersing myself in the genre as a reader and writer of text I am able to reflect on my own process while establishing goals that will guide the work throughout the study. Such goals are essential in order to maintain a focus on what is really important.

Table 1.1 Sample Yearlong Progressions in an English/Language Arts Classroom

Progression 1	Week	Progression 2	Week	Progression 3
Establish literacy workshop	1	Establish literacy workshop	1	Establish literacy workshop
	2		2	
	3		3	
	4		4	
	5	Short story study	5	
	6		6	
	7		7	Biography study
	8		8	
Memoir study	9		9	
	10		10	
	11		11	
	12	Response to literature:	12	
	13	Book review	13	Strategy study: Inference
	14		14	
Establish nonfiction workshop	15	Establish nonfiction workshop	15	
	16		16	Fairy tale study
	17		17	
	18	Editorial study	18	
Feature article study	19		19	
	20		20	
	21		21	Response to literature:
	22		22	Analytical essay
	23	Test preparation	23	
	24		24	Test preparation
Response to literature:	25	Theme study: Holocaust	25	
Letter to the Editor	26	literature	26	Poetry study
Test preparation	27		27	
	28		28	
Multigenre exploration	29		29	
	30		30	
	31	Multigenre exploration	31	Multigenre exploration
	32		32	
	33		33	
	34		34	
	35		35	
	36		36	

To set goals that are rigorous and appropriate to the genre, it is necessary to consider two essential questions: What do I want students to learn, understand, and be able to do as a result of this study? and What about this genre is worthy of an "enduring understanding" (Wiggins 1998)? When establishing goals I do not initially consider students' abilities or their needs. The expectations that are established for the genre study depend primarily on the genre itself and should reflect the structures and processes that proficient readers and writers of the genre use.

Only after goals are established do I begin to consider how to move students toward those objectives and how their eventual success might be measured. Long-term learning goals are broken down into discrete instructional focuses that may be the emphasis of a single lesson or a series of lessons. These instructional focuses are designed to be the bridge between where students are and where I want them to be. Wiggins (1998) refers to this process as "backward planning." He argues that only by starting with the long-term goals and then moving to the day-to-day focuses can we hope to teach students the complex ideas and strategies that are worthy of enduring understanding.

When establishing goals and breaking them down into more discrete instructional focuses, I have found it helpful to think in terms of four distinct learning categories. These categories have been adapted from materials developed by the Denver-based Public Education and Business Coalition under the leadership of Ellin Oliver Keene.

Reading Workshop Learning Categories

Comprehension Strategy Study Students must be taught the strategies that will allow them to successfully understand and interact with texts in various genres. They need to learn what to expect from text, how to approach it, and what to take away from it.

Accountable Talk Study   Although not specifically a reading goal, talk is absolutely necessary to understand text. Humans are social beings, and good readers share, debate, and discuss great texts with one another. Of course, students are all familiar with the concept of talk, but literate conversations are another matter entirely. Students must be taught how good readers discuss text, and they need to be taught the discussion formats and approaches appropriate to specific genres.

Writing Workshop Learning Categories

Text Structure Study The way that a text is put together changes dramatically from genre to genre. Knowledge of these conventions is, at times, useful for readers, but it is essential for writers. Students must be taught to analyze the structure of a text, determine the conventions of a genre, and recognize how authors use and adapt these conventions to fit their purposes, so that they may then use this knowledge when crafting their own texts.

Writing Process Study Writers in different genres go about their craft in unique ways. A poet and a journalist will look at an experience through dramatically different lenses and transform that experience into text through dramatically different processes. It is important to recognize how writers adapt the standard "gather ideas, outline, draft, edit, revise, publish" process to fit their genre, and then engage students in a process appropriate to the genre being studied.

What About Spelling, Grammar, and Vocabulary?

Aren't these aspects of reading and writing worthy of study also? Yes and no. Certainly, these are very important elements of literacy. They should be studied in the classroom before, during, and after a genre study, and teachers should set goals for their students in these areas. However, I have not included them in the preceding goal categories because they are usually student-, not genre-specific. There are exceptions to this generalization—times when vocabulary or grammar is very much tied to a genre style. In the following chapters I have included samples of lessons that respond to such a need as appropriate.

It is only once I am in the study with the students that I plan the actual lessons themselves. Before beginning, I've found it helpful to map out a rough schedule, to estimate how long particular instructional focuses will take and to make sure that holidays and vacations will not pose significant problems. But individual mini-lessons, discussion prompts, and workshop expectations are typically planned on a week-to-week or day-to-day basis. So much depends on what is observed about student learning—how students react to a particular text, how they apply (or fail to apply) a strategy, what else is going on in their reading and writing. Flexibility is essential in order to adapt to meet the needs of students.

Teaching is a constant balancing act between the immediate and the long-term. In planning a genre study, my objective is to allow myself enough flexibility to respond to the immediate needs of students while simultaneously providing enough structure so that I am constantly moving students toward essential long-term learning goals.

Teaching the Unit

No two genre studies look alike. Because they respond to the particulars of the genre and the needs of students, differences exist from genre to genre, year to year, and even period to period. However, there are some general guidelines and tools that I have found to be consistently helpful in teaching genre studies.

Classroom Structure

Hallmarks of the literacy workshop model are the structural elements of mini-lesson, workshop, and the share. These pieces remain essential in the genre study. Mini-lessons allow for a common focus as students and teacher work together to develop a community understanding about key concepts of the genre. They are a time for modeling reading and writing processes by both the teacher and other students, for sharing common difficulties as well as suggestions for overcoming those difficulties, for analyzing our own processes and pushing our expectations further. Mini-lessons provide an ideal opportunity for teaching new concepts.

Within workshop, students have the time and opportunity to try out for themselves the concepts presented in mini-lessons. During workshop, students typically have more control over the content of their work, choosing their books as well as the topics of their writing. I find it helpful to spend much of this time conferring individually with students to help them apply strategies taught during mini-lessons to their own materials. Occasionally, it is helpful to try out a new or difficult strategy on a common text or topic during workshop time, either with the whole class or in a small group. These strategy practices can be a very helpful transition between the teacher-led mini-lesson and truly independent student application. Additionally, I like to set aside some time during workshop to encourage student reflection, either written or oral, on their process and progress.

Although short, the end-of-class share can be remarkably valuable. The share can be as simple as asking students to comment on what worked and what didn't, a simple question that can spark a remarkably insightful discussion. Or students may be asked to share responses to one or two more focused questions—questions that are not text-specific but directly reflect the mini-lesson focus. This time can also be used to clear up confusion or for students to share samples of their reading responses or original written work.

A sample schedule is shown in Table 1.2. It should be adjusted according to the specific purpose in the individual classroom. There will be some days, for example, when mini-lessons extend a bit longer to allow for more student discussion or to clarify a confusing point. Other days, it may be appropriate to skip the mini-lesson altogether so that more time can be spent in conference or small-group work. No one single pattern works in all instances; the structure of the lesson must be adjusted to fit the purpose of the day.

Pacing

Most genre studies last between four and eight weeks, although the first time I try out a new genre it can take longer. Within that time frame, I like to allow signif-

Table 1.2 Sample Schedule

	Reading Workshop	**Writing Workshop**
10–20 minutes	Mini-Lesson *Possibilities* Model reading strategy Practice reading strategy with common text Model discussion Analyze discussion transcript Study genre-related vocabulary	Mini-Lesson *Possibilities* Analyze text structure Analyze author's craft Model element of writing process Practice writing process with common prompt Analyze grammar or spelling convention
20–40 minutes	Workshop *Possibilities* Independent reading Independent practice with common text Teacher-student conferences Small-group strategy practice Reflection in reading response journals Student-to-student discussion	Workshop *Possibilities* Independent writing: seed collection, experimentation, organization, drafting, editing Independent or small-group text analysis Teacher-student conferences Small-group process practice Peer review and editing
5–10 minutes	Share *Possibilities* Discuss what worked? What didn't? What was easy? hard? Discuss responses to focused questions Share samples of student reading responses	Share *Possibilities* Discuss what worked? What didn't? What was easy? hard? Discuss responses to focused questions Share samples of student writing

icant latitude to adjust to student needs. Sometimes students will grasp a concept quickly and be ready to move on to a new focus the next day. Other times, it will take longer than expected, and multiple days will need to be spent modeling, practicing, and experimenting. Some concepts will need to be brought back up several times over the course of a study, with each refocus taking students to a deeper level of understanding. Students must be observed carefully to ensure that a delicate balance is maintained. If the pace is too fast, I risk losing an appreciable portion of the class to confusion; if the pace is too slow, I may lose a similarly sized portion of the class to boredom.

The balance between reading and writing during the literacy workshop demands similar judgment calls. In general, I spend a larger percentage of time on reading workshop at the start of the study, shifting more toward writing as the study progresses (see Figure 1.1). The initial focus on reading is necessary to allow students time to become acquainted with the genre. Before they can even begin to

Figure 1.1 Balance Between Reading and Writing in Literacy Workshops

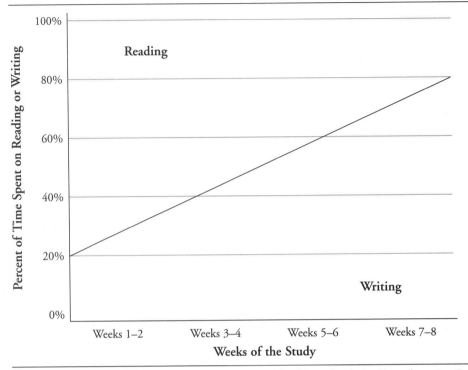

Adapted from a chart developed by a colleague, Steve Ford.

think about writing, they need to feel truly comfortable with the genre as readers, to have a general sense of what that genre looks and feels like, its purpose and its possibilities. However, once this has been achieved, students are ready to think as writers. They'll need increasing amounts of time in writing workshop to go back and analyze familiar pieces and to develop their own writing. By the end of the study, it is writing workshop that occupies the bulk of the time in my classroom. Editing, rereading, and reshaping are time-consuming and intense, and students are likely to insist that they be allowed the time to produce their best work.

Texts and Materials

Using well-selected texts in a genre study is essential. Nothing can cripple a lesson faster than a text that is not age-appropriate, reading-level-appropriate, or above all, engaging for students. And having an inadequate supply of interesting and accessible independent reading texts can ruin even the best-laid plans for workshop. The following are text and material guidelines that I have found helpful for building a well-supplied and well-organized genre study classroom.

Common Texts Short, high-quality texts exemplifying the genre are invaluable. As readers and writers, the students need models of outstanding texts. As a community, the class needs to build a common vocabulary and understanding of the genre. And as a teacher, I need texts that will allow me to create short, focused lessons that communicate ideas succinctly. Unfortunately, such texts can be hard to find. However, an infinite supply is unnecessary. A great genre study can be built around eight to twelve outstanding examples. Moving through a study, I want to be able to refer to texts used earlier, to remind students of the lessons learned from those texts, and to build upon an earlier understanding. This is particularly true when analyzing texts for author's craft. If students have not already had a chance to understand and enjoy a text as readers, it is very difficult for them to turn around and analyze that text as writers. Reusing great texts—studying them through multiple lenses—is an extremely powerful teaching and learning tool.

Independent Reading Texts A strong collection of texts for independent reading is essential. For each genre that my classes study, I provide bins of texts representative of the genre that students can read on their own. However, I am loath to limit students' independent reading to the narrow focus of the genre. Students, especially if they are struggling students, need to be continually reading compelling texts, and not all genres have enough possibilities available. Consequently, I typically also make available a wider selection of books that are similarly structured, for instance, during a memoir study, a large range of first-person narrative texts, or during a feature article study, lots of nonfiction books. During some studies (for instance, an editorial study), when texts are particularly unfamiliar to students or difficult to find, I set aside a time for independent reading that is distinct from the genre workshop.

Reader Response Journals A carefully worded prompt that is linked to the minilesson can transform reading workshop from sustained, silent reading into more focused learning. Asking students to respond to these prompts in a reading response journal serves three purposes. It allows time at the end of the workshop for students to reflect on their reading and consider it at a deeper level than they might otherwise. Independent reflection makes for better sharing or peer discussions because students have had a chance to clarify their thoughts before opening their mouths. Glancing through reading response journals provides me with a quick assessment, and reading samples in greater depth helps me to know what students have mastered and what they still struggle with so that I can shape future lessons accordingly.

Writer's Notebooks The writer's notebook for a genre study simply builds on the writer's notebook that students should be keeping throughout the year anyway. (For ideas about setting up a notebook, see Fletcher 1996 or Bomer 1995, ch. 4.) I encourage students to use previously collected ideas and information, and then to experiment with form and style appropriate to the genre being studied. As students move into drafting complete pieces, their work needs to come out of the notebook. However, in the meantime, the informality of the notebook allows them to try out various ideas and approaches in response to model texts or process lessons. Furthermore, the writer's notebook, like the reader response journal, serves as a great means of assessment so that I can gauge student understanding and need.

Text Collection Folders Three-pronged folders are a simple organizational tool for collecting and reusing common text samples. I require students to keep these easily accessible and well organized. This not only makes it easier on me when I want to use a text a second or third time during a mini-lesson but also allows students to quickly reference these models as they work on their own reading and writing.

Assessing and Evaluating Student Work

Before a study even begins, I consider how I am going to evaluate the final outcomes. What will be the measurement standards? What evidence of student achievement will be used to evaluate their progress against those standards? What are the consequences of failing to meet standards? By considering these questions up-front, I am able to align the evaluation standards with the learning objectives that I set for the study. All of the work that we do together should move students forward toward those learning objectives, and their progress should be measured accordingly.

In the classroom, I find it helpful to differentiate between assessment and evaluation. To me, assessment is what I do all day every day. It is the informal measuring of student progress for purposes of adjusting my instruction to better support student learning. I want to be constantly aware of student needs in relation to the learning objectives. Evaluation, on the other hand, is the final, end-of-the-unit measuring of student abilities against a rigorous standard. This is when I take off my coaching hat and become a critic: Did they meet the learning objectives, or not?

Assessment and evaluation should go hand in hand. The standards that are used for assessment must also be used for evaluation. I am assessing the students' progress toward, and evaluating their abilities against, the same set of standards.

The process of assessment and evaluation should be transparent. I want students to be well aware of the goals and their progress toward them throughout the study. Self-assessment is encouraged; students should reflect on their own learning, assess their strengths and weaknesses, and seek out appropriate support.

For purposes of assessment and evaluation, rubrics are my favorite tool. Midway through a study, when students have a meaningful understanding of the goals of the work, I begin the process of developing a rubric with the class. Together, based on what they have experienced and observed, the students decide on the categories that should be assessed, the criteria that should be used, and the evidence that is appropriate. Often several drafts are necessary. I like to develop a rubric for both reading and writing workshops. When I collect drafts of student writing, those drafts are assessed on the rubric. When I sit down for a reading conference with a student, we discuss his progress using the rubric. Students are encouraged to reflect independently, to place themselves on the rubric and identify ways in which they could improve their work. Finally, at the end of the study, achievement is evaluated using the same rubric. This process is clearly focused and transparent; it serves as a great motivator for students and helps to keep me focused on the goals of the study. The appendix provides samples of rubrics and further suggestions about evaluation.

Publication Celebrations

Student achievement needs to be celebrated. Publication is a public process, and student publication needs to be celebrated accordingly. Hosting a memoir reading, publishing a class magazine, or celebrating the send-off of student-written editorials reinforces the idea that students' work is valuable, and it's fun! I invite parents and administrators in, allow students from other classes to visit, encourage the class to dress up, speak out, and show off. Knowing that a public celebration of their work is expected encourages students to take greater ownership of their writing and to put more effort into their work. Furthermore, participating in a celebration at the completion of one study often motivates students to work harder during future studies.

Professional Collaboration

Teaching a genre study well is remarkably hard work. It requires a willingness to take risks and to become a learner alongside students; constant observation, assessment, and readjustment in response to student needs; and continual determination to push students further in their learning. Though rewarding, it can be very time-consuming. My best strategy for surviving and thriving during a genre study is collaboration. Classrooms of collaborating teachers will not (and should not) look exactly alike, but the opportunity to share lesson-planning ideas, texts, and samples of student work is invaluable. More important, the chance to talk with a colleague who is struggling through the same choices, successes, and frustrations can provide both inspiration and consolation.

Introduction to the Genre Chapters

The chapters that follow describe genre-based units of study set in real-life class-rooms with real-life kids. Each chapter describes an individual genre study, moving from planning through publication and evaluation. All apply the same general principles of genre study, yet each is uniquely tailored to fit the needs of the students in the classroom in which it is set. The classes range from fifth through tenth grade, urban to suburban, advanced to significantly below grade level. Teachers range from novice to experienced; all are comfortable with literacy workshop, reflective about their own practice, and generous in allowing me into their classrooms. With each teacher, I worked as a colleague and co-learner. We set goals, planned, and assessed student work together; I visited classrooms two to three times a week, observing, conferring, and occasionally co-teaching. Our work and learning together is reflected in these chapters.

Each chapter begins with a sample text in the appropriate genre and a discussion of that text. This is followed by a more detailed description of the genre and the merits of its study in the classroom. Goals are set, classes are introduced, and then the studies themselves begin. Sample lessons are interspersed with descriptions of the thinking that went into the planning of a lesson, how that lesson tied to what came before and what would follow, and how the lesson responded to observed student needs. Each chapter ends with a reflection on student progress, samples of their work, and a list of suggested texts.

Each of the profiled classes did good work, and each study has a great deal to offer. However, the classroom teachers and I would be the first to tell you that no study is perfect and none of the studies written about here should be applied in cookie-cutter fashion to other classrooms. These chapters are designed to show the process of planning and guiding students through a genre study; they are not step-by-step how-to manuals. Each offers many ideas about the nature of its focus genre, possibilities for approaches to mini-lessons and conferences, and model uses of texts. Each sets out goals that could be broadly applied and instructional focuses that could be readily adapted. However, each is grounded in the classroom setting and responds directly to the needs of the students in that classroom. The needs of these students are discussed repeatedly because we know that individual classrooms of individual students will have different needs, and as teachers we adapt our plans accordingly. The questions, considerations, and responses that the classroom teachers in these studies exhibited are models of the type of reflective, student-centered thinking that all teachers should apply when planning for their own classrooms.

This is designed to be a book for and about classroom teachers. It is designed to take theoretical concepts and illustrate how they can successfully (and, at times, not so successfully) be implemented in real classrooms. It is designed to be one more voice in the conversation about good teaching. Take from this text what you will; adapt, expand, and refine as you see fit; and make it your own. My hope is that this book will illuminate possibilities and inspire creativity.

CHAPTER 2

Memoir

From *An American Childhood*

Annie Dillard

After I read The Field Book of Ponds and Streams *several times, I longed for a micro-scope. Everybody needed a microscope. Detectives used microscopes, both for the FBI and at Scotland Yard. Although usually I had to save my tiny allowance for things I wanted, that year for Christmas my parents gave me a microscope kit. . . .*

All that winter I played with the microscope. I prepared slides from things at hand, as the books suggested. I looked at the transparent membrane inside an onion's skin and saw the cells. I looked at a section of cork and saw the cells, and at scrapings from the inside of my cheek, ditto. I looked at my blood and saw not much; I looked at my urine and saw long, iridescent crystals, for the drop had dried.

All this was very well, but I wanted to see the wildlife I had read about. I wanted especially to see the famous amoeba, who had eluded me. He was supposed to live in the hay infusion [that came with the kit], but I hadn't found him there. He lived out-side in warm ponds and streams, too, but I lived in Pittsburgh, and it had been a cold winter. Finally, late that spring I saw an amoeba. The week before I had gathered puddle water from Frick Park; it had been festering in a jar in the basement. This June night after dinner I figured I had waited long enough. In the basement at my micro-scope table I spread a scummy drop of Frick Park puddle water on a slide, peeked in, and lo, there was the famous amoeba. He was as blobby and grainy as his picture; I would have known him anywhere.

Before I had watched him at all, I ran upstairs. My parents were still at table drink-ing coffee. They, too, could see the famous amoeba. I told them, bursting, that he was all set up, that they should hurry before his water dried. It was the chance of a lifetime.

Father had stretched out his long legs and was tilting back in his chair. Mother sat with her knees crossed, in blue slacks, smoking a Chesterfield. The dessert dishes

were still on the table. My sisters were nowhere in evidence. It was a warm evening;
the big dining-room windows gave onto blooming rhododendrons.

Mother regarded me warmly. She gave me to understand that she was glad I had
found what I had been looking for, but that she and Father were happy to sit with their
coffee, and would not be coming down.

She did not say, but I understood at once, that they had their pursuits (coffee?)
and I had mine. She did not say, but I began to understand then, that you do what
you do out of your private passion for the thing itself.

I had essentially been handed my own life. In subsequent years my parents would
praise my drawings and poems, and supply me with books, art supplies, and sports
equipment, and listen to my troubles and enthusiasms, and supervise my hours, and
discuss and inform, but they would not get involved with my detective work, nor hear
about my reading, nor inquire about my homework or term papers or exams, nor visit
the salamanders I caught, nor listen to me play the piano, nor attend my field hockey
games, nor fuss over my insect collection with me, or my poetry collection or stamp col-
lection or serious rock and mineral collection. My days and nights were my own to plan
and fill.

————◄○►————

It was a late afternoon in October when Jennifer Roberts, a seventh-grade
humanities teacher, and I sat down with Annie Dillard's wonderful memoir
about finding private passion through the lens of a microscope. The richness of
Dillard's language had triggered many happy childhood memories for both of
us: our own science investigations, basement experiments, and adventures in
backyard puddles. For a time we lost ourselves in sharing our experiences, but a
nagging concern kept bringing Jen back to the reading: "I like this piece, but I'm
having trouble making sense of it. I keep wondering . . . Wasn't Dillard disappointed? It seems as though she and her parents were close, and yet when she
went to them immediately after making a major discovery, they refused to join
in her excitement. How was it possible that she was able to return to that basement with a sense of freedom and independence rather than disappointment
and loss?"

When selecting the reading, I had not considered this angle, but I appreci-
ated Jen's concern. I realized that I might not have been able to bounce back as
resiliently as Dillard in the face of parental apathy. We discussed the text further,
and understanding grew. Jen and I realized that, as kids, we both had had projects
that were ours alone, and while our parents did not try to dissuade us from these
pursuits, they did not actively encourage them either. Although neither Jen nor I
could recall an Aha! moment of independence such as the one Dillard describes so
poignantly, neither could we recall feeling lonely or sad at being left on our own—

indeed these were projects in which we took great pride precisely because they were truly ours. Recognizing the joy we had found in our private childhood pursuits, we could better appreciate the meaning of Dillard's memoir and the role our own parents had played in "handing us our own lives."

I glanced at the clock and realized that I had been there longer than expected. We'd built a lot of understanding around this memoir, but I knew that Jen still had lots to do before she would be able to leave for the day. I started to gather my things, but Jen wasn't finished: "You know, as we've been talking," she said, "I keep relating the image of her alone in the basement with her microscope to my own role in the classroom teaching. In the classroom I am isolated from other adults, and sometimes I am really disappointed that no one is there to witness and celebrate successes with me. But thinking about that now, I realize that I am usually quite pleased to be alone with my students. I think of the extra hours that I have spent working in my classroom, just because I want to, and I realize that Dillard is right—When you do what you do for private passion, it really doesn't matter who else cares. I'd never thought of it in quite that way before." She smiled at me wryly. "I guess I am able to make sense of this memoir."

Thinking Through the Genre

Making sense of memoirs enables us to make sense of our lives. We read and write memoirs to figure out our own experiences and to connect with the experiences and wisdom of others—to learn the stories of other individuals and share our own. Unlike biographies, memoirs allow us to get inside the heads of other people, to experience a moment in their lives from their perspective. A good memoir will provide the reader with the opportunity to connect with the experience—to feel the emotions, empathize with the response, appreciate the learning that took place, and find community in what can be an isolating world. A great memoir will cause readers to reflect upon and better understand their own lives and experiences. Jen's insights about her own passion for her teaching, prompted by Dillard's memoir, are a prime example of this potential.

My own passion for memoir surfaced after my first son was born. I was among the first of my friends to have a child, and the experience, while wonderful, was overwhelming and isolating. Parenting books tended to reduce the experience of mothering to a series of checklists. Friends and family adored the baby but couldn't relate to my woeful sense of inadequacy, moments of sheer terror, and bouts of laughter and tears. It was in memoir that I finally found understanding. Anne Lamott's *Operating Instructions: A Journal of My Son's First Year* and

Christina Baker Kline's collection of memoirs *Child of Mine* provided me with comfort. In these texts I found other women who were going through the same struggles and frustrations. Their experiences helped me see the humor and grace in my own.

By bringing memoirs into the classroom, we provide students with the opportunity to grow as readers and to become more reflective and grounded individuals. Finding similarities between their own experiences and the experiences described in memoirs allows adolescents, who often feel estranged and confused as they muddle through the transition between childhood and adulthood, to know that they are not alone in their struggles. Further, by asking them to recognize the learning that is often revealed in memoirs, we lead them toward wisdom that can help them make sense of their own experiences and prepare them to deal with future situations. Bomer (1995) describes the self-learning that memoirs can prompt in students:

> Reading, after all, like writing, is an act of composing meaning, and reading memoir, like writing memoir, involves a student in the act of composing meaning from his own life. . . . Reading can be a process of discovering the deep structure of what matters to me. Literature can unlock corners of my own experience that before seem to have been inaccessible.

Teaching students to write memoirs builds on their natural self-interest while simultaneously nurturing habits of disciplined introspection and purposeful writing. The act of writing a memoir allows students to explore experiences of their own choosing—to reflect on, examine, and uncover the meaning of events that evoke significant emotion. Nancie Atwell (1998) describes the writing of a memoir as follows:

> Memoir is how writers look for the past and make sense of it. We figure out who we are, who we have become, and what it means to us and to the lives of others: a memoir puts the events of a life in perspective for the writer and for those who read it. It is a way to validate to others the events of our lives— our choices, perspectives, decisions, responses.
>
> Memoir recognizes and explores moments on the way to growing up and becoming oneself, the good moments and the bad ones. It distills the essence of an experience through what a writer includes and, more important, through what a writer excludes. Memoir celebrates people and places no one else has ever heard of. And memoir allows us to discover and tell our own truths as writers.

Although a memoir must start with emotion, the writing itself is far more complex than simply recounting an event, and much more restrained than the sloppy "gush out every feeling that passes through one's head" writing that too often can be found in student journals or diaries. A good memoir demands the disciplined use of language and structure. Writing a memoir will challenge students to develop strong narrative technique and disciplined planning, drafting, and revision skills. William Zinsser (1998) explains the meticulousness with which a memoir writer must work:

> Memoir isn't the summary of a life; it's a window into a life, very much like a photograph in its selective composition. It may look like a casual and even random calling up of bygone events. It's not; it's a deliberate construction. Thoreau wrote seven drafts of *Walden* in eight years; no American memoir was more painstakingly pieced together. To write a good memoir, you must become the editor of your own life, imposing on an untidy sprawl of half-remembered events a narrative shape and an organizing idea. Memoir is the art of inventing the truth.

In classrooms, the study of memoir presents a powerful opportunity. By its very nature, memoir provides a fertile ground for students to make connections with text, to reflect on and make sense of their own lives, and to communicate meaning deliberately through their writing. These skills are essential for readers and writers of memoir. But they are not unique to memoir. All types of literature are better understood when we find and connect with the meaning in text. All forms of writing are stronger when we are thoughtful in our planning and deliberate in our processes. Teaching students these skills and strategies through a relatively accessible genre, memoir, empowers them with knowledge that they can apply throughout their literate lives.

Envisioning the Unit

Jen's seventh-grade students were a diverse bunch. Their reading test scores ranged from third grade to post–high school, with the majority falling in the fifth- to seventh-grade range. About 20 percent were second-language learners. Some had been designated as high achievers. Many students walked to their school, Kroc Middle School, from the surrounding Clairemont neighborhood, an ethnically mixed working- and middle-class suburb, with a sizable minority being bused in from more urban areas. They varied in religion, ethnicity, family background, socioeconomic status, and prior educational experience.

But, despite all this diversity, they had a great deal in common. Academically, nearly all of them had large gaps in their ability to thoughtfully analyze and construct meaning from text. While most enjoyed reading and could regurgitate a summary of a book quite well, few believed that the books they read had any relevance to their own lives. Writing was viewed from a utilitarian perspective; it was done because it had to be done. Most were quite competent at writing a summary or a description but struggled when asked to go beyond these standard prompts. They wrote for practical purposes, and their writing reflected this; it was quick, to the point, and dull.

In addition, these students were all adolescents, struggling to make sense of their place in the world. Many expressed feelings of loneliness and anxiety, and nearly all had a sense that "you just don't know what it's like. . . . No one understands." Despite the fact that they were together in the same classroom for two hours each day, most felt isolated. They had a healthy sense of respect for one another but were not part of an authentic classroom community.

Academically and socially, these students would be well served by a memoir study. The very personal nature of memoir would encourage a shift in attitude about the purpose of reading and writing—a shift that Jen and I hoped to capitalize on to encourage greater understanding of both the genre and the students themselves. We wanted students to see the value of reading and writing literature as a means of making sense of their own lives. We wanted them to learn to interact with text in a more meaningful way, to connect with common emotions, experiences, and ideas, and to learn from the wisdom of the authors. We wanted them to learn the habits of reflection that, when coupled with disciplined planning and thoughtful narrative craft, can lead to the writing of great memoirs. And we wanted students to find community, both through their reading and writing and within the classroom itself.

Teaching the Unit—Reading Workshop

Jen's students entered her classroom as literal thinkers. Most were quite competent at reading narrative text, and many could easily recognize the structural elements of a story: the setting, the main characters, the events. But few had moved beyond this superficial level of understanding.

As we moved into our study of memoirs, Jen realized that our first objective would be to move students from thinking concretely about the *events* in a memoir to more insightful consideration of the *experiences* that are represented in a memoir. The following lesson represents the beginning of that process.

Reading Workshop—Memoir
Goals and Instructional Focus Progression

	Reading Comprehension Strategy Study	Accountable Talk Study
	Goal: Students will learn to recognize the experiences and meaning in memoirs, to analyze universal themes, and to use the truths uncovered in memoir to reflect upon and gain understanding of their own experiences.	**Goal:** Students will learn to have meaningful memoir discussions with a peer partner. Discussions will enhance students' understanding of memoirs.
Weeks 1–2	**Recognizing the Author's Experience** Students will learn to recognize the author's unique experience of the events described in the memoir. <ul><li>What is happening in the memoir? What are the events?</li><li>What is the author's experience of those events? How does the author feel about what is happening?</li><li>Use text evidence to support your understanding of the author's experience.</li></ul> **Connecting to the Author's Experience** Students will learn to connect the author's experiences to events in their own lives. <ul><li>Have you experienced similar emotions or reactions?</li><li>How were your experiences the same? different?</li><li>How does your connection help you to better understand the memoir?</li></ul>	**Developing Appropriate Attitudes and Behaviors for Peer Partner Discussions** Students will learn what is appropriate to do and say when discussing a memoir with a peer. <ul><li>Preparing for a discussion</li><li>Using appropriate behavior during a discussion</li><li>Developing appropriate language</li><li>Getting started. Sharing your own understanding of and connections to the memoir</li></ul>
Weeks 3–4	**Recognizing the Memoir's Meaning** Students will learn to recognize the meaning in memoirs. <ul><li>Why is this experience important to the author?</li><li>What did the author learn from his/her experience? about him/herself? other people? the world?</li><li>Support your understanding with text evidence.</li></ul> **Connecting to the Memoir's Meaning** Students will learn to connect the memoir's meaning to their own experiences. <ul><li>Reflect on your connection. Does the author's learning apply to your own experience? Explain.</li><li>Do you agree with the conclusions that the author came to? Why, or why not?</li></ul>	**Listening to and Learning from Peers** Students will learn to listen, understand, and learn from the ideas and experiences of their peers. <ul><li>Paraphrase. Explain what your partner said in your own words. Check. Is this accurate?</li><li>Clarify confusion. What should you do when you don't understand?</li><li>Compare. How are your partners' ideas and experiences similar to yours? different?</li><li>Learn. What can you learn from your partner's ideas and experiences?</li></ul>
Weeks 5–6	**Exploring Universal Themes** Students will connect authors' experiences and learning across memoirs. <ul><li>Are there connections between the experiences and/or learning in this memoir and the experiences and/or learning in other memoirs?</li><li>How are the memoirs the same? different?</li><li>How does text-to-text connection help you to better understand the memoir(s)?</li><li>How do these themes apply to your life? Which memoir do you find most relevant? Why?</li></ul> **Evaluating Reading Progress—Self-Reflection and Teacher Evaluation**	**Reflecting on the Value of the Conversation** Students will reflect on their conversations to understand how the discussions improved their understanding of the memoir and/or their own experiences. <ul><li>How did the conversation help you to better understand the memoir?</li><li>How did the conversation help you to better understand your own experience?</li></ul> **Evaluating the Discussion—Self-, Class, and Teacher Evaluation**

SAMPLE LESSON: ## Week 1—Reading Workshop

AREA OF STUDY:	**Reading Comprehension**
FOCUS:	**Recognizing the author's experience**
TEXT:	**"Everything Will Be Okay," by James Howe, in *When I Was Your Age*, edited by Amy Ehrlich**
RESPONSE:	**Margin notes describing the author's experience**

Jen gathered her students onto the rug at the front of the room and said, "During the past several days, we've begun exploring memoirs, and I'm thrilled that many of you are finding them entertaining and enjoyable. But memoirs are often written to do more than entertain. They are written to share the author's experience with us so that we might learn from that experience and make better sense of our own lives. Now, some of you may be thinking that the experiences in memoirs are not at all like your own. And to some extent that's true. A lot of memoirs are about events that you or I may never have lived through. But, as readers, we need to consider more than just the *events* in a memoir; we also need to think about the author's *experience* of those events. As you learn to do that, I suspect you'll begin to find memoirs much more familiar and valuable." Students looked skeptical. Undaunted, Jen continued, "Let me show you what I mean."

On the overhead she placed the first page from James Howe's "Everything Will Be Okay." In this touching memoir, ten-year-old Howe falls in love with an abandoned kitten. The kitten is extremely ill, and despite Howe's promises to care for the animal, his family decides that it is best to put it to sleep. In his pain and anger after the kitten dies, Howe realizes that he does not want to be like his father and older brothers, who treat the lives of animals so callously; instead, he declares, "I will decide for myself what kind of boy I am, what kind of man I will become." This text contains a range of emotions that are relatively easy to recognize. It is a good choice for a lesson introducing students to the concept of author's experience.

With the students following along on the overhead, Jen read the first section of the text.

The kitten is a scrawny thing with burrs and bits of wood caught in its hair, where it still has hair, and pus coming out its eyes and nose. Its big baby head looks even bigger at the end of such a stick of a body. I found it in the woods at the end of my street where I play most days with my friends. This time I was alone. Lucky for you I was, I think to the kitten. Otherwise, David or Claude might have decided you'd be good practice for their slingshots. Those two can be mean, I think to myself. I don't like playing with them really, but they live at the end of the street and sometimes you just play with the kids on your same street, even if they're mean, sometimes even to you.

The kitten makes a pitiful noise.

"Don't worry," I tell it, stroking its scabby head until the mewing is replaced by a faint purr. "Everything will be okay. I'm going to take you home, and my mom will give you a bath and some medicine."

I tuck the kitten under my jacket and run out of the woods, across the street, down the sidewalk toward my house. I feel the warmth of the kitten through my shirt and start thinking of names.

At the conclusion of the reading, Jen paused, appeared to think for a moment, and then explained her understanding of the text to the students: "In the text I've read so far, the *events* are that a boy has found a kitten and decides to take the kitten home. This could make for an interesting story, but what I really find intriguing is the author's *experience* of those events. He feels an immediate sense of empathy toward this kitten. He wants to protect it. His devotion to the kitten is intense." Jen made note of her findings in the margins of the overhead transparency, writing, "Feels empathy toward kitten. Wants to protect it."

Then she turned to the students and asked, "Do you think everyone would feel the same way if they found a scrawny, scabby kitten like this? What are some other reactions that people might have?" "Some people would just want to leave the kitten alone because they might think it was diseased or something," one student said. Another commented, "I would want to help it by finding someone who could take care of it, because it seems too sick for me to deal with."

"So what you're telling me," Jen observed, "is that different people might experience the same event in different ways. Some people might be angered by finding a cat like this, others might be disgusted, others might just be sad." Students nodded in agreement. Jen continued, "What you've just described is the difference between events and experiences. An event is something that happens. In this case, a boy finds a kitten. An experience is how the author feels about what is happening; as a boy, Mr. Howe felt an intense devotion to, empathy with, and desire to protect the kitten. We're used to picking out the events of a story. When we read memoirs, we also need to recognize the author's experience. Are you ready to give it a try?"

After receiving somewhat grudging consent (these were seventh-graders, after all), Jen continued. She placed a transparency of the next short section of Howe's text on the overhead, and read it aloud. At its conclusion, she paused. "Okay," she prompted, "what are the events that are described in this section of the text?" A student quickly summarized the events: "His mom takes the kitten and puts it in a box. Then she makes him take a bath. He cries." "Good," Jen agreed. "Now, tell me about the author's experience." "I think he feels really scared for his kitten," one student volunteered. Jen gently coaxed the student to explain further: "What in the text makes you think he was scared?" The student took a moment to review the reading. "That part right there, where it says, 'I feel in the pit of my stomach what the future of that kitten is. The feeling spreads through me like a sudden fever.'" "Good," Jen said. "But what exactly makes you think that he feels scared?" Again the student paused to think, then haltingly responded, "When I feel something in the pit of my stomach, it is usually because I'm really scared, so I think that he must be, too." Jen nodded in agreement, underlined the lines that the student had quoted, and wrote in the margin of the transparency, "Really scared for kitten."

Another student raised her hand. "I think he feels helpless, too," she offered. Jen encouraged her to refer to a specific part of the text as well. "He says, 'But that kitten is mine' when his mom takes the cat away, and then he starts to cry. I think that shows he wants to protect that cat, like you said, but his mom just takes over, and now he's helpless to protect it." Satisfied with the student's explanation, Jen underlined this line as well and wrote, "Helpless" in the margin of the transparency.

This pattern of teacher-student exchange continued through several additional observations about this section and into two further sections of Howe's memoir. Together the class would read a short excerpt of text from the overhead. Jen would then ask questions prompting students to consider (1) the events described in the text, (2) the author's experience, and (3) direct text evidence that would support their understanding of the experience. As they worked, Jen continued to underline appropriate evidence and take notes in the margins reflecting student observations of the author's experience.

It was only when Jen was confident that most students understood the concept of recognizing the author's experience that she released them to continue the work independently. She passed out copies of Howe's text and instructed students to read the remaining sections on their own: "As you read, follow the same process in your head that we've been using together. Stop regularly and follow the plan on this chart."

Recognizing the Author's Experience
1. Consider the events.
2. Consider the author's experience.
3. Make notes of your understanding of the author's experience in the margins.
4. Underline appropriate text evidence.

Students scattered back to desks and comfortable reading chairs. For the next twenty minutes they read, reread, scribbled notes in the margins, and underlined the occasional sentence. As they worked, Jen and I made the rounds, reading margin notes over students' shoulders, asking questions about individual interpretations, pushing students to dig deeper, and providing support for those who were confused.

When students reconvened on the rug at the end of the period, they were eager to share their understanding of the text. They shared first with a peer and then with the whole class. Then Jen asked students to consider the effect of using this reading strategy: "How did thinking about the author's experience, rather than just the events, change your understanding of the memoir?" "It made it more interesting," one student commented. Others noted, "It made it seem more real." "It made it into a story I could relate to even though I don't even like cats." "It made me think that the story was about more than just a cat. It kinda seemed like it was about growing up."

————◄○►————

Jen and I were delighted with students' achievement during this first comprehension lesson. However, as we would discover over and over during the course of this study, it would take considerable practice for students to comfortably incorporate a new strategy into their regular reading behavior. Several days of additional modeling, conferring, and practice using a range of texts were needed. It would take until the end of the week before most students began to feel genuinely comfortable with the concept of recognizing the author's experience.

However, despite their increasing confidence, Jen noticed that many students' use of the strategy remained superficial. They repeatedly used bland words such as *happy, sad,* and *mad* to describe an experience, and consequently their understanding of the memoirs was bland as well. In student conferences it became clear that they were capable of developing a more nuanced understanding, but in order to do so, they would need to be able to describe their interpretations more precisely. Hence, Jen decided that some instruction on vocabulary was in order.

SAMPLE LESSON: ## Week 2—Reading Workshop

AREA OF STUDY:	**Word study**
FOCUS:	**Using specific terms to describe emotions found in texts**
RESPONSE:	**Synonym chart; revision in reading response journal**

To introduce the focus on the lesson, Jen placed two sample reading responses on the overhead:

Sample A

James Howe is sad when the kitten dies because he really liked it.

Sample B

James Howe is devastated when the kitten dies because he felt very protective of it.

She turned to the students and asked, "Which of these two samples more accurately describes Howe's experience in 'Everything Will Be Okay'?" The answer was designed to be obvious, and students quickly recognized that sample B was a better representation of Howe's experience. "Why is that one better?" Jen prompted. Several students volunteered explanations: "It really shows how important it was to him." "It explains why it mattered." "It shows how he really felt." "Good," Jen agreed. "Now, analyze the responses. What is the difference between A and B?" "They are basically the same," one student observed. "It's just a few of the words that are changed. Like, the second one says *devastated* instead of *sad,* and *very protective* instead of *really liked.* They don't really seem that different; it's just the language that's different."

"Right," said Jen. "The structure isn't different; it's the language. The words that we use to describe an author's experience make a big difference. Words such as *sad* and *like* are words we use all the time. There are lots of times that we've been sad, but only a few times when we've felt devastated. Using more precise language to describe an author's experience helps us better understand what that experience was really like. So, today, we're going to do a little work on vocabulary; we're going to develop our abilities to use precise language." Groans erupted from the class. "Don't worry," Jen assured the group. "This will be fun."

On a sheet of chart paper she drew two columns: one on the left, labeled General and one on the right, labeled Specific. In the General column, she listed the word *sad.* "All right," she challenged the students, "what are some other words that could more precisely describe how you feel if you are sad?" They began, of course, with *devastated,* which quickly led to *brokenhearted, despondent,* and *depressed.* As they brainstormed, Jen pushed the students to define the words more exactly: "What does it mean to be despondent?" "When might you be brokenhearted?" "What's the difference between being devastated and being depressed?"

Specific words that could be accurately defined were recorded in the right-hand column of the class chart, across from the general word to which they corresponded. Within minutes, Jen's students had generated twelve synonyms for *sad.* Shortly thereafter, they were able to come up with fourteen for *happy.*

Confident that her students were now ready to work on their own, Jen instructed, "I've written up on the board a list of words that I find over and over in your descriptions of the author's experience in your journals." The board held a list of about twelve adjectives that included *mad, upset, nervous, surprised.* "I'm going to assign you to a team, and I want you to work with that team to repeat the process [see following list] we've just been working on together."

Generating Specific Words

1. Choose a general word that needs to be defined more precisely.
2. Brainstorm other, more specific terms that better describe an author's experience.
3. Carefully consider the meaning of each specific term. Challenge one another by asking, "What does it mean?" "When would you use it?" "How is it different from some of the other terms?"
4. Record your work, using a two-column chart. Be prepared to share.

Rarely have I seen such active student participation in a vocabulary lesson. Students had a great time building their lists, arguing over definitions, and debating which words belonged in which column. And their lists demonstrated that they knew a lot of words (see Figure 2.1). Why hadn't they used them before? Melissa spoke for many when she admitted, "I wasn't sure exactly what *irate* meant, so I didn't want to write it down. It was easier to just say that she was *mad.*"

After thirty minutes of small-group vocabulary work and a five-minute debriefing, that excuse was no longer valid. Jen ended the lesson by sending students back to their desks to revisit their memoir folders. "Find at least five places where you can use more precise language to describe an author's experience, and rewrite your margin notes accordingly," she instructed. For nearly every student, it was now easy to meet this demand. And it made sense to do so. As one student explained, "This is something that seems so small, but it makes a big difference."

―◄○►―

Learning to use more precise language did indeed make a big difference in students' ability to develop and articulate a sophisticated understanding of the author's experience. And soon they were ready to move on to the next challenge: making meaningful connections with the text.

As with the other learning objectives in this study, teaching students to make meaningful connections with the text required time, modeling, and practice. We wanted students to go beyond connecting to the concrete details of a memoir. It is relatively easy, but not particularly useful, to recognize superficial commonalities ("I have a cat, he had a cat"). Instead, we wanted students to make thoughtful connections that would enhance their understanding of the experiences and learning described in the text ("I can appreciate Howe's sense of devotion to that

Figure 2.1 Student's Synonym Chart for Emotion Words

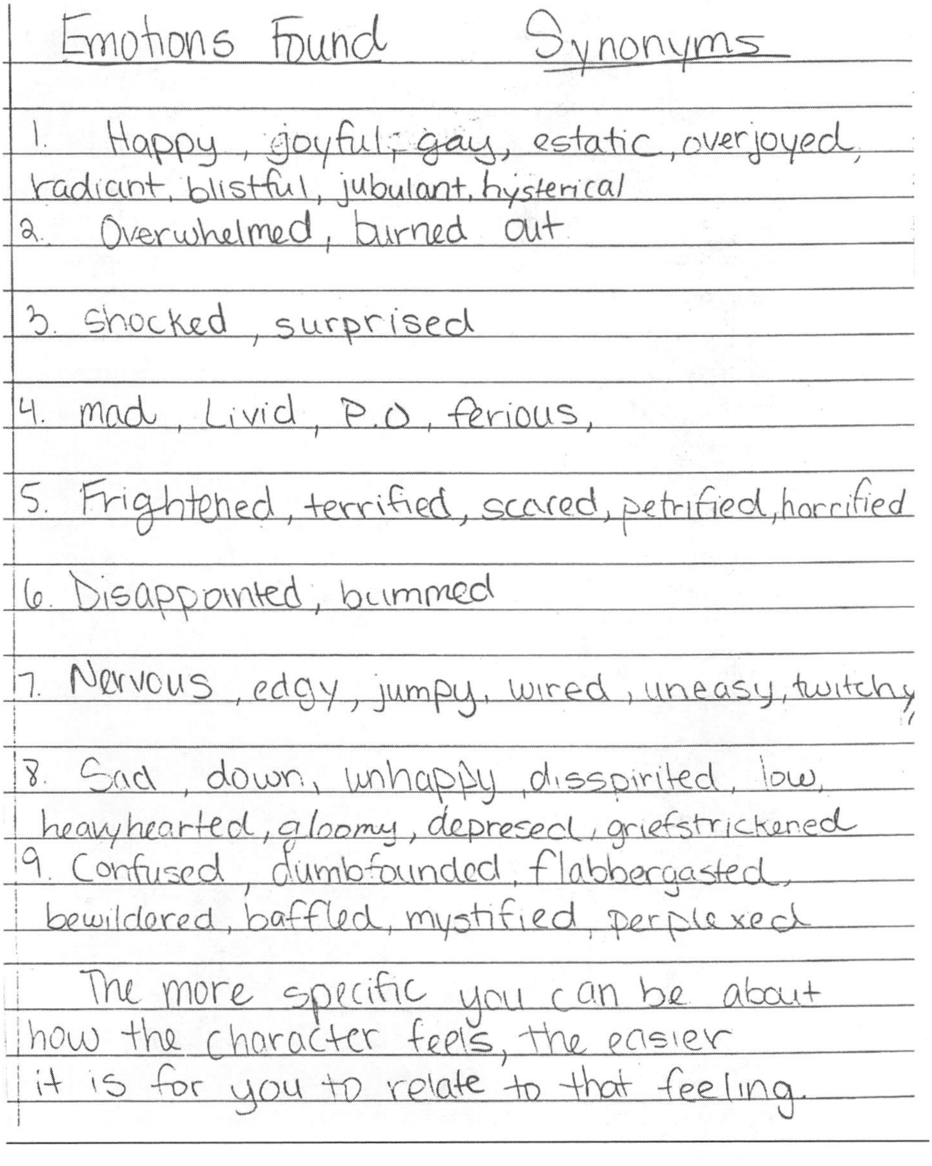

Emotions Found   Synonyms

1. Happy, joyful, gay, estatic, overjoyed, radiant, blistful, jubulant, hysterical
2. Overwhelmed, burned out

3. shocked, surprised

4. mad, Livid, P.O, ferious,

5. Frightened, terrified, scared, petrified, horrified

6. Disappointed, bummed

7. Nervous, edgy, jumpy, wired, uneasy, twitchy,

8. Sad, down, unhappy, disspirited, low, heavyhearted, gloomy, depresed, griefstrickened
9. Confused, dumbfounded, flabbergasted, bewildered, baffled, mystified, perplexed

The more specific you can be about how the character feels, the easier it is for you to relate to that feeling.

cat. I felt the same way when I held my baby sister for the first time. I, too, would have been enraged if anyone had tried to hurt her.")

One of the most valuable supports that students were provided during this phase of the study was the opportunity for them to talk with one another. Throughout our work, peer talk was an important component, but particularly during the weeks when students were learning to connect memoirs to their own lives, peer conversations proved to be essential. Given the unique nature of individual connections, most students found it was not enough to listen to a few examples. They needed to know if *their* connections made sense; they needed someone to listen and then follow up with questions that challenged their understanding. Jen and I had come to better understand our individual connections with Dillard's memoir as a result of our conversation; our students needed similar opportunities.

Jen organized students into peer partners and allotted class time for peer partner talk two to three times per week. Students were instructed to come prepared to discuss an assigned memoir, and they were given guidelines about expected behavior and potential discussion topics. Initial conversations seemed to flow well. Students enjoyed the opportunity, most came prepared, and the majority stayed on task. However, despite this veneer of success, Jen and I grew increasingly concerned as we observed the students in their discussions. We noticed that they typically did a very good job of sharing but that their listening skills were sorely lacking. Now, there is an inherent benefit in sharing something aloud even if no one is listening, but we wanted students' memoir conversations to be more than one-sided sounding boards. We wanted them to challenge and learn from one another, to form connections between their individual experiences, to find community in common understanding. To do this, they would need to learn to listen to one another.

SAMPLE LESSON: ## Week 3—Reading Workshop

AREA OF STUDY:	**Accountable talk**
FOCUS:	**Listening to and learning from peers**
TEXT:	**"I Am Not the Center of the Universe," in *Bad Boy,* by Walter Dean Myers**
RESPONSE:	**Student conversations**

Jen began by reading a short excerpt from Myers's memoir "I Am Not the Center of the Universe." The text describes young Myers's excited anticipation of an upcoming birthday, and then his frustration and disappointment when a distant uncle dies on the day of the intended celebration, resulting in the cancellation of his party. The class had enjoyed reading and responding to the memoir earlier in the week; now Jen wanted to capitalize on their earlier responses to demonstrate the power of paraphrasing. She began calling on students one at a time.

"Jorge, tell me about your response to this piece," Jen requested. She listened politely to Jorge's description of his response—a thoughtful connection to Myers's sense of isolation after his uncle's death—then asked, "So, did you like the story? I did!"

"Linh, how did you respond to this memoir?" Jen asked. Again, she listened politely as Linh described her connection. But the moment Linh was finished, Jen jumped right in with her own, very independent thoughts. "Well! My connection was totally cool."

Jen continued with these types of comments for a while, long enough so that students shifted uncomfortably in their chairs and avoided making eye contact. (After all, if you don't look at the teacher, she won't call on you, right?) Jen was never rude, just self-involved. Her behavior mirrored that of the students.

Finally, she called on Shayne: "How did you respond to this memoir?" Shayne, somewhat reluctant to share after watching his classmates' answers be disregarded, gave a brief summary of his response. This time, Jen paraphrased his statement and actually responded to his ideas: "So, what I hear you saying is that you can relate to Myers's feeling of resentment because you have felt similarly when you were treated differently from your brothers. I think that Myers felt guilty at the same time he felt resentful. Do you sometimes feel that way? Guilty and resentful at the same time?" Shayne (and the rest of the class) looked up in surprise; this was a different Mrs. Roberts. He thought for a moment and then thoughtfully answered her questions. Again, Jen paraphrased and responded to his comments. A conversation!

"Tell me," she asked the rest of the class a few minutes later, "was I a good conversationalist?" Most weren't quite sure how to respond. Not only had Jen's responses been varied, but they were wary of insulting their teacher. Tiffany tried to be diplomatic. "Sometimes you were," she said. "But other times you were a little rude." Other students chimed in, saying that the more abrupt responses had made them feel uncomfortable, stupid, and unimportant. "It made me not want to say anything," Linh admitted. Jen apologized for hurt feelings and went on to explain that often, listening in on student conversations, she heard similar kinds of remarks and they bothered her, too. "When you don't respond to somebody's comment, it devalues what they've said and limits the conversation."

The students then turned to Jen's exchange with Shayne. "What was different?" Jen asked. She had been careful during the model to paraphrase Shayne's comments every time, and that intentional demonstration had had an impact. "You said back to him what he'd just said to you," a student immediately pointed out. Why was that important? "It showed that you were really listening." "It made you make sure that you understood what he said." "It helped you respond back to him instead of just talking about yourself."

"When you are in the middle of a conversation, it is not always easy to listen to and understand everything that is being said," Jen acknowledged. "Paraphrasing, which means repeating something back in your own words, is a great way to help both participants in the conversation keep track of what is going on and build on each other's ideas." The students agreed that applying such a technique to peer partner discussions might be worthwhile. Jen gave them some initial paraphrasing practice, sharing a few connections of her own and asking students to turn to a partner and paraphrase. Once they were comfortable with this, students were sent to try out the strategy in their own conversations.

Jen and I wandered around the classroom observing. Students huddled with their partners, sharing connections and responses to "I Am Not the Center of the Universe" (a somewhat ironic title, given the instructional focus of the day). Many struggled; some students were in such a hurry to express their own thoughts that it was hard for them to take the time to paraphrase the ideas of others; a few students had gotten so accustomed to not listening that they had to repeatedly ask, "What did you say?" before they were able to paraphrase back. Conversations didn't exactly flow yet but, for the first time in some cases, there was some back and forth. Students were making an active effort to respond to what their partners said, paraphrasing and then connecting their partner's ideas to their own. Sometimes these efforts were simply an exercise in following directions. But other times they paid real dividends in supporting student understanding. "You said that you connected the time when the boy feels small and unimportant to when you felt that way at your aunt's wedding," Kelly paraphrased. "You said you felt small then because everybody was busy looking at the bride and no one paid attention to you, and that helped you understand the way Mr. Myers felt." Pause. "Oooo, that idea reminds me of Christmas at my Grandma's. After the gifts are opened, the adults start talking, and it's like they want the kids to go away and play with their toys. It feels like we're just in the way. I hadn't thought of that before."

———◄○►———

Stronger conversations helped students develop stronger connections, which in turn supported greater understanding of the author's experience as described in the memoir. But listening to students' conversations and reading students' entries in their reading response journals, we found that while they had made great strides in their ability to understand memoirs, they were still missing an essential piece. They recognized, and could relate to, the author's experience in the memoir, but when asked, "Why was this experience meaningful to the author?" most were unable to deliver an insightful response.

It is the meaning of the experience that is at the heart of a memoir. Memoirs are often written about events long past, moments that have stuck in the author's mind because they represent important growth in understanding oneself and one's world. In relating those events through a memoir, an author is not just sharing an experience but also communicating the wisdom gained from that experience. Jen and I wanted students to be able to recognize the importance of the experiences that are described in memoirs. Doing so would certainly promote a stronger understanding of the text, and it would help students gain wisdom that might be applied to their own lives.

SAMPLE LESSON: Week 4—Reading Workshop

AREA OF STUDY:	**Reading comprehension**
FOCUS:	**Recognizing a memoir's meaning**
TEXT:	**"The Great Rat Hunt," by Laurence Yep, in *When I Was Your Age,* edited by Amy Ehrlich**
RESPONSE:	**List of "memoir lessons" developed in small groups**

Students arrived on the rug for this day's lesson with texts they had already read. Jen had passed out copies of the memoir the day before and asked students to read it on their own. "Mark it up," she had instructed. "Use all the strategies that we have been working on, taking notes in the margins that describe the author's experience, underlining evidence of that experience in the text, considering your own connections, and using your reading response journal to reflect on those connections. Come prepared, because you'll need to have thoroughly read the text in order to participate in the next lesson."

The text that they were to read, "The Great Rat Hunt," is an amusing, endearing memoir by Laurence Yep. It describes young Yep and his father hunting for a rat in the family's apartment. Yep, asthmatic and often ill as a child, longs for approval from his strong, athletic, and seemingly perfect father. His fear of failure is palpable during the fruitless search for the rat. In the end, despite having been driven out of the apartment by fear of the "huge" rat, Yep's father declares the experience a victory for them both. Through his actions, he reveals both his own imperfections and his unconditional love for his son. This memoir is rich in meaning—a perfect text for this day's purpose.

"As you know," Jen began, "memoirs are about the experiences in people's lives. But they aren't just about any experience. They are about experiences that are *meaningful.* As readers, we need to infer the meaning of the memoir, to figure out why the experience is important to the author. That's what we're going to work on today." Students looked slightly fearful. It had taken each of them a considerable amount of time to learn to recognize the experience in text. Would inferring meaning be as much of a challenge?

"One of the best ways to figure out meaning in a memoir is to look at places where the emotions change," Jen continued. "When that happens, it is often a clue that the author has learned something important." She called their attention to "The Great Rat Hunt." "For example, a place where I think the emotions change in this memoir is right here, on the second-to-last page, when his father admits that sometimes he is scared, too:

> It was the first time I'd ever heard my father confess to that failing.
>   "But you're the best at everything."
>   "Nobody's good at everything." He gave his head a little shake as if the very notion puzzled him. "Each of us is good at some things and lousy at others. The trick is to find something that you're good at."

"Before that, young Yep had idolized his dad," Jen said. "He had really believed he was perfect. After this discussion with his dad, he starts to see him as more human, less perfect. As a reader, I can really feel that shift in emotions, from fearful reverence to relaxed companionship. That's a big change, and it's important. It helps me to understand that the boy learned something: his dad wasn't perfect. That realization is part of why this memoir is meaningful."

Jen looked at her students. It was their turn. "What else makes this memoir meaningful?" she asked. "What else has the boy learned? Take a moment, look back at the text and at your notes. Find a place where the emotions change. Think about the significance of that change. What was it like before? after? What did he learn?"

We waited while the students reviewed the memoir. Would they be able to find meaning in the text? Hands began to creep up. "I think one thing he learned was that he doesn't have to be perfect for his dad to like him," a student volunteered. Jen nodded in encouragement but challenged the student to provide an explanation of her inference. "Why do you think that is what he has learned?" she asked. "What evidence from the text supports that understanding?" "Here." The student pointed at the following passage:

> "I'm lousy at sports," I confessed.
>   Slowly his knees bent until we were looking eye to eye. "Then you'll find something else," he said and put his arm around me. My father never let people touch him. In fact, I hardly ever saw him hug mother. As his arm tightened, I felt a real love and assurance in that embrace.

The student continued, "Before he kept saying how he always felt left out or unloved, but now he says that he feels 'real love' when his dad hugs him, even after he admits that he's bad at sports. That makes me think that he's learned that his dad loves him even though he's not perfect."

Other students spoke up to volunteer their interpretations of Yep's memoir. Each time, Jen challenged them to support their interpretation with text evidence and to explain the relevance of that evidence. Together, they generated an impressive list detailing meanings in Yep's memoir:

- His father loves him.
- Don't be so hard on yourself.
- Give other people credit for recognizing your strengths as well as your weaknesses.
- Father was proud of him.
- Father accepts him for who he is.
- Father isn't always perfect either.
- He doesn't need the approval of others.
- It's okay to be different.
- He's worth more than he thought he was.

Discussion was cut short by an unplanned fire alarm. So it wasn't until the next day that Jen was able to regroup and ask students to apply their learning on their own. She divided students into groups, assigned each group a previously read memoir to revisit, equipped them with chart paper and markers for creating a list of their findings, and sent them off to reread, analyze, and discover the meanings in the texts. "Don't be shy about challenging one another," Jen reminded the students. "Make sure there is evidence in the text that supports each interpretation. Everyone in the group should agree with an interpretation, and be able to defend it, before you write it on your list."

When the groups came together thirty minutes later, they brought with them lists of thoughtful interpretations of the memoirs. Listening as each group shared its findings, Jen and I were impressed with the students' insightful understanding of the text and their ability to support their interpretations with text evidence. When Jen asked students, "How will this lesson change the way that you read memoirs in the future?" one student explained, "I'll read more slowly because I'll want to think about not just the experience, but why the experience is important." Another said, "I'll have to think about it more after I'm done with the reading, maybe even reread parts." My favorite response came from Shannon, who commented, "I think it'll make me think about my connections more carefully, to see if the meaning of the memoir fits with my experience."

———◄o►———

During the final weeks of the memoir reading workshop study, Jen pushed students to further engage with memoirs by focusing on two additional learning objectives.

Reflecting on Text-to-Self Connections As Shannon had suggested, the meanings contained in a memoir have the potential to teach us a great deal about our own lives. So, once students were comfortable inferring meaning in memoir texts, we pushed them to consider the application of the author's learning to their own experience: "Does the author's learning apply to your own experience? Why, or why not?" "What did you learn from your experience?" "Do you agree with the conclusions that the author came to? Why, or why not?" In some cases, students discovered that there was little relevance between the memoir's meaning and their own experience. But, in other cases, the connection resonated deeply and prompted students to understand events in their own lives with increased clarity.

Exploring Text-to-Text Connections With the help of a few leading questions ("Do you notice anything similar about the meanings in these two memoirs?" "Doesn't this learning sound familiar? Haven't we encountered a similar learning by another author?"), students were able to recognize that many memoirs explore similar themes. Jen applauded this recognition and encouraged them to analyze how various authors treated these themes. Howe and Yep, for example, both discussed their relationships, as children, with authority figures. Both came to realize that they did not need to be like their fathers in order to be of value. What prompted this realization? How were their experiences the same or different? How were their relationships with their fathers affected by this learning? Which experience do you relate more closely to? Discussing these questions with students, and teaching them to ask similar questions, encouraged thoughtful reflection and insightful responses to the literature they were reading. The following is one example of such a response:

Response to *Billy Elliot,* by Melvin Burgess
Marc C., Grade 7

Text: In the chapter that I read today, Billy is hanging around the ballet class that is in the same building as the boxing class that his dad wants him to go to. He's really fascinated by the dancing and desperately wants to give it a try, but he knows that his father would be very upset if he did.

Connection: I've only read the first part of the book, but so far, a lot of the experiences seem like the ones in "The Great Rat Hunt." Billy really respects and sort of fears his father, just like Yep does. But he wants to do something that is really different from what his father wants him to do, also like Yep.

Reflection: I'm wondering if Billy will find out the same thing that Yep discovered, that he can be his own person and his father will still love him. Of course, it could be more like that other memoir, the one where the kitten dies and the author pushes his father and brother away. Either way, I think that this book is really about finding your identity, which is good because I think that's a struggle that a lot of people go through. I know I can relate to it!

Teaching the Unit—Writing Workshop

Memoir is not a genre with which students are generally familiar. Consequently, getting started in writing workshop presents a special set of challenges. Not only do we need to help students develop ideas for their own writing, but we also need to teach them about the genre in which they'll be writing.

Although it would have been more expedient to simply give students a definition of memoir, Jen chose instead to expose them to a variety of sample texts and have them develop their own understanding of what a memoir is. This path was chosen in part because it was more engaging for students, in part because she wanted to establish early the expectation that students would be analyzing published texts as a means of gathering ideas for improving their own writing, and perhaps mostly because it is hard to pin down an exact definition of memoir. For teaching purposes, Jen tends to define a memoir narrowly: a short text focused on a single incident that is meaningful to the author. But even within that narrow definition things can be confusing. How long is a single incident? What makes it meaningful? For whom is it meaningful? These are questions that only the author of a memoir can really decide. By giving students the responsibility of analyzing texts and developing their own understanding of memoir, we were asking them to think like authors—necessary preparation for becoming authors themselves.

SAMPLE LESSON: ## Week 1—Writing Workshop

AREA OF STUDY:	**Text structure**
FOCUS:	**Defining a memoir**
TEXT:	***The Circuit,* by Francisco Jimenez; *Voices from the Fields,* edited by S. Beth Atkin; various other texts**
RESPONSE:	**List of memoir characteristics**

Jen called students together on the rug and told them that she was going to read them two texts: one would be a memoir and the other would not. Their job was to identify which one was the memoir and be able to explain why. The first text was "The Circuit," a memoir in Jimenez's book of the same name. It describes the experience of a migrant child during one circuit of crop harvesting—his feelings

Writing Workshop—Memoir
Goals and Instructional Focus Progression

	Text Structure Study	Writing Process Study
	Goal: Students will learn to recognize and use the structure and techniques of narrative text in order to communicate meaning through their memoir.	**Goal:** Students will learn to reflect on experiences and understand their significance in order to plan and craft a meaningful memoir.
Weeks 1–2	**Defining a Memoir** Students will construct a clear definition of a memoir. • What are the defining characteristics of a memoir? What must a memoir have? What may a memoir include? • What is the purpose of a memoir? Why are they written? • How are memoirs unique from other types of fiction and nonfiction text? • What kinds of topics, lengths, purposes, and writing styles are appropriate for memoir?	**Gathering and Nurturing Seed Ideas** Students will develop habits of reflection and intro-spection in order to identify and develop seed ideas for their memoirs. • What memories are most important to you? Why? What quirky, funny, or strange memories have stuck in your head? • What are the moments within the important events that are meaningful? • What makes that moment meaningful? What learning does it represent? Is it small enough to be appropriate for a memoir? Do you want to write about it?
Weeks 3–4	**Understanding the Structure of a Memoir** Students will learn to recognize and use the struc-tural elements of a memoir. • What are the main text events in a memoir? • What is the purpose of each event? What do they show the reader? • Are all of the events necessary? How does each contribute to the meaning of the memoir? **Crafting Narrative Text** Students will analyze and learn to use narrative techniques in order to show, don't tell, the meaning of their memoir. Among the techniques to include: • Internal thoughts • Dialogue • Character actions • Descriptive language • Comparisons • Narrative voice	**Planning Your Memoir** Students will learn to plan out their memoir using an appropriate memoir structure. • What is your "memorable moment"? What meaning do you want to communicate through your memoir? • What events and ideas do you need to include before your memorable moment? after? • What is the purpose of each event? How do these events work together to show the signifi-cance of your experience? **Drafting** Students will use appropriate narrative techniques to draft a memoir that shows their meaning.
Weeks 5–6	**Ending the Memoir** Students will analyze the endings of memoirs to learn appropriate methods for completing the story and reinforcing the learning. • Which endings do you find most compelling? Why? • How do authors show the significance of their story at the end of their memoir? Is it stated? alluded to? not mentioned? Which method is most effective? Why?	**Review and Revision** Students will learn to reread and revise their mem-oir to ensure that it all works together to communi-cate meaning clearly. **Evaluating the Writing** • Establish a set of evaluation criteria • Measure your final published piece against established criteria • Reflect on learning

of frustration and isolation as he is repeatedly uprooted to follow the harvest. The second text was a short introduction from *Voices from the Fields*. It describes in general terms, using formal, third-person language, the difficulties of growing up as a migrant farmworker—similar material but from a very different genre.

After reading both texts, Jen asked, "Okay, which one was the memoir, and why?" Students almost instantly recognized that "The Circuit" was the memoir. Their exposure to texts they knew to be memoirs during the previous few days had made this the obvious choice. But it was much harder for them to explain why. After a few faltering efforts at a definition, Jen asked the students to do a bit of research. They were told to review the memoirs that they had previously read and collected in their folders and to compare them while asking, "What do these texts have in common?" and "What makes them memoirs?"

As students worked, Jen and I made our way around the room, gently nudging students toward recognition of the attributes of a memoir. "What do you notice about who is narrating the story?" "Are they all told in first person?" "Why do you think that might be?" "What do you notice about the scope of the memoirs?" "How many days do they usually span?" "Why do you suppose it looks at such a short time period?" These questions helped students consider the characteristics of a memoir and also ensured that they were active in considering why such characteristics were present.

Once students had had a chance to consider the attributes of a memoir on their own, they compared their findings with their neighbors' lists and finally gathered on the rug to develop a class definition. In response to Jen's initial question, "What are the characteristics of a memoir?" students listed the following:

Characteristics of a Memoir
- A memory; a description of an event from the past
- Written in the first person; told from one person's point of view
- Based on the truth
- Reveals the feelings of the writer
- Has meaning; shows what the author learned from the experience
- Focused on one event; about one point in the author's life
- About the author's experience more than about the event itself

Then came more challenging questions: "What is the purpose of a memoir?" "Why would someone sit down and write about an event in their own lives?" Students quieted down again. Some stared at the list of memoir characteristics, others flipped back through their folders, considering the purpose of individual memoirs. Finally, a quiet voice in the back spoke up, "I think that people write a memoir about something because they felt like the experience was important and they wanted to share it with other people." "Good," Jen encouraged. Then she pushed further: "But what makes it important? Is it the event itself that is important, or is it something else?" The first student to respond to this question put forward his opinion that it was the event itself, but another student quickly contradicted that idea: "It can't just be the event, because some of the memoirs are about events that really don't seem all that important, like going to a movie or to a normal day of school. I think people write memoirs because they learned something from that experience and that is what makes it important to them." "Yeah," another voice chimed in, "they are writing to share what they learned." "Or maybe," a final voice added, "they are writing because that event stayed with them and they can't figure out why. Maybe writing a memoir is a way of making sense of your own experiences."

————◄○►————

When it came time for students to choose seed ideas for their own memoirs, Jen repeatedly emphasized two primary aspects of the class's definition of a memoir: it has to be small, and it has to be meaningful. These criteria ran contrary to students' instincts. When first encouraged to consider ideas for possible memoir topics, they immediately latched onto big, glorious events: going to Disneyland, summer camp, elementary school graduation. These were events that students viewed as important, in part because other people had told them they were important. But when pressed, "Why was this event meaningful?" "What did you learn from this experience?" "What lessons do you want to communicate by writing about this topic?" students struggled to explain the significance of the experience. Their struggles stemmed from two difficulties: the events they had chosen were too big and unwieldy, and most students were unaccustomed to reflecting on the value of particular events in their lives.

To address these issues, Jen decided to teach students to use webbing. Teaching students to brainstorm ideas in an associative fashion would help them to find smaller moments, within their big important event, that could potentially serve as memoir seeds. Teaching them to question and reflect on the significance of those moments would help them choose a seed that could produce a meaningful memoir.

SAMPLE LESSON: # Week 2—Writing Workshop

AREA OF STUDY:	**Writing process**
FOCUS:	**Gathering and nurturing seed ideas**
RESPONSE:	**Webbing of seed ideas in notebooks**

Sitting at the front of the class, Jen thought aloud through her process of finding a seed idea for her memoir. She explained that as she had reviewed her writer's notebook, the entry that she was most drawn to was one about her wedding. She had decided that she wanted to write about that special day but knew that topic was too big and unwieldy: "I can't just write an essay about the whole wedding. That wouldn't fit our definition of a memoir. I need to make it smaller and more meaningful. So I started to think about what aspect of the wedding was most meaningful to me, and eventually that led me to a seed that I can develop into a memoir. I'm going to share the process that I went through with you now, and in a few minutes, I'm going to ask you to try a similar process as you work to develop your own seed ideas."

She turned on the overhead and wrote the word *wedding* in the middle of a blank transparency. She then began a process of free association, writing down the people, places, and events she associated with the occasion. Quickly, *Kris, mom and dad, the bay, photographer, Leslie,* and *Grandma's fall* were recorded in a web around her main focus. As she wrote, Jen talked aloud about each of these elements, briefly describing what they were and thinking through whether they might work as a seed for the memoir. She kept her discussion brief but focused on two primary criteria: Is it small enough? and Is it meaningful enough?

When she had filled the screen, Jen paused. She decided that none of her associations thus far was appropriate for a memoir but that the most interesting possibility was her association with "Grandma's fall." Her grandmother had slipped and fallen shortly before her wedding. The event tore Jen—she felt she wanted to go take care of her grandmother but realized that her many guests and her future husband were waiting for her. Jen explained that, for her, "Grandma's fall" was rich with memoir possibilities. She then removed the now-filled transparency and wrote "Grandma's fall" on the center of a new one and began her web of associations again (see Figure 2.2).

It took three webs before Jen eventually found the moment she was looking for. It was the moment that the sirens from the ambulance faded in the distance and she shifted her attention from her grandmother's injury to her wedding. Neither Jen nor her family had been sure that she would be able to pull herself together in order to walk down the aisle, but somehow at that moment she found the strength to move forward. This was a moment that was both small and meaningful—perfect for a memoir.

Jen revised her process with her students: "What did I do to find a seed idea for my memoir?" Their observations became a list of guidelines that they would soon apply themselves:

Finding a Seed Idea for a Memoir
1. Review your writer's notebook to find an interesting topic.

Figure 2.2 Jen Robert's Association Web for "Grandma's Fall"

2. Build from that topic. What people, places, or things do you associate with that topic?
3. Record your associations using a web.
4. For each association, consider:
   • Is it small enough to make into a memoir?
   • Is it meaningful enough to make into a memoir? Did I learn something from this experience?
   • Would I want to write a memoir about it? Why, or why not?
5. If the answers are no, continue developing ideas.
6. Once you find a moment, write an explanation of why it will make a good memoir.

Students were then sent to work on their own seed ideas. As they worked, we monitored their process, questioning, probing, and making the occasional suggestion. Webbing proved to be a great aid for many, moving them away from grand topics and focusing them on specific, meaningful moments. Brandon moved from wanting to write about "scuba diving" to deciding to write about a moment when he and his dad were crouched on the ocean floor as a shark passed overhead. This moment, he explained, was both terrifying and exhilarating; it taught him to respect the ocean. Kelly decided to write about the first time that she successfully rode a wave on a surfboard. She explained, "After spending several days in angry frustration, feeling like I was a failure, the thrill of success taught me that sometimes it's sweeter when you have to work to get something."

Not all students were able to successfully focus their topic on this day. Some required individual writing conferences to find a meaningful moment. Others would continue to focus and find meaning in their topic throughout their drafting process. But this lesson did a great deal to help the majority of students develop seed ideas for their memoirs. As one student explained, "Before I was trying to find some big thing that everyone would think was important. But after webbing, I have a couple of moments that probably no one else would care about but they are important to me." This was exactly what we wanted for a memoir.

<hr>

Once students had successfully found a seed idea, many were champing at the bit to start writing. But Jen knew from experience that it is important for students to have a solid plan in place before they begin drafting their memoir. In the previous lesson and the many conferences that followed it, we had worked with students to help them understand the significance of their "memorable moment." Now we needed them to understand how to communicate that significance to others. Writing a memoir is more than just detailing the moment and telling why it is important. Writing a memoir requires that the author show the meaning of a particular moment by carefully selecting and describing events that precede and follow that moment. Meaning needs to be carefully revealed through story, and in order for that to work, the story needs to be carefully planned.

SAMPLE LESSON: ## Week 3—Writing Workshop

AREA OF STUDY:	**Text structure**
FOCUS:	**Understanding the structure of a memoir**
TEXT:	**Excerpt (pp. 43–47) from *Bad Boy*, by Walter Dean Myers**
RESPONSE:	**Plan of "text events" and "purposes" for individual memoirs**

"Most of you have now found one significant moment that you want to capture in your memoir," said Jen. "We've talked through its importance, and you know the meaning that you want to convey to your audience. Now it is time to think about how to communicate that meaning. Today we are going to consider how authors select and use the events in their memoirs to show the significance of that one memorable moment. We'll analyze a published text first, and then you'll be asked to begin developing your own plans."

Students were then instructed to open their memoir folders to a previously read excerpt from Walter Dean Myers's *Bad Boy*. This brief memoir describes Myers's discovery of the power of books. In it, he goes from being the sulky, sullen student being punished at the back of the room to being an avid reader who discovers the "more real me" in the world of books. The memoir was short, it was familiar, and it clearly developed its meaning through a succinct series of text events. It fit our purposes perfectly.

Students reread the text once on their own to reacquaint themselves with it. Then Jen began the process of analysis: "This memoir contains several different events. What are they?" Together the class identified five major text events, which Jen recorded in a column on a sheet of chart paper. Once they were all reasonably satisfied with this list, Jen asked, "What is the purpose of each of these events? What do they show the reader?" This question was a bit more challenging, but with support students were able to identify the purpose of each of the events. The finished chart looked like this:

Text Event	Purpose
Description of Myers's behavior in class	Shows how unhappy he is at school
Fight with one of the other boys	Shows how nobody thinks he is smart; shows that he is a "bad boy"
Punishment by teacher	Shows his bad relationship with teacher and how unhappy he is at school
Reads "East o' the Sun and West o' the Moon"	Shows how he learned to like books: "I realized I liked books, and I liked reading" (*memorable moment*)
End-of-year report card	Shows how his love for books helped him to do better in school

After the chart was completed, Jen pushed students to analyze Myers's work further. "Are all of these text events necessary?" she asked. "How does each contribute to the meaning of the memoir?" This question was too big for students to take in all at once, so Jen broke the analysis into smaller pieces: "Which event is most important here?" After a short debate, students agreed that the time when he is reading the fairy tale "East o' the Sun and West o' the Moon" is most important. "Why?" Jen pushed. "Because that's when he learned that he likes books," explained Mario, "and that's the point of the whole memoir." Mario was absolutely right—the experience of sitting in the back of the room reading (and enjoying) "East o' the Sun and West o' the Moon" was the moment on which Myers's entire memoir was based. That experience was what was truly meaningful—it was his "seed idea."

Jen agreed with Mario's explanation but then went on to ask, "If that is the memorable moment, why are the other things included? Why do we hear about his bad behavior in class, his fight with the other boy, and his punishment by the teacher? Why not just start with his reading the book?" Students puzzled over this for a few seconds before Alliena volunteered an explanation: "We needed to see how much he disliked school at first in order to understand why it was important that he found a book he liked." The rest of the class breathed a collective "Ohhhh!" of understanding. Jen allowed a few more students to contribute their ideas before turning the class's attention to the final text event. "What about the end?" she asked. "Why is it necessary to include the part about the report card? Why not just end with his response to 'East o' the Sun and West o' the Moon'?" Nicole jumped right in: "Because he has to show why what he learned made a difference in his life, that it wasn't just one book he liked. He had to show that learning to like reading helped him get along in school, since that was where he had so many problems at the beginning of the memoir."

"So what can we learn from our analysis of Myers's memoir?" Jen asked as the students' discussion of the text itself wound down. Their findings:

Planning a Memoir
- Every text event has to have a purpose.
- The memoir needs to show attitudes or feelings *before,* so that the reader understands the author's learning at the end.
- The memoir needs to show the *before* part several times, not just once.
- The memoir needs to show the *after*: How did the learning change the author's life? Why was it significant?
- Every text event needs to build toward, show, or explain the significance of the author's learning. If it isn't doing one of those things, it shouldn't be included.

This was a great list. It represented a firm theoretical understanding of the structure of a memoir. But Jen knew that if students were to apply this list of guidelines to their own planning, she would need to show them how to do so. She also realized that the students had been together for more than fifteen minutes now. She didn't have a lot of time, so she opted for a quick model.

"Kelly," Jen called, "your memoir is about how thrilling it was to learn how to surf, right? How can we apply some of these things to your memoir outline? If you want to show how sweet the success was, then you're going to have to show some of the failures, too. Give me some examples. What about after your memorable moment? What can you do to show the significance of this event in your life?" Kelly responded to Jen's questions with ideas. Other students added their input, and in a relatively short amount of time an outline emerged:

Text Event	Purpose
Getting thrashed by waves	Shows how miserable she was
Watching others make it look so easy	Shows how she felt like a failure
Getting cold, deciding to go in after one more try	Shows that she was ready to give up
Successfully riding first wave to the beach	Shows her excitement and disbelief at success (*memorable moment*)
Staying out and continuing to surf	Shows how success totally changes her attitude about surfing and belief in herself

After Jen finished recording Kelly's outline on the chart paper, she turned around to a room full of raised hands. Everyone else wanted to work on their outlines, too. They ran through a couple more together, but then students were growing restless, a sign that it was time to let them apply their learning to their own outlines. So Jen quickly summarized and sent them to go and apply their learning independently. Some were able to get right to work, immediately outlining a series of purposeful text events. These were mostly students whose topics were similar to the ones worked on by the whole class; hence they were able to readily make appropriate adjustments. Others needed more time and support to think through different possibilities. The idea of shaping their own history to fit their purpose was a new concept, and it took some getting used to.

As Jen and I circulated, we encouraged students to be creative in their use of events. They could reference an event from days, weeks, or even years earlier to show how they had felt before their memorable moment. They could compare their own experience to someone else's response to the same events to show why the event was meaningful to them. Or (and this was perhaps the most shocking for students), they could rearrange, adjust, or even make up pieces of their story in order to convey the larger meaning. A memoir doesn't need to be completely true to actual events in its details; what matters is its ability to communicate the significance of an author's experience.

————◄○►————

The outlining expectations that Jen had set were rigorous. She was requiring every student to thoughtfully select and understand the purpose of each part of his or her memoir before drafting. This required introspection and creativity on the part of the students, and it took considerable time and support in the classroom. Thus, it wasn't until the end of the third week that the actual drafting process began. Students were sent home with outlines in hand to work on their drafts over the weekend, and on Monday morning Jen and I waited in eager anticipation. However, as we read through the first round of drafts, we were often disappointed.

Some students had done an excellent job. They had internalized the style and structure of the memoirs they had read, and they had employed appropriate narrative techniques to craft meaning into their text. But more often, students' writing came across as distant retellings of events—lists of what happened accompanied by brief add-ons that explained the purpose of the event: "I was in shock." "This made me feel really angry." Or (my favorite) "The purpose of including this in my memoir is to show you that I felt really alone." As we read through students' work, Jen and I realized that a lesson on "show, don't tell" was needed. Students needed to learn that the best memoirs reveal meaning through the actions, thoughts, and dialogue of the characters. By showing rather than telling the importance of the events, authors bring their characters into the story, making the memoir more interesting and meaningful for the reader as well as the writer.

SAMPLE LESSON: **Week 4—Writing Workshop**

AREA OF STUDY:	**Text structure**
FOCUS:	**Crafting narrative text; show, don't tell**
TEXT:	**"Everything Will Be Okay," by James Howe, in *When I Was Your Age*, edited by Amy Ehrlich**
RESPONSE:	**Creative response to common prompt**

On the overhead Jen placed an edited version of the first piece of James Howe's memoir:

> I found a kitten. I picked it up and petted it. It purred. I took it home. I felt really protective of the kitten.

Jen asked the students, "What do you think? Why was this event important to the author?" Students mumbled a few attempts at response. Obviously it was important because he says it made him feel protective, but most students agreed that this wasn't very effective. "He says he felt protective," explained one student, "but he doesn't really convince us. It's hard to connect to."

Then Jen placed the real excerpt from "Everything Will Be Okay" on the overhead (see Reading Workshop, Week 1). The class read through the text, and then Jen asked again, "What do you think? Why was this event important to the author?" Students were able to respond much more readily now. They pointed out Howe's physical response to the kitten, his desire to take care of it, the connection he felt to the kitten's hurt, and his obvious love for the kitten. Jen interrupted, "But wait a minute. This example and the first example describe the same basic events, so why is it that this time you find it so much more meaningful?" Students hadn't realized the connection between the two pieces, and it took them a moment to check and make sure that their teacher was right, but they recovered nicely. "The second one gives a lot more information about what happened," explained one student. "It helps you see what is happening," said another. And then the gem, "The first one just tells you how the author felt; the second one actually shows you."

Jen seized on the opportunity: "Yes! The second one shows the reader why what is happening matters to the author. The first one doesn't; it just tells us. As writers, we need to write more like the second; we need to show our audiences why what we are writing about is important to us. You've all thought through the importance of each of the events that you are writing about in your memoir. That was the 'purpose' part of your outline. But many of you are not *showing* that importance in your writing. Many of your memoirs read more like the first example than the second. So that is what we are going to work on today—learning to show, not tell."

Seeing that most students were satisfied with this explanation, Jen pushed them into analyzing the excerpt from Howe's memoir. Sentence by sentence and word by word, the students examined the text and considered the techniques that Howe had used to show the importance of the events to the audience. Their findings:

Ways to Show Meaning in Text
- *Through the character's actions.* "I tuck the kitten under my jacket and run out of the woods."
- *Through the character's dialogue.* "'Don't worry,' I tell it, stroking its scabby head until the mewing is replaced by a faint purr. 'Everything will be okay.'"
- *Through the character's thoughts.* "I feel the warmth of the kitten through my shirt and start thinking of names."
- *Through comparisons.* "This time I was alone. Lucky for you I was, I think to the kitten. Otherwise, David or Claude might have decided you'd be good practice for their slingshots."

- *Through descriptive language.* "The kitten is a scrawny thing with burrs and bits of wood caught in its hair, where it still has hair, and pus coming out of its eyes and nose."

"You need to employ these same techniques in your own writing," Jen instructed. "You need to use actions, dialogue, thoughts, comparisons, and descriptive language to show, not just tell, why the events you describe are important. Now, I know that some of you are writing about events that are from a long time ago, and you may not remember all of the dialogue or exactly what you were thinking. That's okay. You are allowed to adjust or invent details in order to show your meaning."

Looking at her students, Jen realized that this was a lot to take in. Students had just been introduced to five different narrative techniques. They weren't ready to try to apply them to their own memoirs yet; they needed a chance to experiment, to try out these techniques without having to worry about what to replace in the original draft or how to adjust the details of their own experiences. So Jen provided students with an original common prompt that was similar to the style of writing many had used in their own memoirs:

The papers were passed back. I got mine. I turned it over. I saw my grade. It was an F. I was disappointed.

"Try adding actions, dialogue, thoughts, comparisons, or descriptive language to this memoir," she instructed. "Put yourself in the place of this author. Instead of telling me that you were disappointed, show me. You don't have to use all the techniques, but choose the ones you think are most appropriate. And, obviously, you don't have to use actual dialogue or thoughts. Make up what you need to, but make the memoir realistic, and make sure it shows your disappointment."

When students returned to the rug twenty minutes later, they brought with them a wide range of writing samples. All showed disappointment, but the reasons behind that disappointment were wide-ranging. Some were disappointed in themselves because they hadn't tried their best; others were disappointed with their teacher because they thought that she was being unfair; others feared disappointing their parents. Listening as their peers shared, students became aware of the variety of uses of narrative techniques and the remarkable difference that can be made by showing rather than telling your meaning.

———◆◇◆———

During the days that followed, students worked to show meaning in their own memoirs. This required considerable support. Jen modeled the process of rereading and revising using a sample student memoir. Students took turns reading each other's work to identify places where their peers were telling, rather than showing, the importance of events. We reviewed other published memoirs to examine individual narrative techniques in greater depth. Students were encouraged to constantly refer to their outlines in order to remind themselves of their purpose for each of the text events, and to ensure that their revisions fit their purpose. And Jen and I spent a great deal of time conferring individually with students about their writing, the significance of the events included in their writing, and how their narrative could be adjusted to communicate meaning to others.

It took time, but gradually students' work improved, so much so that we began to notice some of the grammar, spelling, and punctuation difficulties that plagued their writing. Of course, these difficulties had existed all along; the students didn't suddenly forget how to use punctuation. But during the early stages of the writing process, Jen and I had intentionally ignored such mistakes. It was much more important that students initially focus on learning to write fluently and to convey meaning through their writing; grammar, spelling, and punctuation were secondary. We wanted students to be free to experiment with inserting dialogue, for example, without worrying about the exact uses of quotation marks or capitalization. However, as students' memoirs improved and we moved toward publication, these niceties became more important. In order for writing to be effective in communicating its meaning to an audience, grammar, punctuation, and spelling need to be strong enough so that they don't impede appreciation of the content. To address students' struggles with these elements, Jen chose several of the most common areas of difficulty and taught specific lessons, including the following lesson on dialogue punctuation and formatting. Of course, not all such mistakes could have been addressed through mini-lessons. Small-group writing tutorials, individual conferences, and good old written feedback were also used to address difficulties that smaller numbers of students had in their writing.

SAMPLE LESSON: ## Week 5—Writing Workshop

AREA OF STUDY:	**Conventions of the English language**
FOCUS:	**Dialogue punctuation and formatting**
RESPONSE:	**Revision of common text sample; review and revision of individual memoirs**

Before students arrived, Jen copied a sample piece of dialogue onto chart paper. It was short but successful in its use of punctuation and formatting, conventions that many students were struggling with.

"Nick! I want you to take out the trash," yelled my mom.

"Do I have to?" I asked.

"Yes," she replied, "or else you don't get your allowance."

"Okay," I sighed, "I'll be right there."

Once the kids had arrived and were settled, Jen gave them a moment to read the chart, then explained simply, "Many of you are struggling with punctuating and formatting your dialogues correctly. This person has used perfect punctuation and formatting on his dialogue. Tell me what you observe."

Some observations were immediate. Others took longer. Even though (or perhaps because) they had been reading dialogue for years now, many students struggled to see the obvious. However, with a bit of prompting, they gradually developed a fairly extensive list of rules for dialogue:

Rules for Punctuating and Formatting Dialogue
- There are quotation marks around the parts that are spoken.
- The first letter of each spoken part is capitalized.
- There are dialogue tags that explain who is talking each time the speaker changes.
- A new paragraph is started after the speaker changes.
- The dialogue tags can go before, after, or in the middle of dialogue.
- The first letter of the dialogue tag is not capitalized unless it is a name or at the beginning of a sentence.
- There's always punctuation—a comma, a period, a question mark—at the end of the spoken parts. It goes inside the quotation mark.
- There's always a period or comma at the end of the dialogue tag.

Wanting to cement the class's understanding before sending them off to hunt down and correct dialogue mistakes in their own memoirs, Jen then presented the students with a common prompt. Their job was to rewrite it, correcting the punctuation and labeling the corrections in their notebooks.

I want ice cream she said.

Yes I said I do too. Then she said we should go get some.

Okay I said let's do that. Then we left to go get the ice cream.

Watching students struggle to fix the dialogue prompt was illuminating. They had been able to identify the punctuation and formatting in the model dialogue piece fairly easily, but now many were confronted with indecision. Students repeatedly raised their hands to ask, "Where do I put the comma?" "Does this have to be capitalized or not?" "When do I have to start a new paragraph?" Rather than simply respond, Jen and I typically answered their questions with more questions, encouraging them to look at the model, to consider the rules they had developed, and to talk to their peers. By the time the whole class came back together to fix the prompt, most students had successfully identified and corrected the mistakes.

We were just about to send students off to apply their learning to their own memoirs when Casey spoke up from the back: "Ms. Roberts, there's another problem there that you didn't fix. In the first dialogue sample, they don't use the word *said* once. But in the second it is used four times. That makes it boring. It needs to be fixed." He had us there! When Jen and I had made up the samples, we hadn't consciously limited our dialogue tags to *said* but had simply tried to write basic, incorrectly punctuated dialogue. But our unintentional word selection provided a great opportunity. Many students similarly limited themselves to the word *said* when writing dialogue. And Casey was right; it was boring and needed to be addressed.

With some classes we might have waited for another day, but we knew this class would be able to handle a bit more instruction. "So, what are some other words that we can use for *said?*" Jen asked. Students eagerly brainstormed a list. It included *pleaded, answered, exclaimed, replied, cried, responded, screamed, explained, complained, whined, yelled, demanded, announced, asked, questioned, sighed, blurted, mumbled, implied, inquired, proclaimed,* and *wondered.* Then, pulling from this list, they replaced *said* in the dialogue prompt so that it read

> "I want ice cream!" she demanded.
> "Yes," I sighed, "I do, too."
> Then she exclaimed, "We should go get some."
> "Okay," I replied, "let's do that." Then we left to go get the ice cream.

After we had finished, Casey, satisfied with the efforts, explained, "See, that makes it much more interesting. It gives the conversation more life!" Right again! Jen added an additional instruction to the list of dialogue rules:

- There are lots of different ways to show who is speaking. You don't always have to use the word *said.*

Then she sent the students off to apply their learning to their own memoirs.

———◄o►———

In the final weeks of the memoir study, students were allowed blocks of time to work independently on improving their memoirs. By now they had very much taken ownership of the work and the experiences that were described in their writing. They all knew what they wanted to communicate, and each worked effectively to do so. Jen supported their work through writing conferences and by making resources readily accessible; charts from all the previous lessons had been posted where they could easily be referenced. A class-developed memoir rubric allowed students to assess themselves and identify additional areas that needed work. And peers were encouraged to draw on each other's strengths; more often than not, our writing conferences ended with a suggestion to "go take a look at ——'s memoir and ask him/her about how he/she used ———." Encouraging students to use the resources of the classroom on their own served multiple purposes: (1) It provided individual students with the tools they needed to write strong memoirs; (2) it freed up the teacher to focus on students with the greatest needs; and most important, (3) it nurtured the reflective, resourceful, and self-reliant habits of good writers.

Evaluating Student Progress . . .

By the time the study of memoir drew to a close, the class had become a much closer-knit community. Reading, talking, and writing about their own experiences had enabled students to reflect and learn from published memoirs, their own experiences, and each other. As they learned together, they developed an appreciation and respect for the value that each member brought to the classroom.

This was perhaps most in evidence during their final memoir celebration. Jen had booked the library for the day, and the students had invited their parents and other classes to hear memoirs read aloud by their authors. It was a lovely celebration in many ways, but the most impressive part, for me, were the responses that students wrote to each other's memoirs. Each student had placed a folder with a copy of his or her work and a page for comments on one of the tables that stood around the room. Although it was not required, nearly all of Jen's students took the opportunity to read and respond to their peers' memoirs. Among the comments: "You were really brave to share this experience. I admire you." "Thank you for writing about your brother's death. It helped me to understand how I felt when my cousin died." "Your memoir inspires me to want to face my own fears. Thank you." This class was no longer a group of isolated, angst-ridden teenagers. It was a community of people who protected and supported one another.

. . . in Reading Workshop

For the most part, students had met the goals that Jen and I had set out for them. Everyone in the class was now able to recognize the author's experience in a memoir. All could find meaning in memoirs and support their interpretation of that meaning with text evidence. (Not all interpretations of meaning were of equal quality, however. A few students struggled to move beyond trite clichés, whereas others were able to thoughtfully recognize multiple layers of meaning.) Most students were able to purposefully connect with memoirs, recognizing commonalities between their own experiences and those described in the memoirs and using the connections to better understand the text as well as their own experiences. They were able to thoughtfully discuss memoirs, their interpretations, and their connections with peer partners. And many had demonstrated considerable skill in developing text-to-text connections as they explored themes that ran through different memoirs.

Jen and I were pleased with students' growth in developing effective reading strategies. But what pleased us more was the appreciation that most students now had for the genre itself. As the following comments indicate, these seventh-graders had come to see the value of reading memoirs:

> A memoir is a person's heart and soul on a piece of paper. Reading it can release emotions that you have never thought about before and help you to understand something that you never have before.
> —*Shayne P.*

> I like thinking about the author's learning because it helps me to understand the whole memoir, not just see it in little bits and pieces. When I do that, I understand why the author wrote it and why it is important. It helps me learn about life and know what to do and what not to. A lot of the learnings are things that my mom already taught me, but they are more meaningful when they come from a person's own experience, not just as instructions.
> —*Nicole W.*

> Reading memoirs helps me to understand why I do things the way I sometimes do them. Like, when we read *The Invisible Thread,* I saw myself in that experience. I had walked away in a similar situation, but I didn't understand my actions then. Now I do. Reading a memoir helped me know why I did things before, and it will help me make decisions in the future.
> —*Linh H.*

. . . in Writing Workshop

Students had groaned, complained, dug their heels in, and rebelled at various times during the writing process, but in the end they had produced some wonderful memoirs. They had learned to find a seed idea from their own experience, reflect on its significance in their lives, and craft their memory into a meaningful memoir. Of course, some of the work still suffered from grammar flaws, breaks in meaning, or a disproportionate focus on events rather than the author's experience. However, listening to students discuss their work and describe its strengths and weaknesses quickly revealed that even if they had not mastered the craft of writing memoir, they understood its objectives and its applications. This understanding was most clearly exhibited by Ana. Two days before the memoir celebration she decided to change her topic. Needless to say, this made Jen and me very nervous—Ana had struggled for weeks to produce a mediocre memoir about friendship, and we were concerned about what she would be able to create in two days. But our worries were groundless. Ana ended up with a wonderful memoir about her estranged father's death. She had recognized that this was a subject with much greater personal meaning for her than her previous subject, and that it was therefore a more appropriate topic for her memoir. She had had the courage to begin the writing process again, and as she wrote, she had employed all the craft elements and writing techniques that Jen had been discussing during the preceding weeks. She had internalized the knowledge and found the strength to use that knowledge to share a painful but very meaningful experience.

Here are representative samples of the memoirs that students wrote.

A Sorrowful Good-bye
Andrea W., Grade 7

The phone rang louder than ever as I opened my sleepy eyes. I heard my grandmother's voice that sounded like constant jabbering to me. When she hung up, she walked lethargically back into her room. Even from where I slept, on the floor next to her bed, I knew something was wrong. She blinded me as she clicked on the lamp above me.

"Get up. It's happened." She spoke quickly and quietly in Chinese. I wanted to ask what had happened, but I knew it would have been a foolish question. Somehow, some way, I already knew she was gone. My mother was really gone.

She had fought leukemia for most of her life. Every time there was a breakdown in her system she mended herself with strength and luck.

I dressed silently and gravely. Everything felt numb as I walked out to the car. It was four in the morning and the drive to the hospital was endless. There weren't any sympathetic words exchanged between my grandmother and me. We were lost in our own painful thoughts. The blanket of silence wrapped around us and it felt so cold I couldn't stop shivering.

When the car finally came to a halt, I didn't want to get out. I never liked the hospital. To see all the people within the hospital who were harmed in some way hurt me, too. I pressed my nose gently against the window of the car. It was still dark outside and all I could see was the hazy outline of Presbyterian Hospital.

"Ai ya! Come on!" my grandmother hissed exasperatedly at me. "Do you not want to see your mother?"

At that moment, I wasn't sure if I did. I was scared to see what my mother would look like. People told me that death was like sleeping for a very long time, but I wasn't dumb. I knew that death was when you don't move, you don't breathe, and you'll never wake up. It's *nothing* like sleep.

My footsteps echoed loudly throughout the corridors of the medical center. The nurses that worked the late-night shift looked weary and had dark circles under their eyes. Still they walked in a brisk pace, going from room to room.

My father and brother came out to meet us with grim faces. I felt tears cloud my vision, but I refused to let it all out before even confronting my beloved mother. My brother saw how uncomfortable I was. He put his hand upon my head and gave me a small but reassuring smile. I tried to give him one back, but failed.

A doctor and his nurse stood outside my mother's room. From a distance, the nurse leaned over to the doctor and murmured something. The doctor nodded in response. At that point, I was pretty sure she had said, "Poor girl." I clenched my hands into tight fists. I wanted to scream that I wasn't poor and my mother would live forever, but I would have just been kidding myself. I walked past them in silent anger.

The moment I stepped into the room, an eerie silence took place. It was as if my whole surrounding had changed. The room was dimmed and my three tired and grief-stricken uncles sat alongside of my mom. One held a string of beads and prayed softly.

My father pushed me a little from behind.

"Say your farewells," he instructed meekly. I proceeded forward and stopped when I stood next to the bed where my mom seemed to lie so peacefully. She had always eluded the grasp of death. Her fight was long and hard but in the end, she wasn't the victor.

My eyes were transfixed on her and I hesitated slightly as I took her hand in mine. No longer could I feel her gentle grip of comfort. Now I was hoping she could feel mine. It was then I felt how badly my heart was hurting. My tears slid down my face and I didn't think that they would ever stop flowing. My eyes fell on the oxygen mask that cradled her delicate head.

"Why won't it work?" I yelled silently to myself. I remembered my father telling me that the words I spoke then, she would take to heaven with her. I slowly set my head down next to hers. Shutting my eyes, I whimpered a little. I gave her hand a reassuring squeeze and managed to whisper, "I love you so much, Mommy."

After my good-bye, a nurse led me to a room with toys scattered all over the floor. I sat down and picked up a plastic cube. I put pressure onto it, and let out air softly. As I let go, it sucked the air back in. Like breathing. Something I wished my mother could do again.

My father came in the room with red swollen eyes. I had never seen my father cry and it twisted my heart to see him do so. I couldn't take any more. I leapt up running to him and just let all the pain, the anger, come together and burst. I tried to muffle my sobs but the pain didn't muffle at all. I wanted the nightmare to stop. It didn't take me long to realize that it wasn't a horrible dream at all.

The Jumps
Casey M., Grade 7

The bike jumps in the canyon were so huge my cousin Blake and I couldn't even see over them. I would never be able to make this, I thought as I gazed upward. They were bigger than any jump I'd ever seen.

Blake said, "Wanna try them or do you wanna go home?"

I took a deep breath and answered, "I'll go first."

I went up the hill a little distance so I could get some speed. I zoomed down the hill. When I hit the jump I launched up into the air. It felt like being on top of the Empire State Building. I thought I was going to make it, but instead I crashed like a rock being thrown off a roof and smacking the ground.

At first I thought my leg was broken. I couldn't believe I was able to get up after that fall. This jump was like a monster trying to scare me away, but I refused to let it scare me.

"We're not leaving until one of us makes it," I told Blake as I got up.

"Not unless it gets too late," Blake mumbled.

"I know one of us will make it before we have to leave," I answered back.

Next Blake tried the jump. He launched off the jump like he was being shot out of a cannon. I thought he was going to make it but instead his front tire hit the beginning of the landing. He hit so hard that he flew over his handlebars and SMACK! Face first into the dirt.

"Oh, man that oughta hurt," I howled as he crashed.

He just lay there, so I ran up to him and asked, "You all right?"

"Yeah, I'm fine," he answered. "That try was awful though."

"At least you got closer than I did," I replied.

"Are you sure you don't wanna go home?" Blake asked.

"No," I answered simply.

I tried the jump again. My nervous energy made my hands all sweaty. Right then my handlebars slipped out of my hands, so I jumped off and landed on my knees.

"Lucky me," I groaned.

"Watch out!" Blake screamed.

I looked back and right then I saw my bike tumbling right behind me. I screamed and ducked. The bike bounced right over me. I just lay there for a moment, stunned.

"The monster hill is out to get you," Blake laughed as he ran over.

"Man! I would've had that if I didn't lose the handlebars!" I exclaimed. Now this hill was making me mad.

Blake was still hurt from his first try, but I was not ready to give up. This time I thought I had it so I held on. I was almost there . . . and then the bike started leaning to the side and BAM! I crashed.

Blake laughed hysterically. "You look like a squashed bug," he called, making fun of how I looked on the ground. "Why are you still trying? Let's go."

"Shut up and help me get untangled," I grumbled.

After all those tries I was bruised and cut up from head to toe. It was getting late. There was time for only one more try.

I started rolling on my bike down the hill with my heart pounding in my ears. I launched. Once I was in the air I knew that I was going to make it. My handlebars were straight and I was in control. I had so much air I felt like I was Superman—I was flying! I hung there for what seemed like forever. And then I was down. My front tire hit first and then my back came down. I finally had my perfect landing!

I was screaming, shouting. I was exhilarated! My body was covered with bumps and bruises but none of that mattered. I had made it. I made the jump!

As we left, I looked back over my shoulder. The jump was no longer a monster. Now it was just a big hill.

Suggested Texts

In recent years it has become very popular to publish one's memoirs. This trend has resulted in some fascinating books and some not so fascinating ones. Fortunately for teachers and students in the secondary classroom, many outstanding children's and young adult book authors have published their own memoirs, providing us with rich material for a study of the genre. The following books are among Jen's and my favorites. However, don't limit yourself; pull together as many memoir texts as you can find so that both you and your students have access to plenty of authors and subjects. One word of caution: Depending on the age of your students, you may want to be careful with the content of adult-level reading texts.

Memoirs

Picture Books

Aliki, *Christmas Tree Memories*

Barbara Cooney, *Miss Rumphius*

Lauren Mills, *The Rag Coat*

Patricia Polacco, *My Rotten Redheaded Older Brother; Thunder Cake; Uncle Vova's Tree*

Allen Say, *Grandfather's Journey*

James Stevenson, *When I Was Nine*

Grades 3–6

Alma Flor Ada, *Under the Royal Palms: A Childhood in Cuba*

Aliki, *Christmas Tree Memories*

Beverly Cleary, *A Girl from Yamhill*

Barbara Cooney, *Miss Rumphius*

Tomie de Paola, *26 Fairmount Avenue; Here We All Are; On My Way*

Amy Ehrlich, ed., *When I Was Your Age: Original Stories About Growing Up* (2 vols)

Jean Fritz, *Homesick: My Own Story*

Lauren Mills, *The Rag Coat*

Gary Paulsen, *Guts; Harris and Me; My Life in Dog Years; Woodsong*

Patricia Polacco, *My Rotten Redheaded Older Brother; Thunder Cake; Uncle Vova's Tree*

Allen Say, *Grandfather's Journey*

Gary Soto, *Living Up the Street; A Summer Life*

Jerry Spinelli, *Knots in My Yo-Yo String*

James Stevenson, *When I Was Nine*

Stanley "Tookie" Williams, *Life in Prison* (mature content)

Grades 6–10 (Young Adult)

Roald Dahl, *Boy: Tales of Childhood; Going Solo*

Amy Ehrlich, ed., *When I Was Your Age: Original Stories About Growing Up* (2 vols)

Sid Fleischman, *The Abracadabra Kid: A Writer's Life*

Mary Frosch, ed., *Coming of Age in America: A Multicultural Anthology*

Frank Gilbreth, Jr., and Ernestine Gilbreth Carey, *Belles on Their Toes; Cheaper by the Dozen*
Francisco Jimenez, *The Circuit*
Anita Lobel, *No Pretty Pictures: A Child of War*
Adeline Yen Mah, *Chinese Cinderella: The True Story of an Unwanted Daughter*
Walter Dean Myers, *Bad Boy: A Memoir*
Gary Paulsen, *Guts; Harris and Me; My Life in Dog Years; Woodsong*
Johanna Reiss, *The Upstairs Room*
Sara Shandler, *Ophelia Speaks: Adolescent Girls Write About Their Search for Self*
Gary Soto, *Living Up the Street; A Summer Life*
Yoshiko Uchida, *The Invisible Thread: An Autobiography*
Laurence Yep, *The Lost Garden*

Grades 10+ (Adult)
Maya Angelou, *I Know Why the Caged Bird Sings*
Jean-Dominique Bauby, *The Diving Bell and the Butterfly*
David Faber, *Because of Romek: A Holocaust Survivor's Memoir*

The following texts approximate memoirs; they are fictional accounts written as if they were true memoirs. While purists may want to use only true memoir texts, we found that these texts were very helpful and that students were able to understand the differences and use the fictionalized memoirs appropriately.

Grades 3–6
Paul Fleischman, *Seedfolks*

Grades 6–10 (Young Adult)
Sandra Cisneros, *The House on Mango Street*

These texts are not memoirs, but they are a great help to students writing memoirs:

Grades 6–10 (Young Adult)
Melvin Burgess, *Billy Elliot*
Ralph Fletcher, *A Writer's Notebook: Unlocking the Writer Within You*
Lois Lowry, *Looking Back: A Book of Memories*
William Zinsser, ed., *Inventing the Truth: The Art and Craft of Memoir*

Grades 10+ (Adult)
William Zinsser, "Writing About Yourself: The Memoir," ch. 14 in *On Writing Well*

CHAPTER 3

Feature Article

From "Death of an Innocent: How Christopher
McCandless Lost His Way in the Wilds"

Jon Krakauer

*James Gallien had driven five miles out of Fairbanks when he spotted the hitchhiker
standing in the snow beside the road, thumb raised high, shivering in the gray Alaskan
dawn. A rifle protruded from the young man's pack, but he looked friendly enough; a
hitchhiker with a Remington semiautomatic isn't the sort of thing that gives motorists
pause in the 49th state. Gallien steered his four-by-four onto the shoulder and told him
to climb in.*

*The hitchhiker introduced himself as Alex. "Alex?" Gallien responded, fishing for
a last name.*

*"Just Alex," the young man replied, pointedly rejecting the bait. He explained that
he wanted a ride as far as the edge of Denali National Park, where he intended to walk
deep into the bush and "live off the land for a few months." Alex's backpack appeared to
weigh only 25 to 30 pounds, which struck Gallien, an accomplished outdoorsman, as
an improbably light load for a three-month sojourn in the backcountry, especially so
early in the spring. Immediately Gallien began to wonder if he'd picked up one of those
crackpots from the Lower 48 who come north to live out their ill-considered Jack London
fantasies. Alaska had long been a magnet for unbalanced souls, often outfitted with
little more than innocence and desire, who hope to find their footing in the unsullied
enormity of the Last Frontier. The bush, however, is a harsh place and cares nothing for
hope or longing. More than a few such dreamers have met predictably unpleasant ends.*

*As they got to talking during the three-hour drive, though, Alex didn't strike
Gallien as your typical misfit. He was congenial, seemed well educated, and peppered
Gallien with sensible questions about "what kind of small game lived in the country,
what kind of berries he could eat, that kind of thing."*

Still, Gallien was concerned: Alex's gear seemed excessively slight for the rugged conditions of the interior bush, which in April still lay buried under the winter snowpack. He admitted that the only food in his pack was a ten-pound bag of rice. He had no compass; the only navigational aid in his possession was a tattered road map he'd scrounged at a gas station, and when they arrived where Alex asked to be dropped off, he left the map in Gallien's truck, along with his watch, his comb, and all his money, which amounted to 85 cents. "I don't want to know what time it is," Alex declared cheerfully. "I don't want to know what day it is, or where I am. None of that matters."

During the drive south toward the mountains, Gallien had tried repeatedly to dissuade Alex from his plan, to no avail. He even offered to drive Alex all the way to Anchorage so he could at least buy the kid some decent gear. "No, thanks anyway," Alex replied. "I'll be fine with what I've got." When Gallien asked whether his parents or some friend knew what he was up to—anyone who could sound the alarm if he got into trouble and was overdue—Alex answered calmly that, no, nobody knew of his plans, that in fact he hadn't spoken to his family in nearly three years. "I'm absolutely positive," he assured Gallien, "I won't run into anything I can't deal with on my own."

"There was just no talking the guy out of it," Gallien recalls. "He was determined. He couldn't wait to head out there and get started." So Gallien drove Alex to the head of the Stampede Trail, an old mining track that begins ten miles west of the town of Healy, convinced him to accept a tuna melt and a pair of rubber boots to keep his feet dry, and wished him good luck. Alex pulled a camera from his backpack and asked Gallien to snap a picture of him. Then, smiling broadly, he disappeared down the snow-covered trail. The date was Tuesday, April 28, 1992.

More than four months passed before Gallien heard anything more of the hitch-hiker. His real name turned out to be Christopher J. McCandless. He was the product of a happy family from an affluent suburb of Washington, D.C. And although he wasn't burdened with a surfeit of common sense and possessed a streak of stubborn idealism that did not readily mesh with the realities of modern life, he was no psychopath. McCandless was in fact an honors graduate of Emory University, an accomplished athlete, and a veteran of several solo excursions into wild, inhospitable terrain.

An extremely intense young man, McCandless had been captivated by the writing of Leo Tolstoy. He particularly admired the fact that the great novelist had forsaken a life of wealth and privilege to wander among the destitute. For several years he had been emulating the count's asceticism and moral rigor to a degree that astonished and occasionally alarmed those who knew him well. When he took leave of James Gallien, McCandless entertained no illusions that he was trekking into Club Med; peril, adversity, and Tolstoyan renunciation were what he was seeking. And that's precisely what he found on the Stampede Trail, in spades.

For most of 16 weeks McCandless more than held his own. Indeed, were it not for one or two innocent and seemingly insignificant blunders he would have walked out of the Alaskan woods in July or August as anonymously as he walked into them in April. Instead, the name of Chris McCandless has become the stuff of tabloid headlines, and his bewildered family is left clutching the shards of a fierce and painful love.

———◄◊►———

So I don't get it, am I supposed to feel sorry for the guy?" Carolyn Sommer looked at me with frustration. She and I had sat down with this article during spring break as we met to plan for a nonfiction feature article study with her students. "I mean, here's a young man who, from the sounds of it, has everything going for him and he walks into the woods, and dies. What a waste!"

I couldn't help but agree. It was a waste. But there was a reason that I had dragged out this article. It is a decade old now, but Krakauer's account of McCandless's life and death continues to have a grip on me. This haunting story of a young man who gave up everything to pursue an ideal that benefited absolutely no one is perplexing and troubling. A former young idealist myself, it makes me question my own pursuit of idealistic objectives; as a teacher of young people it disturbs me; as a mother of two young sons, it scares the heck out of me. But more than anything else, it makes me think.

Despite Carolyn's initial frustration, it was clear as we discussed the article that "Death of an Innocent" made her think as well. We talked about the fine line between brilliance and craziness, between idealism and obsession. We discussed the difficulty of following one's ideals in our society and the ridicule that individuals who choose to do so often face. Where was McCandless in this balance? Should he be admired or admonished? Krakauer's article opens the door for these questions but leaves the answers unclear. He presents a portrait of a complex young man. He tells of the hurt that McCandless caused but also the friendship that he easily engendered among those he met. He describes McCandless's search to find his way in terms that anyone who has been through adolescence and young adulthood can relate to. The article becomes about more than just one young man; it becomes a query into our own understanding of our individual relationship with the world around us.

As our coffee grew cold and our time ran out, Carolyn pushed back from the table and sighed. "You know, if that had been a simple, straightforward newspaper article that just told the facts I probably could have dismissed it fairly easily. I could have simply chosen to believe that McCandless was a crazy person who had no relation to my reality at all. But Krakauer doesn't allow me that comfort. He's taken those facts and shown me the story behind them. He's humanized McCandless. And now I'm not going to be able to forget the story either."

Thinking Through the Genre

Good nonfiction shouldn't let readers forget. It should capture readers' fascination and spark within them an intense desire to learn, not just about interesting people and places, but about ideas and perspectives. This is what a feature article is all about. Feature articles and similarly styled nonfiction texts take information about people, places, events, or phenomena in the world and seek to explain it. And, as readers, it is this explanation that we crave. We now live in a society where multiple twenty-four-hour news stations and Web sites constantly update us about the latest events. The Internet gives us instant access to an almost unlimited supply of facts on every imaginable topic. But despite this, magazines like *Newsweek, Time, National Geographic, People, Smithsonian, Vanity Fair, Esquire, Atlantic Monthly,* and *Rolling Stone* continue to thrive. Why? Because we like to have the facts explained to us; we want to learn from other people's perspectives and appreciate their insights.

Tracy Kidder wrote a best-selling book entitled *House*. The entire text is essentially a collection of feature article–style essays about the aspects of building a house. To most of us, the idea of reading several pages about the creation of a wooden plank would seem remarkably boring. However, Kidder's gifted style and unique understanding of the wood and its significance hold readers spellbound. What Kidder offers is not really the wood or the paint of the house itself, but his own transparent presence. Zinsser (1998) writes,

> Ultimately, the product that any writer has to sell is not the subject being written about, but who he or she is. I often find myself reading with interest about a topic I never thought would interest me—some scientific quest, perhaps. What holds me is the enthusiasm of the writer for the field. . . . This is the personal transaction that's at the heart of good nonfiction writing.

Introducing a feature article study into the classroom provides students with the opportunity to understand the fascination that can be found in reading and the enthusiasm that can be communicated through writing great nonfiction. Too often the nonfiction that students encounter in the classroom is driven by facts, not ideas. This is unfortunate, because it limits appreciation for both the text and the subject. Most of us would balk at reading an entry about the Civil War from a U.S. history textbook—too dry, too filled with boring facts, too bossy. I don't want a committee-designed textbook telling me "everything I need to know in five easy lessons." But an article about counterespionage efforts by the Confederate army or about sunken Union warships would fascinate me. These articles examine the same time period but offer a more specialized focus. They don't try to be authoritative; instead, they put forth a unique perspective that readers have the opportunity to assimilate into their own understanding of the War Between the States. Yes, such texts do offer facts, but they also encourage thought, raise questions, and inspire interest in the topic. These are the texts that we need to put in front of students.

As a teacher, I want my students to understand that the world is not just about facts, it is truly about ideas—individual understandings of how facts are put together based on one's own experience and knowledge. I want them to know that they have the power, as readers, to interact with a nonfiction text, to do more than simply dig for facts. Students need to be able to see the ideas in texts, to understand the author's perspective or bias, and to connect the understanding of the author with their own outlook on the world. Reading feature articles in the classroom provides students with an outstanding opportunity to achieve these goals.

Teaching students to write feature articles presents them with a vehicle through which to communicate their own unique understanding of the world. Too often students feel that the "experts" are much more learned and far away. Teaching them to write a feature article empowers them to recognize that their voices have power, that their perspectives are valid and important. It supports recognition of the fact that the world beyond their immediate community may be different and that what seems commonplace to them may be a revelation to a potential audience. This understanding, in turn, encourages more thoughtful observation of the writer's own environment. Writers of feature articles learn to find fascination in the commonplace as well as the remarkable. They learn to pursue that fascination to uncover new worlds of understanding. Lucy Calkins (1994) explains, "Living like a nonfiction writer, then, means watching for surprise and perplexity and mystery. It means knowing that even the subjects we know very well can be endlessly new to us."

Furthermore, teaching students to share their understanding of the world with others through the genre of a feature article ensures that they will articulate their ideas in a thoughtful and rigorous format. Feature articles require research, analysis, synthesis, organization, and good, strong writing. This is not simply a "put the facts in the right box" report; this is literary journalism. Writers of feature articles need to be aware of their craft and their voice. They are writing to share their own understanding with an audience, and as such, the manner in which they write matters.

Envisioning the Unit

Put simply, Carolyn's students didn't like nonfiction. These were fifth- and sixth-grade students at Wilson Academy, a school located in one of San Diego's poorer neighborhoods. In general, they were a good group. The class had been identified as high-achieving; most students read two to three grade levels above expectations;

they engaged in wonderful discussions; and they had a great relationship with their teacher. But all of that changed when the fiction books were set aside. Suddenly, the students went from being happy and engaged to being grumpy, reluctant readers.

This transformation is not unusual. It comes from the belief that nonfiction texts are all boring. It is the fear of having to write a report or research paper—dull, scary assignments that students hate to write and teachers hate to read. And it comes from loss of confidence. Most students' comfort zone is with fiction; it is what they are familiar with and consequently what is easiest to read. Nonfiction offers a different structure and style, and for many it is intimidating.

Carolyn understood her students' reluctance to read and write nonfiction, but wisely she decided to forge ahead. She knew that her "babies" would soon be entering the big, bad world of middle school. In history or science class, they would be expected to read and respond to expository text. They could groan all they wanted, but this was a reality they wouldn't be able to avoid. Furthermore, Carolyn knew that as adults her students would absolutely need to be able to read and write nonfiction texts; this is a prerequisite for success in our information-driven society.

As Carolyn and I worked together to plan a nonfiction study, we decided to focus primarily on feature articles. The articles are short and engaging, and pictures, illustrations, and a wonderful variety of topics would help to pique students' interest. The style of text would allow us to push students beyond the "scan-and-dip" style of reading that had previously characterized their interactions with nonfiction (Calkins 2001). Thoughtful, idea-driven feature articles would provide the opportunity for students to see, understand, and respond to the ideas inherent in nonfiction text. Furthermore, the unique and at times quirky variety of topics appropriate for feature articles would ensure that every student would be able to write as an expert about something important to them. This would move students away from the perception that writing nonfiction necessarily means hours and hours of book research that results in putting the correct facts in the correct boxes. Instead students would be pushed to recognize their unique understanding of familiar people, places, events, and phenomena, and then share that perspective with others using appropriate writing structures and processes. Through a study of reading and writing feature articles, Carolyn and I hoped to capture students' interest, not only in the genre but in exploring and thinking deeply about the world around them.

Teaching the Unit—Reading Workshop

We began the study by filling the classroom with the sight and sounds of feature articles. Carolyn filled baskets with current and back issues of *National Geographic*

Reading Workshop—Feature Article
Goals and Instructional Focus Progression

	Reading Comprehension Study	Accountable Talk Study
	Goal: Students will learn to read and understand feature articles. They will recognize the ideas in text and understand the relationship between information and ideas.	**Goal:** Students will learn to share nonfiction articles with peers through informal discussion and formal presentation.
Weeks 1–2	**"Reading" Text Features** Students will learn to use titles, photos, section headings, illustrations, captions, etc. to gather relevant information before reading the text. • What do you see on the page? • What information can you learn from the features? • How do you think this information might help you as you read the article? **Predicting the "Big Idea"** Students will synthesize prereading information into a larger understanding, or "big idea," that will guide their reading. • Why do you think the author or editor chose to include these features and this information? • What do you think the author wants you to understand about this topic? • What can you expect as you read the article?	**Developing Appropriate Attitudes and Behaviors for Peer Talk** Students will learn what is appropriate to say and do when discussing nonfiction text with a peer. **Discussing an Article** Students will learn to effectively discuss nonfiction articles with peers in order to better understand a common text. • What is your understanding of the article? What is your partner's understanding? • How are your ideas the same? different? • Does evidence from the text support both of these ideas? If not, why not? • Can your ideas be synthesized into a larger understanding?
Weeks 3–4	**Developing Your "Big Idea" as You Read** Students will use their "big idea" as they read, continuously developing and expanding their understanding in response to new information and ideas. • Stop and think. What new information have you learned? • How does this new information fit with what you already knew? • How does this new information change your understanding of the text? What's the "big idea" now? **Outlining the Ideas and Information in Text** Students will learn to thoughtfully organize the ideas and information in text in order to better understand the article. • What are the most important pieces of information within each section of text? • What is the main idea of each section? • How do the section ideas fit together? What is the "big idea" of the article overall?	**Presenting an Article** Students will learn to prepare and present an independently read article to peers. • What are the most important information and ideas to share? • How can information and ideas be organized to make things clear for your listeners? • How should you begin your presentation? • How can you adjust your presentation to suit your audience? • How should you conclude your presentation?
Weeks 5–6	**Responding to an Article** Students will learn to respond appropriately to the ideas and information in nonfiction feature articles. • How do the ideas and information in this article connect to what you already know? • Do you have questions or concerns about the ideas or information explored in the article? • Do you think that the author treated this issue appropriately? Was he or she biased in the presentation of information? Explain. **Evaluating Reading Progress—Self-Reflection and Teacher Evaluation**	**Responding to a Peer Presentation** Students will learn to listen and respond appropriately to a peer presentation. • What do you learn from the presentation? • What questions do you have? about the article? about the presentation? • What did the speaker do well? • What would you suggest he/she do differently during future presentations? **Evaluating Peer Presentations—Self-, Class, and Teacher Evaluation**

Explorer, Time for Kids, World Magazine, Ranger Rick, Scientific American Explorations, Muse, Sports Illustrated for Kids, and *Discovery Girls.* She pulled particularly engaging articles out, stapled them to bulletin boards, and hung them from a clothesline. In addition, she began to read nonfiction aloud. Choosing carefully, she would begin each morning with a funny, scary, or disgusting article about shark attacks, human anatomy, or beauty queens. These articles not only helped to build student interest but helped students' ears become familiar with the sounds and structures of nonfiction. Lucy Calkins refers to this as developing students' "internal containers."

Read-alouds and a classroom filled with great texts provided a wonderful start. It got students to the table. They loved listening to and talking about each day's read-aloud article. They loved looking at the magazines. But they still weren't reading the articles. Instead they were flipping from page to page, admiring the pictures and perhaps vaguely skimming the captions. A few students would try their hand at the text, but even these adventurous souls didn't manage to get very far. After observing this behavior for a couple of days, Carolyn called me, concerned. "I thought for sure that students would be able to read these magazines. I know that the vocabulary is not too hard, but they just don't seem to be able to sustain an interest. Many don't understand what the content is about. They don't have the background knowledge to be able to read and understand the text. I don't know, maybe this study is too hard."

Carolyn was right. Her students had neither the content knowledge nor the strategy tools for accessing most nonfiction articles yet. But this didn't mean that the texts were too hard or that she should give up. It meant that we needed to teach students how to scaffold nonfiction articles for themselves. Scaffolding is something that we often talk about doing for students; science and history teachers spend hours and hours developing creative ways to scaffold textbooks so that students can access them. But ultimately our goal should be to provide students with the tools so that they can scaffold texts for themselves, to help them build a content and structural knowledge to be able to read a wide range of nonfiction articles.

We decided to begin by focusing on background knowledge. Given the wide range of student interests and article focuses in the classroom, there was no way that we could introduce students to every topic. But we could teach them to use the features on the page to build an understanding of the content before they even began reading the text. Titles, pictures, captions, fact boxes, section headings, and so on reveal a lot about an article. Good readers use that information to develop content expectations that guide their reading of the text itself. The following lesson demonstrates Carolyn's introduction to the use of text features.

SAMPLE LESSON:	Week 1—Reading Workshop

AREA OF STUDY:	**Reading comprehension**
FOCUS:	**"Reading" text features**
TEXT:	**"Paid to Play Games," by Robert Sullivan, from *Time for Kids***
RESPONSE:	**Gathering information from text features and recording findings on Post-it notes**

Carolyn gathered her students on the rug. They each sat in their own chair with a highlighter, pen, stack of Post-it notes, and a copy of the most recent *Time for Kids* magazine in their laps. "So, how are feature articles going?" Carolyn asked. After a few minutes for responses, Carolyn added her own observations to the conversation: "As I've been working with you while you are reading, I've noticed some really good things and some not so good things. One thing you are all doing that I think is fantastic is you are looking at the pictures in the magazines. Some of you may think that this is just fluff and not really part of reading, but you'd be wrong. Good nonfiction readers look at pictures all the time. But, I've noticed that many of you aren't getting all the information you can out of the pictures and the other features. That's a problem because good readers don't just look at the pictures, they 'read' them, trying to learn all the information they can from each picture. You can also read captions, titles, maps, graphs, anything that the author or editor put on the page to support the text itself. And then you can use all that information to help you read and understand the article."

Students opened their copies of *Time for Kids* to the center article, "Paid to Play Games." This two-page article discussed the astronomically high salaries of professional athletes and compared the salaries of Shaq and Alex Rodriguez to those of teachers and the president. We had chosen it to use today because it contained a rich variety of text features, everything from digitally altered photos to bold statistics to an eye-catching border at the top of the page. "Tell me," Carolyn began, "what features do you see on the page?" For now the names of the features didn't matter (this would come much later in writing workshop when students were working on publishing their own articles); what was important was that students *notice* the features. Too often, young readers have been trained away from looking at the features, told to skip right to the text, and frequently students won't even see the features on the page. "A picture of Shaq," one student shouted. "A piggy bank," said another. As students described what they saw, Carolyn highlighted the features themselves on the transparency of the article that she had placed on the overhead; she encouraged students to do the same in their magazines. Gradually, with a few well-phrased questions ("What about around the outside of the text? Notice anything?"), students were able to notice all the features on the page.

"Okay," Carolyn said, "now let's go back and 'read' these features more carefully. What information can we get from each of them?" Faces that had become relaxed and open took on a blank look. Many felt they had just "read" the features. "It's a picture of Shaq, what more do you want to know?" one student asked. "Well, if I were 'reading' that picture," Carolyn modeled, "I would see that Shaq (and I know that's his name because it says so in the caption) is wearing a basketball uniform, but he's not holding a basketball, he's holding a coin. And the way the picture is placed makes it look like he is tossing the coin into a piggy bank. I also notice that the coin Shaq is holding is a one-dollar coin, the largest denomination of coin that exists. All of that suggests to me that Shaq is a basketball player who is paid a large amount of money to play a game, and that he is able to deposit that money into his own bank account." Carolyn recorded some of her observations on a transparent "Post-it" (also known as a cut-up transparency and a bit of tape) and placed it on the appropriate feature on the overhead. Understanding dawned and hands began to go up. Together the class went through the rest of the article, reading the features and recording their observations on Post-it notes.

Before she sent students off to practice reading features independently, Carolyn made sure they understood the purpose of the strategy: "Look at all the information we have gathered. How is all that going to help me once I start to read the text of the article?" One student volunteered, "You already know some of what you are going to read." "You know what the article is about," explained another. "You can connect what you read to the pictures and headings." All true. We would need to push the point further at a later date, but for today the students understood their task and the reasons behind it.

Carolyn equipped students with Post-it notes and sent them off to read the text features in articles of their own choosing. She and I circulated, pointing out additional inferences that could be drawn from a photo or title and encouraging students in their work. Most understood their task well and were able to come up with some great insights into the text based solely on the features. Despite the fact that students were "just" looking at the features, many spent perceptibly more time with each article on this day than they had on previous days, when it was expected that they would be reading the whole thing. Of course, a few students did read the text itself after completing their prereading activity (which was fine; we had not forbidden it, just not encouraged it). Several explained that it was hard to resist after they'd gotten interested in the article from their work with the pictures and titles; they wanted to find out more. My favorite comment came from Angelica, a bright little girl who had remained sulkily silent throughout Carolyn's mini-lesson: "At first I thought this was really stupid. I mean, it's so obvious. But once I started reading the features I found other stuff that I hadn't noticed at first.

And then when I read the article, it was easier to understand. Maybe it's not such a stupid idea after all." High praise from a sulky sixth-grader.

◄◉►

It took several days of practice for students to become truly adept at using text features to gather information. Carolyn found herself teaching lessons about charts, graphs, and maps—graphics found frequently in feature articles that were not familiar to all students. But over time students became more comfortable recognizing and using features. They began to point out similarities across texts, patterns found in certain publications, and occasional inconsistencies between the work of authors and that of the copy editors who put together the page layout. An additional finding that was noticed by a couple of the students was the use of puns in titles. Double meanings, alliteration, homonyms, and puns were frequently used to engage the audience and support the ideas of the article. For most students, however, this word play went right over their heads. Although understanding the word play in nonfiction articles is not absolutely crucial to understanding the text, it does make the text more enjoyable and supports language development as well. Consequently, Carolyn and I decided to teach a lesson about this aspect of feature articles.

SAMPLE LESSON: ## Week 2—Reading Workshop

AREA OF STUDY:	**Word study**
FOCUS:	**Recognizing and understanding the word play in titles**
TEXT:	**Various**
RESPONSE:	**Identifying word plays in previously read articles**

On chart paper at the front of the room, Carolyn had listed several titles taken from magazine articles that students had not previously seen. "Going the Distance," "A Head Start," "It's About Time," "The Heat Is On," "The Mane Attraction." Each of these titles had double (or in some cases, triple) meanings related to the article it headlined. Students did not have the articles in front of them. Carolyn knew from experience that photos and captions caused students to see only one aspect of a title; by taking away that context, she wanted them to see additional possibilities.

"You have become awesome feature readers," Carolyn said. "And you know that titles and subtitles are a great way to get information before reading. So, we have some titles up here, and without your seeing the article, I want you to tell me what the article will be about." Heads nodded in agreement; these kids were confident in their abilities. "So, what do you think an article titled 'Going the

Distance' will be about?" Student response was immediate: "Going someplace far away, like maybe Alaska or Antarctica." "Working hard on something for a long time . . . what's that word? . . . perseverance." "I think of distance as about racing, so maybe it's about a marathon or something." "But, it's gotta be about going, too. Maybe going a long way to run a marathon?" Carolyn recorded their responses on the chart paper and then revealed the article from which the title had come. It was a story about international athletes who come to the United States to compete. It profiled Martina Navratilova, Manute Bol, and Mark Plaatjes, describing their decisions to leave poverty or oppressive governments to pursue opportunity despite meeting some difficulties in the United States. Carolyn talked a bit about the article and then asked, "So, who was right about the meaning of the title?" "I was!" was the immediate response from five different directions. Carolyn let the students debate their own correctness for a few minutes before interrupting, "Yes, you were all right. The article is about traveling a long distance, and it is about perseverance, and it is about running or other types of athletics. That is the point. Authors often use titles with multiple meanings to get readers thinking and draw them into the ideas of the text. Let's try some more."

This felt like a game, and students delighted in challenging one another to discover additional meanings of titles. They worked through Carolyn's list of titles, sharing their ideas first with a partner and then with the whole class before briefly viewing the articles to see if their ideas fit. Title interpretations became more and more creative. Some suggestions were way out of the ballpark, but students also came up with ideas that Carolyn and I had not considered but that added a whole new dimension to understanding the article. Once it was clear that students understood expectations, Carolyn sent them on a hunt. "Go back to some of the articles that you have already explored. Take a look at the titles, and see if you can catch any word play. If you find multiple meanings, highlight that title and write the possible meanings down on a Post-it."

For some students, the Post-its flew onto the page; they were able to immediately recognize multiple meanings. Others stared at titles for a long time before recognizing the word play. A few referred to dictionaries, and most compared notes with a friend, alternately competing and collaborating. For a small number, divorcing their title interpretation from the pictures on the page seemed nearly impossible; they couldn't find more than one meaning because their mind immediately went to the obvious and then shut off. Carolyn matched these students with a partner and encouraged them to read titles to one another, holding the magazine so that the listener couldn't see the article. This roughly simulated the mini-lesson and encouraged struggling students to stretch their minds beyond the obvious.

By the time Carolyn called students back together to share their findings, everyone was bursting with title ideas. They shared intentional misspellings, rhymes, oxymorons, and word repetitions. Some had found three, four, or five different interpretations of titles. A few had extended their search to subheadings and captions. Perhaps more important, students also found a purpose in their search. In response to Carolyn's standard, "What did you discover today?" students commented, "Words can mean different things, depending on how you use them," "Authors sometimes try to trick you to make you think," "You can't just look at something and think you're done; you have to really think about it," and, my favorite, "Looking at feature articles can be fun."

The fun with word play lasted throughout the study. Students were challenged to add new findings to the class "Tricky Titles" board (with friendly competition quickly developing to add the most or the most original tricky titles), and especially intriguing titles served as whole-class brainteasers. These activities very much encouraged students to pay close attention to language, not only in feature articles but in other aspects of their lives as well. Students contributed "tricky titles" from history texts, science articles, their parents' newspapers, and even their favorite Internet chat rooms.

———◦———

From the first days of the study, Carolyn had been laying the groundwork to encourage students to think about feature articles in terms of ideas. Rarely did she ask students about cool facts or interesting information in their reading; instead she would query, "What is this article about?" or "What idea is the author communicating?" Simple questions but very hard to answer. Students were not used to thinking about nonfiction text as containing any ideas. Many had been trained to read articles and informational texts for the purpose of picking out facts; they had been taught to break the information down rather than put it together. Over and over again students collected wonderful insights and detailed facts from the features of the text and engaged in lengthy and animated discussions, only to shut down when asked to synthesize their findings. Suddenly their vocabularies were reduced to two- or three-word phrases. "It's about space," they would report, or "The main idea is wild ponies." These abbreviated responses were not ideas, they were just topics, which would provide little help for making sense of the reading itself. After all, an article about "space" could go in any number of directions. It could describe space travel in the future, its possibilities and its risks. It could advance new theories about the origins of the universe. It could compare the fantasies of science fiction writers with the realities of the limits of science. To simply say that the article is about space tells the reader little about what to expect from the article or how to connect the facts and ideas encountered during a reading of the text.

Students needed to see that information necessarily breeds ideas, and that, in the case of feature articles, much of the work of developing an idea or understanding of the information has already been done by an author. Feature article writers have sorted through the available information, organized it, and written about it in such a way that a coherent understanding is developed. As readers, it is our job to recognize that understanding. We need to stop and consider, "How is the author organizing these facts?" "What does he or she want me to understand about this information?" "What's the main idea of this article?"

Carolyn had modeled her own responses to these questions with several articles, and during shared readings students could, with considerable guidance, find the ideas in text. But on their own, they were having tremendous difficulty. After a week without much progress, everyone was getting frustrated. So Carolyn and I decided to try a different approach. Instead of waiting until students had read all or part of an article to ask about the main idea, we decided to use just the information that students could read from the features. This approach would provide a limited but focused set of data. It would eliminate the need for understanding the text, instead allowing students to predict a main idea based on photographs, titles, captions, and charts. Synthesizing this information into a prediction would force students to move beyond their literal interpretation of the text and into the realm of ideas and concepts.

SAMPLE LESSON: ## Week 3—Reading Workshop

AREA OF STUDY:	**Reading comprehension**
FOCUS:	**Predicting the "big idea"**
TEXT:	**"Dancing with Pride," by Steph Smith, from *Scholastic News***
RESPONSE:	**Class chart of "big ideas" for "Dancing with Pride"; individual development of "big ideas" for independently selected articles**

"Today we are *not* going to look for the main idea," Carolyn announced, much to everyone's relief. It was time to reframe students' thinking, and changing the language of the classroom was a part of that goal. "Instead, we are going to think about the facts." The anxiety visibly eased from students' faces. They were good at facts. "I want you to take a look at this article and just think about the features for now. What are the facts that you can see or infer from the features?" Students spent several minutes looking over "Dancing with Pride," an article about two Native American boys and their participation in the dances of their culture. Soon students' papers were filled with notes and highlights, and Carolyn had filled a chart at the front of the room with their observations.

She took a deep breath; here was the make-or-break question: "Now, why do you think the author chose to include these facts with this article? What does she want you to understand?" The students puzzled over the question. They looked at the chart. They looked at their papers. Finally, Victor spoke up: "I think the author wants me to understand that Native Americans have a strong culture." Carolyn and I mentally let out big sighs of relief. "That's a great idea, Victor. Why do you think so?" "Well, because she uses really positive words to describe the culture, like *pride* and *beauty* and *celebrate*. And also the biggest picture on the page is of the two kids dancing in their costumes. So it seems like the culture must be really strong and important."

Victor had got it! Carolyn recorded his response on the chart paper and then encouraged other students to share their ideas. "What else might the author want you to understand?" Responses ranged from "I think the author wants us to understand that Indian kids have to go between two cultures" to "I think the author wants us to understand that Native Americans have a cool dance." All were able to support their ideas with evidence from the text, and no one gave the brief answers that had been typical when we had talked about main ideas in the past. We had found the right question to ask.

After recording a variety of student responses, Carolyn let the students in on a little secret: they had just found the main ideas of the article! The reaction was a mixture of delighted surprise at their success and shocked indignation at having been tricked. "What was different this time?" Carolyn wanted to know. "Your question made me think about it different," Vendric explained. "Before, I was thinking about the topic, but now I'm trying to figure out what the author wants me to know about the topic." "It's like this way you're thinking about the ideas behind the facts, not just the facts themselves," Ashley said. Together the class agreed to rename this kind of thinking. Gone was the term "main idea"; from here on out, students would be looking for the "big idea" and focusing on the question "What does the author want me to understand about this information?"

To cement their understanding and capitalize on their renewed enthusiasm, Carolyn instructed the students to go back to the articles that they had previously examined: "Review your notes, reread the features, and think, 'What does the author want me to understand about this information? What is the big idea?'" Changing the terms of the question dramatically changed the level of student understanding. Certainly, as Carolyn and I roamed the room, we continued to need to nudge a few students in the right direction. But now all were beginning their response with the phrase "I think the author wants me to understand . . . ," and all were completing their response with an idea. At the end of the workshop we called students back together and created a Before-and-After chart to display their learning. Linda then summed up the new attitude of the class with the challenge, "Okay, feature article, bring it on! We're ready for you!"

———◅○▻———

In the days that followed, Carolyn and I built on students' new understanding of the "big idea" concept. We continued to encourage them to develop an initial big idea based only on the text features. Then, as they read the article, they were instructed to pause occasionally to consider the following questions: What new information do I have? How does that new information fit with what I knew before? What is the big idea now? How has it changed? Asking and responding to these questions ("Before I thought that the author wanted me to understand . . . Now I think the author wants me to understand . . .") helped students to synthesize the bits of information in the text, understanding how they fit together and why they were important.

Gradually, we began to introduce longer and more complex articles, replacing articles from *Ranger Rick* and *Scholastic News* with texts from *New York Times Upfront* and *Scientific American Explorations*. These new, meatier texts presented students with a challenge: rather than simply one big idea these texts often contained many. Although still grouped around a single main concept, longer feature articles are typically divided into sections, and each section in the text has a big idea of its own.

To deal with these more sophisticated texts, students needed a more sophisticated approach. Simply pausing occasionally to think, "What's the big idea and how has it changed?" wouldn't provide them with the depth of understanding that these more complex feature articles required. We still wanted students to be able to synthesize a larger understanding, but we needed it to be based on a recognition of the many smaller ideas contained in the article. So we decided to teach students to outline.

Outlining nonfiction feature articles has widespread application. Many history and science teachers encourage their students to outline content readings; study skills classes often teach the technique as an essential study skill. I frequently outlined my own readings during college. Doing so helped me to see the information and ideas through a clearer lens; it helped to crystallize my understanding. Carolyn's students experienced similar learning. After they went through the process of outlining an article, the typical response was "Oh, now I get it!"

However, teaching outlining in the abstract felt somewhat uncomfortable. Yes, there was a long-term learning purpose behind the practice, but we needed a more immediate application. So Carolyn and I turned to talk. Throughout the study students had been sharing ideas with one another informally. That's what you do when you discover a great idea or piece of information, you share. Now we wanted to capitalize on this natural desire to share by making the opportunity more rigorous. Rather than simply "turn to your partner and share," we would require students to formally present articles to one another. Doing so would teach students necessary oral presentation skills and provide them with a great opportunity to use their outlines for an authentic purpose.

SAMPLE LESSON: **Week 4—Reading Workshop**

AREA OF STUDY:	**Accountable talk**
FOCUS:	**Presenting an article**
TEXT:	**"Sudan's Lost Boys Find a Home," by Ritu Upadhyay, from** *Time for Kids*; **various other texts**
RESPONSE:	**Class chart of presentation guidelines; independent text outlines and student-to-student presentations**

Carolyn tacked her outline from the previous day's mini-lesson on the wall:

Ms. Sommer's Outline of "Sudan's Lost Boys Find a Home"

I. The Lost Boys endured tremendous hardships in their struggle to escape war.
   A. Started in 1987.
   B. Families were killed, boys escaped because tending cattle.
   C. Thousands traveled Sudan to Ethiopia, later Ethiopia to Kenya.
   D. Traveling for 10+ years.
II. Coming to America has been a difficult adjustment but will be worthwhile if the education they receive will allow them to someday return home to help their country.
   A. Living in apartments or with families.
   B. All consider school very important.
   C. Older ones work minimum wage jobs.
   D. Adjustment to new culture very hard.

Big Idea: The Lost Boys are an amazingly resilient group, who despite tremendous difficulties retain a remarkably positive attitude and an overwhelming desire to improve their futures and their country's fate.

"You know," Carolyn said, "the first thing I want to do after I read a really interesting article is to share it with someone. But if I just came to you and said, 'There's this really great article about these lost boys from Africa, and they had to travel a really long way, and now they are in the United States, and that's hard, too, but it's cool because they want to go back . . .' you would probably be really confused." Carolyn paused and looked around. Sure enough, there were plenty of confused faces and a few giggles (they were accustomed to Ms. Sommer's acting a bit crazy in order to prove a point).

"When we share an article with someone who hasn't read it," Carolyn continued, "we need to be really organized, and we need to really understand the article. You have been working on outlining articles in order to help make sense of those articles for yourself. But today we are going to put those outlining skills to use in order to present articles to each other. This is the type of thing that professionals do all the time. Doctors, lawyers, pilots, even mechanics need to keep up with the latest advances in their fields, but often there are too many advances and too many articles for everyone to read every article. So they have 'literature reviews,' gatherings where people will present an article that they read to the group so that everyone can understand the important information. Presenting articles to your peers in this classroom will prepare you for when you are a professional someday, and it will be a great opportunity for you to share the articles you've found during our study."

Carolyn turned to the chart revealing her outline of "Sudan's Lost Boys Find a Home." "Yesterday, you helped me create an outline of this article," she said. "Together we thought through each section of the text, considering the main idea of that section and the supporting details. Then we synthesized all of those pieces to reach our understanding of the big idea of the article. Today, I'm going to use these notes in order to clearly present the article. Of course, it would be really boring to just read my notes word for word. When I'm talking to someone, I need to judge by their reaction what they are and aren't understanding and adjust accordingly. If they are obviously really interested, then maybe I'll want to share more details; if they are confused, I might have to rephrase something; or if they look impatient, I may choose only the most important parts to share. But no matter how I choose to adjust things as I speak, having an outline will help me to make things clear. Let me show you."

Carolyn paused for a moment to step into the role of presenter. She gave a short, clear, engaging speech about the ideas presented in the article. As she spoke, she used her finger to point to the notes that she was referring to. Her students were impressed. "You really sound like a professional, Ms. Sommer," Ashley said, "I mean, you could be on TV or something, like an expert!" Carolyn laughed and insisted that her students could do it, too. "But let's think about what 'it' is for a minute," she suggested. "What steps did I take to prepare and present this article?" The class debriefed their teacher's process and, in so doing, created a guide for their own work:

Preparing and Presenting an Article
1. Read and outline the article.
2. Review your notes to prepare.
3. Introduce your article by telling the title and author first.
4. Talk through your outline one piece at a time.
5. Emphasize the ideas. Pause between sections.

6. Use your own words. Don't just read off the outline.
7. Speak slowly and confidently.
8. Look at your audience.
9. Adjust your talk according to your audience's reaction.
10. Conclude by sharing the "big idea."
11. Ask if anyone has any questions.

"Now it is your turn," Carolyn informed the class. Since this was a first try, and since many were still struggling a bit with outlining, Carolyn arranged the activity so that students would have a significant amount of support. She distributed two different articles: an article about cave exploration to half the class and an article about sharks to the other half. Students were instructed to work with a peer who had been assigned the same article as they read, outlined, and prepared their presentation. This opportunity allowed students to get help as they read and outlined the article as well as to practice their presentation on an audience familiar with the subject.

After about thirty minutes of preparation, it was time for the main event. Students were paired with a partner who had read the other article. Carolyn reminded them of the presentation guidelines, made certain that each was seated directly opposite his or her partner, and then set the clock timer for one minute.

Some students raced through their presentations, finishing with plenty of time to spare. Others added many details and didn't make it through the article before the timer went off. We weren't too concerned about time this first day; it would take some practice for students to learn how to adjust their presentations to an appropriate time limit. However, using a timer was a great way to keep students organized and focused.

The timer was reset, and the presentation responsibilities shifted to the other partner. When both had had a chance to share their articles, students debriefed, first with each other and then as a whole class. They shared common difficulties and successes and explained what made listening to a presentation interesting or confusing. Several requested copies of the article they had not read. Nearly all the students agreed that the experience of presenting a text made their own reading more thoughtful. "Before, I would have just read it and thought a little about it and then put it away," Brandon admitted. "But knowing I was going to have to tell someone else about it made me really think about what it all meant and why it was written. Now I'm really gonna remember it."

———◄○►———

Setting up presentation opportunities had a dramatic effect on students' willingness to read and outline nonfiction texts carefully. Suddenly they were reading for an authentic purpose, and because of this they were much more willing to be thorough and thoughtful in their reading. Wanting to make sure that presentations carried weight, Carolyn was careful not to overuse these opportunities. She typically scheduled two or three days for presentations each week, with one of those days including individual presentations to the whole class. She always maintained time constraints and consistently held students accountable by listening in on the conversations herself, getting feedback from peers, and using a rotating set of tape recorders. To support further growth, Carolyn taught students to listen carefully and respond to one another's talks, to ask questions and probe for clarification. For students who struggled with aspects of thinking through an article and preparing a presentation, Carolyn provided small-group support—working step-by-step through a common article together—and individual conferences. As students grew more confident and capable, they were increasingly encouraged to choose more challenging texts to share; this increased their motivation and sent them delving into a huge range of magazines as they sought out the coolest, grossest, or weirdest articles possible.

In the final weeks of the study, students spent much of their time engaged in reading or presenting their texts. Less and less time was spent in whole-class lessons. But difficult though it was to interrupt them, Carolyn wanted to be sure students understood that it is not just the author's understanding of the facts that matters. Yes, the author has interpreted the facts, and that interpretation is presented in the text. And, yes, it is important that we, as readers, understand the author's interpretation. But, as readers, we don't just have to accept the author's interpretation and set it aside. We need to interact with that understanding, to connect it to what we already know, ask questions, and ultimately make the understanding our own. This is a crucial part of reading and understanding nonfiction text. So Carolyn decided to tear students away from their reading for one more important lesson.

SAMPLE LESSON: Week 5—Reading Workshop

AREA OF STUDY:	**Reading comprehension**
FOCUS:	**Responding to an article**
TEXT:	**"Expanded Drug Tests in Schools?" by Peter Vilbig, from *New York Times Upfront***
RESPONSE:	**Class discussion; reading response journal reflections**

Carolyn passed out the latest copies of *New York Times Upfront* and asked students to open to the appropriate article and read it. It was wonderful to be able to sit back and watch as students read, scribbled notes in the margins, highlighted, and outlined portions of the article on their own.

Finally, Carolyn broke the silence: "Tell me about this article." Students readily described the text. "It was about the issue of privacy versus the issue of safety," Linda began. Several other students supported this assertion, detailing important aspects of the case of an Oklahoma high school student who argued all the way to the Supreme Court that being made to take a drug test in order to participate in school activities violated her Fourth Amendment rights. Their explanations were thoughtful and succinct, clearly representing the big ideas of the article. They had come a long way.

Then Carolyn posed a second, newer question. "So, what do you think?" she asked. Then, wanting to make sure that students didn't merely "take sides" on Lindsey Earls's case, she elaborated: "Do you think there really is a conflict between privacy and safety? Can you think of any other examples of this conflict? Do you question the school's decision in this case? What would you do if you were Lindsey Earls?"

It was like opening a can of worms. Suddenly, every hand in the room was up; students were eager to respond. And the responses were good. Because students had thoroughly thought through the article and understood the underlying conflict that was discussed, their responses were not simply "That's horrible" or "Ooo, she had to pee in a cup," reactions that would have been expected a few weeks earlier. Instead students were much more thoughtful as they integrated this article into their larger understanding. Several students connected the experience of Lindsey Earls to a recent "thong check" that a vice principal had conducted at a dance at a local high school. Others saw similarities between school drug tests and airport security checks. Some put themselves into the shoes of the school administration, voicing the pressure from parents and the community to keep schools safe. And a few wondered aloud about the decreased levels of privacy in the wake of September 11.

Twenty minutes later, Carolyn talked the students back through their contributions and gave names to the techniques that they had used naturally. She pointed out the connections, comparisons, questions, concerns, and perspectives they had used. She explained that good readers of nonfiction do all these things when they respond to an article. "Of course, they don't do every one of those things with every article," she said. "But good readers will respond to the text using one or more of these responses. Doing so makes the text real, connects it to their world, and synthesizes it into their own understanding."

———◇———

As the study drew to a close, Carolyn and I worked to ensure that students would be able to broadly apply their learning. We reviewed their growth with the class, pointing out what had been learned and why it was helpful. We brought in samples of texts used in seventh-grade science and history classes. Applying their nonfiction reading strategies to these texts now, while their learning was still fresh, would provide students with the confidence and knowledge they would need to be able to use these strategies successfully during the coming years. And we encouraged students to be aware of the availability and use of feature article–style text in the world outside the classroom.

Teaching the Unit—Writing Workshop

A great feature article begins with a great topic. Of course, feature articles can be written about nearly any topic, but not every topic is appropriate for every writer. In the classroom it is particularly important for students to choose a topic carefully. Topics should be close to the students—things they already know a lot about and for which they can obtain additional information easily. Topics also need to be interesting for the students. As writers, they will grapple with these topics for several weeks, and it is important that they be truly engaged in learning and communicating about those topics. Finally, topics need to be unique: students need to have a fresh understanding of a topic that has not previously been communicated to this audience. As writers, they should feel a pressing need to share their own unique understanding of the world (or some small part of the world) with others through a feature article. This is their big idea.

Carolyn had talked through these goals with her students, encouraged them to comb through their writer's notebooks for ideas, reviewed the diversity of topics in the articles that they had read, and modeled her own process of trying out and discarding ideas. But after several days of digging, reviewing, and modeling, conferences revealed that students were still struggling with topic ideas. Most were stuck thinking about topics that sounded like what they had read in *National Geographic Explorer* or *Time for Kids.* Students wanted to write about sharks or mummies or something similar—big topics that were vague in their focus and distant from most students' experience.

"What am I doing wrong?" Carolyn asked me after class one day. She wasn't doing anything wrong, but coming up with topics in isolation is a challenging process for any writer. Most writers of nonfiction articles work in collaboration with an editor who can help guide their thinking process before, during, and after writing. These students, none of whom had ever written a feature article before, desperately needed an editor to guide them, and they needed one soon, before they got frustrated and gave up. We decided to "fishbowl" an editor-writer conference with the students to help them gain insights into the considerations that typically go into the topic selection process. This "sneak-peek" would support our

Writing Workshop—Feature Article
Goals and Instructional Focus Progression

	Text Structure Study	Writing Process Study
	Goal: Students will recognize and learn to use the structures and techniques of expository text. When crafting a feature article, students will learn to choose structures and techniques appropriate to their topic and "big idea."	**Goal:** Students will learn to share their unique understanding of a familiar topic through the construction of a well-organized and thoughtfully crafted feature article.
Weeks 1–2	**Defining a Feature Article** Students will construct a clear definition of a feature article. • What are the defining characteristics of a feature article? • What is the purpose of a feature article? Why do writers write feature articles? • How are feature articles different from other forms of nonfiction text such as a research paper, investigation, or editorial? **Understanding the Scope of a Feature Article** • What kinds of topics can feature articles be about? • What kinds of information might they include? What are appropriate sources of information for a feature article? • How does the purpose of the article help to determine the kinds of information that are included, and vice versa?	**Finding a Topic and a Purpose** Students will find a topic that is familiar to them but that would prove new to their audience. • Is the topic familiar? Is it interesting?. • Do you have a unique understanding of the topic? Explain. • What do you want your readers to understand about the topic? What is the "big idea"? **Gathering Information** Students will gather appropriate information from easily accessible sources.
Weeks 3–4	**Understanding the Structure of Feature Articles** Students will analyze texts to determine common organizing structures found in feature articles. • How do authors organize their information? • How does the organizing structure support the topic or "big idea"? • How would the reader's understanding of the topic change if the text were organized differently? **Crafting Expository Text** Students will analyze and learn to use techniques appropriate for crafting nonfiction text. Techniques to consider include: • Topic sentences—linking information to ideas. • Introducing speakers and sources of information. • Placement of information within a paragraph. • Organizing paragraphs.	**Getting Organized** Students will organize their information using an appropriate structure. • Which organizational structure works best for your information and "big idea"? Why? • How can your information best be organized within that structure? • How would your article change if you used a different organizational structure? **Outlining and Drafting** Students will outline their article and then draft it in a manner that incorporates appropriate expository text elements.
Weeks 5–6	**Crafting an Introduction, Conclusion, Title, and Text Features** Students will analyze effective strategies for creating introductions, conclusions, titles, and text features that engage their audience and support the "big idea." For each element, students should consider the following questions: • In published texts, which introductions, conclusions, titles, features, etc. are most effective? Why? • What is the purpose of each of these elements? • How do authors shape these elements to engage their audience? • How do authors shape these elements to support the "big idea" of the article?	**Review and Revision** Students will learn to reread and revise their text to ensure that all aspects of their writing are connected to a "big idea." **Evaluating the Writing** • Establish a set of evaluation criteria • Measure your final published piece against established criteria • Reflect on learning

subsequent individual writing conferences with students and empower them to begin to think like editors themselves.

SAMPLE LESSON: # Week 1—Writing Workshop

AREA OF STUDY:	**Writing process**
FOCUS:	**Finding a topic and a purpose**
RESPONSE:	**Topic revision; written explanation of new topic**

Tinika shyly took a seat across from me as the students gathered their chairs into a circle around us. Once they were settled, I turned to the students around us first. "Most of you have been working hard to find topics to write about, and that is great. But I know that it's hard to know if your topic is appropriate. So today I'm going to play the role of magazine editor, and Tinika is going to play the role of feature article writer, and we are going to have an editor-writer conference about her article ideas. This is the kind of conference that many writers would have with their editors before they begin writing. It helps writers to focus their topics, and it helps editors know what to expect as they prepare their overall publication. While we are talking, I want you to keep track of the questions or concerns that I have about Tinika's topic. Write them down in your notebooks, because chances are, you'll need to think about many of the same questions and concerns for your topic."

Once the other students were focused on their responsibilities, I could devote my full attention to Tinika. "I understand that you have an idea for an article. Tell me about it." Tinika quickly outlined her initial idea: "I want to write about TV shows." "Okay, what about TV shows do you want to write? Why should our readers read an article about TV shows instead of simply turning on the TV and watching the show?" "Well, I guess I was thinking that I could write about what goes on behind the scenes; that would be interesting," Tinika replied hesitantly. "Yes, that could be interesting, but do you know what happens behind the scenes?" "Well, I've read a couple of articles about it." "That's a start, but chances are that our readers would have read a couple of articles about that, too. You need to have a new perspective, a new point of view, and in order to do that you need to be able to be close to the topic. Do you know anyone who works behind the scenes at a TV show that you could talk to?" "No," Tinika admitted, "but I do know people who watch a lot of TV!" "Well, maybe that is where we can go with this. Tell me about the people you know who watch a lot of TV. What have you observed about them?" Tinika responded, "I've noticed that sometimes the TV can cause a lot of fights. Like if I want to watch something different than my brother at the same time, or if my brother wants to watch something that our mom doesn't want us to see." "Good, this sounds like it could be interesting. Maybe what you really want to write about is TV's impact on the family. Do you know people outside your family where TV causes stress? Will there be other people you can interview for this article?"

A combination of relief at finding a topic of which her "editor" approved, and excitement about the topic itself, swept over Tinika's face. "Oh yeah! I have plenty of friends that I can talk to and people that I can interview." "Wonderful. Now, before you leave, let's think this through one more time. We know that you'll be able to interview people, but will you also be able to find other resources, like research studies or statistics on TV watching? Will this topic be narrow enough? We don't want you writing a twenty-page article. I think your perspective is unique, and I haven't seen a lot written about this topic in popular magazines, so I think it will be interesting for our audience, but what about you? Will you find this topic interesting? Is this a concept that you feel is important to communicate with an audience?" After each question I paused, and Tinika and I thought it through. As we concluded, she left with a big smile on her face, thrilled with the success of her interview.

I turned to the class and saw a forest of raised hands. Vendric spoke out, "Ms. Lattimer, can I go next?" The other students nodded. They had seen the success of Tinika's interview and now wanted a chance of their own. We took two more. During his conference, Jonathan moved from a general interest in soccer to wanting to write about Mexican-American reaction to the match between Mexico and the United States in the World Cup. Ashley shifted her original interest in "fashion" to a more focused interest on the amount of time and money that teenagers are willing to spend on their appearance. Each of the "fishbowl" conference participants became more focused in their thinking and more aware of their audiences and their potential resources as a writer.

Despite student protests, three conferences were enough. It was time to shift the responsibility to the students. Together we created a list of the most common questions or concerns from an "editor":

Choosing a Topic—Questions from the Editor
- Is the topic interesting to you?
- Who are your readers? Will the topic be interesting to them?
- Is the information new? Explain.
- Is your perspective new? Explain.
- Will you be able to find information about your topic? Where?
- Is the topic narrow enough? Explain.
- What will you want your readers to understand about your topic? What will be your purpose or big idea?

Then we moved into workshop. Carolyn and I instructed students to think through the common "questions from the editor" on their own. They could work in their notebooks or talk with a friend. We would still be available to confer, but they were expected to at least begin the process of narrowing their topic on their own.

Although not everyone came away with a great topic on this day, over the next several days of thinking, conferring, and refocusing, wonderful ideas consistently emerged. As a teacher, it was pure joy to see the excitement on a student's face when he or she found a topic that was truly exciting, something personal that could be shared with others. I thought Elizabeth was going to fall over in amazement when I kept insisting, "Yes, you can write about the difficulties that immigrant children face as translators for their parents." "But I have never read any other articles about it; are you sure it's okay?" Well, it would provide a unique perspective into a phenomenon that is increasingly widespread but infrequently acknowledged. This was more than okay; this was exactly what a feature article was supposed to do.

———◦———

As soon as students were secure and satisfied with their topics, the rush to gather information began. Initially, students put all their emphasis on getting to the Internet. Despite the fact that we had intentionally steered their topic selection toward the familiar, previous experience with research papers told students that they needed hard facts. And, in their mind, the Internet was the best possible source of hard facts.

But this was not a research paper. It was a feature article, and as such, the information needed was different. We didn't want a paper filled with distant facts, we wanted articles that used familiar information in unique ways. We wanted students to learn to shape their own experiences and observations of the world into text. However, when Carolyn and I tried to pull students away from the computer, they looked at us like we were obstructing them. They didn't yet fully appreciate the scope of possibilities for feature articles, and they certainly didn't think of friends or neighbors as legitimate sources of information. The following lesson was designed to expand their understanding of the possible sources of information that can be used for a feature article.

SAMPLE LESSON: ## Week 2—Writing Workshop

AREA OF STUDY:	**Text structure**
FOCUS:	**Understanding the scope of a feature article**
TEXTS:	**"Playgrounds of the Future," by Kendall Hamilton and Patricia King, from *Newsweek;* "Paid to Play Games," by Robert Sullivan, from *Time for Kids*; "Dancing with Pride," by Steph Smith, from *Scholastic News***

RESPONSE: **Analysis of articles to determine types of information used; independent determination of types of information appropriate to individual topics**

On the overhead Carolyn placed a transparency of "Playgrounds of the Future," a feature article that students had read earlier in the week during reading workshop. Their task today, she explained, was to analyze the types of information that were included in this article. Together, the class read through the first few sentences:

> On a sunny Sunday afternoon, seventh-grader Josh Hartley is helping to build a wet-sand dam at Jack Fisher Park in his hometown of Campbell, California. A six-year-old "reinforces" the dam with twigs. Another presses a button that floods a concrete channel with water, to test the structure's mettle. The barrier holds. "It's pretty cool," says Hartley. "You feel like you've accomplished something.

Carolyn stopped. "Okay, what information was in the text that we just read?" Her question was initially greeted with silence. Finally, Edgar spoke for the class, commenting, "Ms. Sommer, there wasn't any information. There was just a story about some kids playing at a playground." "Yes, there was a story about kids playing at a playground," Carolyn responded, "and that, Edgar, is information." On the overhead Carolyn wrote the word *story* next to the sentences she had just read. "Think of it this way," she explained to the class. "Does the story teach us something about playgrounds? Does it support the big idea of the article? If the answers to those questions are yes, then it's a source of information."

"But Ms. Sommer," Karla interjected, "there's a quote there, too, from one of the kids. Is that just part of the story?" "Well, what do you think? Does the quote teach us something about playgrounds? Does it support the big idea of the article?" Karla and others agreed that the quote was important but worried that it wasn't a quote by an "expert." "That's okay," Carolyn said as she wrote the word *quote* on the transparency. "Quotes don't have to be from experts in order to be information."

The class continued to read through the article, stopping every paragraph or so to consider the information that had been presented: what information was there, and what type of information was it? At the end, they agreed that there were essentially four types of information in this article:

Types of Information
- Examples or stories
- Quotes from everyday people
- Expert opinions and quotes
- Facts, laws, and statistics

Carolyn then challenged students to take a look at two other articles on their own. "Most of the information that you'll find will fall into these four categories," she explained, "but not every type of information will be found in every article. The type of information that is used depends on the author's purpose. As you look at these two articles I want you to consider what types of evidence are used, and why the author chose to use that type of information."

Students set to work and quickly discovered the differences. "Paid to Play Games" was filled with statistics. A few expert quotes added flavor, but mostly the article was full of fact after fact about the amount of money that superstar athletes make compared with the salaries of teachers and of the president of the United States. On the other hand, "Dancing with Pride" used the story of two brothers to illustrate the reality of Native American kids today. It recounted anecdotes from their lives and used their own words as a source of information, placing no emphasis on experts or statistics. Very different articles, but both effective.

It didn't take students long to recognize these differences, but the real question was whether they understood the reasons behind the author's use of various types of information. Carolyn called them back together. "Why do you suppose," she asked, "that the authors of these two articles chose such different types of information?" "Well," Ashley said, "the article about professional athletes has to have a lot of statistics because it's all about money, and so they have to show what different athletes make. But in the article about the Indian dancing, it was more interesting to tell the story of the kids instead of just giving statistics about the number of kids that danced and that kind of thing." Carolyn nodded enthusiastically as other students chimed in, explaining that the types of information that were used in each case supported each author's purpose.

"Let's think about that in the context of your writing," Carolyn said. "What type of information will be most effective for your topic? What information will support your purpose?" She presented the question generally, but students considered it individually: "I'm writing about Yu-Gi-Oh," Nicholas began, "how this game is now kind of replacing Pokémon for some kids. I have been trying to find stuff on the Internet, but there didn't seem to be a lot that was really good. It was all just about what the game is. Now I'm thinking that maybe I should be talking with kids instead. I could get some stories and maybe even some quotes from just, like, average people." Nicholas's shift in focus was representative of many students'. After this lesson, many shifted away from worrying about how they were going to get Internet access and instead began considering the resources available in their classroom and community.

◄◦►

As students gathered information, Carolyn and I repeatedly emphasized that it was quality, not quantity, that mattered. We didn't want students to go and interview

Figure 3.1 Organizing Structures for a Feature Article

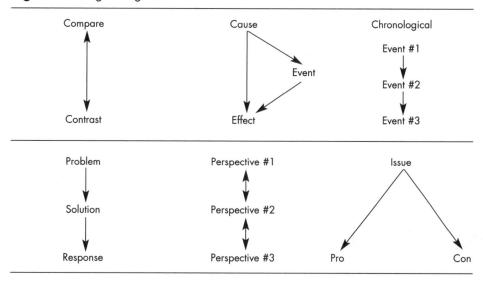

twenty different people and get a survey of opinions on a topic. We wanted them to talk meaningfully to a handful. We encouraged students to find people who would be interesting sources of information or opinions, to explain their topic, and to engage in an in-depth conversation. For those who did decide that more expert input was needed, we encouraged them to find one or two strong references and tried to point them toward some good sources.

Balancing the gathering of information with the development of a purpose can be delicate. On the one hand, you don't want students to determine their big idea too soon. Doing so risks limiting the depth and variety of information available and often prevents them from developing a full understanding of their topic. On the other hand, students need to have a clear direction early in the process. They need to consider what type of information would be most helpful and to find appropriate sources within a reasonable amount of time. Carolyn and I tried to maintain an appropriate balance between open-mindedness and direction. We did ask students to determine an initial big idea right up-front—one that grew out of their own experiences with and prior understanding of their topic. Having a stated big idea allowed them to find better sources of information and ask better questions. However, we also encouraged students to be open to the possibility of reshaping or extending their big idea as they pursued their research and writing. We did this by discussing the growth of our big ideas for our own articles and by consistently asking probing questions during writing conferences: "Have you considered this point of view? How did that information reshape your thinking?"

"What do you want your audience to understand now?" "Which pieces of information best support your big idea?"

By the end of the second week of the study most students had gathered a reasonable amount of information and developed a fairly solid big idea for their articles. They were ready to begin to organize their quotes, stories, and facts into an appropriate structure. The problem, of course, was defining *appropriate.* Feature articles are shaped according to their topic, the information available, and their purpose. There is no one formula; there are many. Together the class reviewed and analyzed the structures of published feature articles, looking for guidance in various models. Six basic structures were found (see Figure 3.1). In the following lesson, Carolyn demonstrates how students can use these structures to effectively organize information for their own feature articles.

SAMPLE LESSON: ## Week 3—Writing Workshop

AREA OF STUDY:	**Writing process**
FOCUS:	**Getting organized**
RESPONSE:	**Independent organization of information into an appropriate structure**

Carolyn pulled the chart with the six previously determined organizing structures to the front of the class, tacked up a couple of pieces of blank white chart paper, and wrote her big idea in large print on the board:

> *Big Idea:* Violence is increasing at youth sporting events. Parents, kids, and officials are all concerned and want something to be done. Even though it may mean training sessions and rules for parents and coaches, most welcome suggestions for reform.

She waited for the students to settle into their seats, and then she took out her notes (enlarged onto half-sheet-sized notecards) and dumped them on the table in front of the students. "As you know, I've been working to do research for my own article. You watched as Ms. Lattimer took me through the process of finding a topic. You helped me to figure out who to talk to for information, and you helped me determine my big idea. Now I need your help again. I have the ten pieces of evidence that I find most compelling here: a story about a violent incident at a hockey practice where one dad killed another dad; quotes from parents, players, and a referee; and two facts that relate to programs being used by leagues to try to curb violence at youth events. How am I going to organize all that information?"

Carolyn paused to let the question sink in, then asked, "What do you think? Which organizing structure makes the most sense for my information and my big idea?" Students were very hesitant to respond. They were used to the teacher's telling them what to do. Carolyn tried from another perspective. "Okay, then which organizing structures *don't* make sense? For example, to me, it doesn't make sense to use a chronological structure. I'm not writing about a particular event or series of related events, I'm writing about something that is happening in a lot of different places and affecting a lot of different people. So I would rule out a chronological structure for my topic. Do you agree?" The students agreed, and following Carolyn's lead, they were able to eliminate three other structures that were also unlikely to work well in this instance: a compare-contrast structure, a pro-con structure, and a cause-effect structure. Although these structures might have worked under other circumstances, given Ms. Sommer's purpose and the information she had collected, they were not appropriate for this article.

That left two remaining choices: (1) looking at the same issue from various perspectives—the player, the parent, the league official, or (2) using a problem-solution structure. Carolyn let them think through the possibilities for a few moments, then suggested they try putting the information into the two structures to see which would be most effective: "Many of you, when you try to organize your own information, will find that there may be more than one option that could make sense. In that situation, the best thing you can do is to try them both out and see which one works most effectively."

Using a black marker, Carolyn wrote the basic outline of the first structure on a piece of chart paper: "perspective #1—players, perspective #2—parents, perspective #3—league." Then, one piece at a time, in no particular predetermined order, she began to go through the information she had gathered. She read each short piece aloud, then asked the students, "Where should we put this in our structure?" Some pieces could be placed easily; others, after struggling, had to be set aside. Carolyn reassured students that not every piece of evidence needs to fit into every structure, but she suggested that if too many need to be left out, then perhaps the structure is not the best one. In the end, seven of the ten pieces of information found a home in the first structure. "What do you think? Does this structure work?" Carolyn asked the students. There was a tepid response. Yeah, there were opinions from players, coaches, and parents, but a lot of them said the same thing, and it might not be that interesting to just say the same thing three different times. Plus, the students were concerned that some of Carolyn's most interesting evidence, like the story about the fight between hockey dads, didn't even make it onto the board.

The class repeated the organizing process with the second structure, Problem-Solution-Response. The same information (Carolyn had cleverly prepared a second set of evidence cards) was reorganized into this new structure. This time information was grouped by content rather than by source. This required more thoughtful processing by students; they couldn't just look at the name on the notecard and immediately know where to place it. As the discussion continued, it became clear that this organizing structure made more sense. Why? "It just makes more sense," explained Brandon. "I mean, the evidence fits better in it, and it will make the article more interesting because you can really describe the problem and then get into the solutions and what people think about it. That one will make it a good article. The other one seems kinda boring."

Carolyn praised the students for their work and then gave them their instructions. "I want you to follow the same process that we used together. Think about your big idea. Look at your information. Consider the structures. Figure out which structures can be eliminated. Then try out your information in the structures that remain—don't be afraid to try more than one—and figure out which one works best. Remember, the structure that I will use is the structure that will work best for my article. You may or may not use the same structure for your article; it depends on your topic and your evidence."

Despite Carolyn's suggestion, most students began by trying to organize their information into the problem-solution-response framework. For a few this worked, but for many it didn't. Fortunately, Carolyn's model had included a failure as well as a success. This helped students realize that when something wasn't quite working, there were other options to try. Because students were so close to their subjects and relatively unfamiliar with potential organizing structures, this process took time. Many had to try out three or four different structures, and the majority required considerable support to determine which structure worked best for their information and their purpose. Fortunately, students were able to try out a new structure simply by moving notecards around (rather than copying notes from paper to paper). This tactile manipulation eased frustration and allowed students to more easily see how their information, their purpose, and the structures could fit together.

—◄◦►—

After students had decided on a basic organizing structure, we encouraged them to define their plans more rigorously by outlining their ideas and information. We asked them to follow a relatively informal outline plan (similar to the one used in reverse in reading workshop), which focused on building their big idea through each section of their organizing structure. Sommer's outline follows:

Ms. Sommer's Outline of "Violence at Youth Sporting Events"
Big Idea: Violence is increasing at youth sporting events. Parents, kids, and officials are all concerned and want something to be done. Even though it may mean training sessions and rules for parents and coaches, most welcome suggestions for reform.

I. The Problem

Idea: Violence is increasing at youth sporting events. Parents, kids, and officials are all concerned.

Information

1. Referee quote
2. Parent quote
3. Story from player

II. The Solution

Idea: No one has found a solution for the problem, but several places have suggested more training and restrictions for violent parents and coaches.

Information

1. Example of training program in Florida
2. Committee suggestions for reform in local league

III. The Response

Idea: Most parents, kids, and officials welcome suggestions for reform.

Information

1. Statistics
2. Player quote
3. Parent quote

Outlining was a challenge for many, but the greater challenge came after the outlines were created and drafting was to begin. Students were stumped about how to proceed. Initially we pointed them back to their favorite feature articles: "Take a look at how 'Dancing with Pride' is written. What does the author do to explain ideas and information?" But students returned from such investigations without many answers. They needed more concrete advice; they needed to hold up an outline and a finished piece of text and see the connections between the two.

SAMPLE LESSON: Week 4—Writing Workshop

AREA OF STUDY:	**Text structure**
FOCUS:	**Crafting expository text**
RESPONSE:	**Drafting paragraphs based on outline**

"Most of you are now finished with your outlines and you're ready to start writing," Carolyn began. "But as I've been talking with you, the question I keep hearing is 'How do I put it all together?' This is a great question, and there is no one right answer. There are lots of ways to put a draft together. But I'm going to share one way with you now so that you'll have some ideas about how to get started."

She turned to two charts posted on the wall behind her. One showed her article outline. The other revealed the first paragraph that she had written for the Problem section of the text.

> Parent and coach anger at youth sporting events is an increasingly common phenomenon. Bill Richardson, a soccer league referee in the Los Angeles area for the past fifteen years, says that he has definitely seen an increase in anger at his games. "In the past few years, refereeing has really not been any fun. I've gotten yelled at by coaches and parents for calls that I've made. Most parents are still really supportive, but some are just out of control. I mean, this is a youth league, not the World Cup.

Together the class read through the charts. Students were impressed with their teacher's efforts. "That sounds like a real article out of a real magazine," commented Julie. Carolyn smiled. "Well thanks. Let's take a look at what I've done and then maybe you can help me come up with some more paragraphs that sound good, too. How did I get from here"—Carolyn pointed at her outline—"to here? How are these pieces put together?"

The class dissected the paragraph and eventually decided that there were essentially three elements present:

- *A quotation.* This was taken directly from the information Carolyn had gathered.
- *An introduction of the speaker.* This was an explanation for the readers of who was being quoted and why his words mattered.
- *A topic sentence.* This connected the main idea of the section to the information.

Carolyn then walked students through the process of using those three elements to create a second paragraph for the Problem section of her article. Together they considered how to introduce the speaker, where to place the quotation, and how to tie the main idea of the section to the information in the quote. The result:

> Parents and players have noticed an increase in the violence also, and for some it has made them rethink their decision to participate. Linda Fuller, mother of an eight-year-old soccer player, explains, "I'm reluctant to enroll my son in sports again next year. He loves the sport, but the coach can get really aggressive with the kids, really yelling at them if they don't win. This should be about fun and exercise. My son shouldn't come home from practice in tears."

When Carolyn read their work aloud, the students were delighted: they sounded like real magazine authors, too! "Now, I've got one more quote that I wanted to use in this section," said Carolyn. "What do you think, can you each try to come up with a paragraph on your own?" Although some were hesitant, most were willing to give it a try. Carolyn read the quotation aloud and posted it where students could see, then stood back to let them try out paragraph development on their own. Some struggled, a few erased more than they wrote, but many were able to produce fairly decent paragraphs. As they compared their work a short time later, Carolyn and I delighted in hearing students explain to one another how their work could have been made stronger. A few brave souls volunteered to read their paragraphs aloud, vividly demonstrating that more than one style could be successful and inspiring everyone by showing just how "professional" students could sound.

◄○►

Once students got started with their drafting, writing a feature article didn't seem nearly as scary as they had initially feared. They learned to connect their thoughts and information, to organize their information in the most effective manner, and to choose their words carefully. The class worked together to overcome some of the common problems: "What are some different phrases I can use to introduce speakers or stories?" "How can I repeatedly refer to the big idea without sounding like a broken record?" Individual issues were addressed in conferences or small groups. Repeatedly, students were sent back to review text models, to see how other authors shaped their information or manipulated their language. An example of one such lesson follows.

SAMPLE LESSON: ## Week 5—Writing Workshop

AREA OF STUDY:	**Text structure**
FOCUS:	**Crafting an introduction**
TEXTS:	**"Monster Pets," by Alexandra Hanson-Harding, from *Junior Scholastic*; various other texts**
RESPONSE:	**Analyzing previously read feature articles to find introductions that work; identifying characteristics of those introductions**

"Monster Pets," an article that had fascinated students, begins with a recounting of a violent dog attack in northern California:

> Diane Whipple had just returned from the grocery store. As she took out the keys to her apartment, two enormous dogs attacked her, crushing her larynx and causing her to bleed to death.

The dogs belonged to a neighbor, Marjorie Knoller, who tried but failed to restrain the dogs. A California jury found Knoller guilty of second-degree murder. She now faces 15 years to life in prison. She and her husband, Robert Noel, were also found guilty of involuntary manslaughter.

Such convictions are rare in the U.S. In fact, never before has a California resident been convicted of murder for a death that his or her pet caused. But the jury's decision raises a key question: Are owners responsible if their pets go bad?

The vivid imagery and dramatic conclusion of this event had very much pulled students into the article as readers. Carolyn and I had decided that it would make a great model for discussing introductions with them as writers.

"Today we're going to look at how authors start their articles," Carolyn said. "We'll look at the introductions to a variety of articles that you've already read during reading workshop. But this time, I want you to think as a writer, to pass judgment on articles as you consider these questions." She pointed to the board on which she had written, "Does this introduction work? Why, or why not?" "What are the characteristics that make for a good introduction?"

Students began their introduction analysis by rereading the opening for "Monster Pets." "Does this introduction work?" Carolyn asked when they were finished. "Why?" Students universally agreed that the introduction worked, but explaining why was more difficult. "It's interesting," Tiffany said. "Okay, but why?" Carolyn pushed. "What makes it interesting?" "Well, it tells about something that was really violent," Tiffany responded. Still not satisfied, Carolyn tried again: "Yes, the incident was really violent, but how does the author make that work for the article? Why doesn't she just say, 'Two dogs attacked a woman and killed her'?" Tiffany was stumped, but Brandon jumped in to help: "That way isn't very interesting; as a reader, I would probably just skip that article. But the way she describes it is really vivid. It has lots of strong language like *enormous* and *attacked* and *crushing*. The words make it come alive."

Now we were getting somewhere. "Yes!" Carolyn exclaimed. "A strong introduction must be interesting to readers, and one way to make it so is to create strong images using strong language. Now, what else does this author do to make this introduction work?" Carolyn's question met with silence. Students weren't sure what else they were expected to find in an introduction. Carolyn redirected the question: "What if we stopped after the first paragraph. It's mostly in the first paragraph that the violence and the interesting description comes. Can we just stop there and then move straight into the body of the text? What do you think?" Students quickly expressed their belief that the second and third paragraphs of the introduction were needed, but, again, it was difficult to explain why. Then Edgar mentioned "the big idea." A lightbulb suddenly went on as students realized that these paragraphs were needed to connect the introductory story to the big idea of the article. "Right," Carolyn agreed. "Authors have to make it clear to readers how all the pieces connect. This is especially true for the introduction, where you are first introducing the reader to your ideas and setting the stage for everything else to come. This author does a great job of building toward the idea that pets can become dangerous and that owners may end up being responsible for the actions of their pets. But think about if, instead, the article was about out-of-control lawsuits. How would you reshape the introductory story? How about if this was about the hazards of apartment living?" We could see the wheels turning as students worked to respond to these questions. Now they were thinking as writers, realizing that language and stories can be manipulated to fit the purposes behind the writing.

Wanting to strengthen students' understanding of the author's power to manipulate text as well as provide them with some additional models of successful introductions, Carolyn asked students to review articles they had previously read. "Go back, look at the introductions, find at least three that you think are successful, and then consider why they are successful. For the 'Monster Pets' article, we agreed that a successful introduction had to be interesting and build toward a big idea. Are there other criteria as well? Are there other ways to make it interesting besides using strong language and a violent example? Take a look and see what you think."

Students combed through their article folders, passing judgment, analyzing author's craft, and making notes about which ones worked. Some students, thinking ahead, made particular note of introductions that worked in articles that were similar, in topic or structure, to their own original articles. When they came back together, students agreed that the two criteria we had established with the "Monster Pets" introduction held for all introductions. They all needed to be interesting, and they all needed to build toward a big idea. But students had discovered many different ways to meet these criteria. Vivid stories were popular, but they didn't all need to be violent. Some were dramatic, others heartbreaking, others were much more average, designed to make you realize that this could happen to you. Hypothetical examples (or "stories about things that could be but didn't really happen yet") were also popular because they made the reader imagine a reality that he or she didn't like. Sometimes the introductory story was connected to the big idea by a connecting sentence or paragraph that explained its relevance. Other times, the big idea was intertwined into the introductory story itself.

"I get that I need to have a strong introduction, and I see how these other people did it," Ashley said, "but how am I supposed to do that myself? Where am

I supposed to find a story that just works so perfectly?" Looking at the other students' faces, it was clear that Ashley wasn't alone in her worry. I spoke up from the back of the circle. "Ashley, your story is about the cost of fashion—how much girls pay, and whether or not it's worth it. Right?" Ashley nodded. "So it seems like a great introductory story would be about a girl who spends a lot of money on a big day, like a prom or a big dance. You could describe what she did, how much she spent, and then her reaction, that day and then the next day. When it was all over, was it still worth it?" "Yeah, that sounds good, but where am I going to find that?" Ashley's voice took on a frustrated note. "You've got a great resource right here," I responded. "Ladies, have any of you ever spent a lot of money to make yourself beautiful for a big event?" Eight hands shot up. A few questions quickly revealed that Karla had a great story that Ashley could easily mold into an introduction. "Ooohhh!" Ashley exclaimed, turning bright red, "I know exactly how to use that! Thanks. I get it now!" Thanks to Ashley's willingness to share her own frustrations, many other members of the class "got it," too.

◄○►

Over the next several days, students built on Ashley's example to find stories or hypothetical examples that they could use for their own introductions. Then we worked to shape these stories appropriately, crafting them to engage the reader and clearly introduce the big idea. During this time Carolyn and I spent a lot of time conferring individually with students about their own articles. But we also encouraged them to share their work with each other, successes as well as struggles. Seeing the ideas of a peer and listening to a classmate explain his or her process can be a powerful tool for any writer.

This pattern of learning repeated itself as the class moved into the final stages of writing a feature article. To determine how best to write a conclusion, craft titles and section headings, select illustrations, create captions, and prepare a layout, students first analyzed published texts and then experimented on their own work. We focused on one element at a time, spending one or two days on each as a class, although individual students were free to spend more or less time, depending on the needs of their article. Throughout this process, Carolyn and I provided one-on-one and small-group support, and encouraged peer collaboration. In addition, Carolyn modeled her own process as a writer as she wrote her conclusion, titles, and so on, and as she reread and revised to ensure that everything worked together to support her big idea.

In the final weeks, the classroom took on the look of a publishing house, with students at different tables working on different steps of the process. A few students were still struggling with the body of their texts. Others searched through old magazines for appropriate photos or tried out their artistic talents and drew their own illustrations. Another table was stacked with dictionaries and the-sauruses that students were using to help them develop clever titles and section headings (the word play lesson from reading workshop kicked in with a vengeance). In another area of the classroom, students sat with the various pieces of their text and features, a blank white 11" x 17" sheet of paper, and a glue stick. They moved the pieces around, trying to determine the best layout. At each of these stages students consistently impressed us by the way they used the resources around them. Carolyn and I couldn't be everywhere at once, so students turned to the texts, the lesson charts, and each other for guidance. In fact, in the last days before the articles were due, students were so engaged and so self-sufficient that Carolyn and I were really no longer needed. A bittersweet moment of success for a teacher.

Evaluating Student Progress . . .

By the end of the study, the change in attitude and ability was remarkable. Many of these students, including some who had been most adamant in their initial resistance, now told us that they liked nonfiction better than fiction. Why? "Because it can still tell a great story, but it's real. So you're entertained, and you are learning about real stuff." "Because it makes you look at the world around you differently." "Because it's just more interesting."

. . . in Reading Workshop

During the final days of the reading workshop study, each student was required to present an article of his or her choosing to the class. These presentations were designed to incorporate all the aspects of the study: reading and understanding feature articles, looking for big ideas in text, outlining ideas and information, and oral presentation. The results were impressive. Students selected a wide range of articles based on their interests and abilities. All students were able to clearly explain the topic and big idea of the article they had chosen. Most were able to explain the relationship between the information and ideas in the article. And the majority could respond thoughtfully to the article's ideas, discussing questions, connections, and comparisons of their own.

Carolyn and I were thrilled with the progress that these presentations revealed. But perhaps more pleasing was the fact that many students were apply-ing appropriate nonfiction reading strategies even when they weren't going to have to present. In their independent reading, many took the time to preview the text features and predict a big idea before they began reading the text itself. During informal reading conferences, students were able to explain their thinking about the ideas and information in the text in an organized fashion. Nearly all wrote notes in the margins or, when reading a textbook particularly, kept a running outline of the text as they read.

Of course, there was still progress to be made. Some students continued to have difficulty recognizing the complexity of ideas in more advanced texts. Second-language students in particular had a great deal of difficulty developing a final synthesis. They could identify the main idea in each section of an article and present a strong summary, but they had trouble stepping back and recognizing the larger concepts that the article explored. Many students remained quite reliant on the title, photos, and captions that appeared in magazine feature articles and had trouble when these aids were removed in more advanced articles and books. But despite these ongoing challenges, the study had succeeded in its most important objectives: getting students interested in reading nonfiction and providing them with the tools to meaningfully interact with the ideas of the text.

. . . in Writing Workshop

On publication day we were greeted with a wonderful variety of feature articles. Students were thrilled to display their work and savored the opportunity to explain the process of writing a feature article to visitors. The room bubbled with phrases like, "You have to really know what big idea you want to communicate," "You should choose a topic that you know a lot about, but other people may not," "Sometimes it's hard to find the right story, but if you have a good topic and you keep asking the right people, then you can find it eventually." It was delightful to listen to students' enthusiasm and to hear their pride in their work, but my favorite, oft-repeated phrase for the day was, "The next time I write a feature article I'm going to. . . ."

Students had discovered the satisfaction that can be gained in communicating an idea through a nonfiction article. They now knew how to find a topic that was close to them, conduct some basic research, organize their evidence, and then put it all together in a way that represented their thinking and their understanding. Feature articles had become a communication tool for members of Carolyn's class, a way to present the writer's understanding of the world to an audience. And on publication day, as students explained their own articles and read through the work of their classmates, new ideas kept cropping up. Now the world seemed full of feature article possibilities.

This growth in appreciating the role of nonfiction writing was perhaps our most important success. Certainly, students also came away from the study with a greater understanding of process and structure in nonfiction informational writing. All knew more about nonfiction organizing structures, and most could use these structures to arrange evidence appropriately. Everyone understood topic development, and nearly everyone could narrow their research focus and make use of easily available resources. The whole class understood the importance of building an article around a big idea. Some still struggled with developing topic sentences, introducing new information, and crafting a conclusion. A few articles were presented with inappropriate titles, missing captions, or spelling errors. Work still needed to be done to improve students' nonfiction writing. But significant progress had been made, and most important, students had found a purpose in writing feature articles.

Here are samples of the feature articles that students created.

In the Middle

Elizabeth V., Grade 5

Kids who act as translators for their parents are caught between childhood desires and adult responsibilities.

Imagine yourself having to tell your parents about your homework habits in a parent-teacher conference. That's what 7-year-old Maria had to do. Her mom didn't speak English and the teacher didn't speak Spanish, so Maria was stuck translating. "I could tell the teacher held back because of me," Maria said. Maria shouldn't have had to be there, but she had no choice. "It was really awkward," she admitted later.

Helping Out

There are many kids who must translate for their parents and are put in a position similar to Maria's. Many adult immigrants arrive in this country not knowing how to speak English. However, in the workplace, government offices, and even in stores, English is needed to communicate. A lot of parents want to go to English classes, but some just don't have the time. They have to work to put food on the table and take care of their kids. Also, it is much harder for a grown-up to learn a second language. As a result, many immigrants come to depend on their children.

Not an Easy Job for Kids

But this dependence can cause problems. "I get mad because my mom tells me to ask someone something in English and I understand and can talk to the person, but then I have trouble translating their answer back into Chinese," says Jennie, 12, whose parents speak only Chinese. In addition to being frustrating, translating can also be scary. "I get scared because my mom's looking at me and depending on me, but it's intimidating to try to do something that I'm not really old enough to do—there's a lot of pressure," explains Monica, age 16.

Hard on Parents

Kids are not the only ones who get frustrated. Sometimes parents do, too. "I get frustrated because I can understand when they speak English, but when I try to speak English, I can't make out the words, and they don't understand me," Noemi, age 36, explained in Spanish. It can also be humiliating to have to depend on your children.

Parents can also be at a disadvantage when their children don't translate correctly. Kids can take advantage by telling their parents to sign permission slips for trips they shouldn't go on or to sign a reading log when they haven't done the reading. "I took advantage of the situation many times," admitted Paul, 16, a Russian immigrant.

Advantages for Kids

Even though translating can be difficult for kids, it can also help them. A recent study by Harvard University's School of Education found that immigrant girls are usually more successful in school than immigrant boys. Part of this difference is caused by the fact that more immigrant girls are responsible for translating for their parents. This teaches them responsibility and helps them to succeed in an adult world.

Many kids of immigrants find themselves in the middle. They are forced to act more mature and at times it can be really difficult. But it is also something that many willingly do because they want to help their families. "It's hard for me to do this," says Francisco, age 13, "but I do it because they're my parents and I want to help out."

Gothic Teenagers: Misguided or Misunderstood?
Linda C., Grade 6

They dress weird, look different, and keep to themselves. . . . Do we need to be worried about these mysterious teenagers?

In the spring of 1999 two teenage outcasts shot and killed thirteen students and wounded twenty-eight others before turning the guns on themselves. This tragedy at Columbine High School was felt across the country. The two students wore black trenchcoats and many in the press immediately labeled them as Goths. This led to widespread "Goth hysteria" with people fearing anything related to the Gothic subculture and the people involved in it.

Misguided

Mainstream America, whose only contact with Goth ideas is usually through the media, believes that Goths are all about strange makeup, depression, and death. Goths are often victims of weird looks, name calling, and even having things thrown at them.

Adults often take the attitude that they are looking out for teenagers' best interests by trying to steer them away from Goth culture. Carolyn Sommer, a teacher at Wilson Academy, explains her concern: "It's one of those doors where you open it and you don't know how far back it goes. I think it is good that [Goths] are finding an identity, but I don't think most people realize that it is centered around death."

Alicia Porter, designer of the Web site "A Study of Gothic Sub-Culture: An Inside Look for Outsiders," explains the mainstream attitude. "Three words best sum up what the Goth stereotype is all about: death, pretension, and angst." She adds, however, "Like any stereotype, the Goth stereotype is a one-dimensional exaggeration and people are not usually so one-dimensional."

Misunderstood

Despite the fears that people have, the Gothic subculture is not really all that bad. "Parents think it grabs hold of teenagers and warps them. It's quite the reverse. Instead of causing suicide and depression, it gives them people to talk to. It's a catharsis," says Gavin Baddeley, author of *Goth Chic: A Connoisseur's Guide to Dark Culture.*

Many teenagers who become involved in the Goth subculture are already depressed and feel that they are isolated from the rest of the world. By getting involved with the Goth community, it gives them people who are feeling the same way to talk to and it makes them feel better knowing there are other people out there like them. "I like the clothes, I like the music, I feel comfortable. It doesn't make you more depressive, it makes you happy," explains Alison Ehrick, 22.

Even the Goth subculture's focus on death can be healthy. "Many Goths say that Gothic represents acceptance of the inevitability of death and the existence of the darker side of life. That does not mean that Goths possess an obsession with either one," explains Porter. Baddeley has a similar perspective: "I think it's healthier to be intrigued by vampires and thinking about ideas of mortality than to watch wrestling."

Coming to an Understanding

Goths are like any other group of people. Some will do bad things, but the majority won't. Dr. Jamie L. Miller, a psychologist in Escondido, explained that in her practice she sees some Goths who get involved for negative reasons and the Goth subculture has a bad influence on them. However, she also sees some who do it to be different. For these patients the Goth subculture may have a good influence, depending on the person.

Many Goths do very well in school, get good grades, and don't have any behavioral difficulties at all. Few Goths are ever involved in crimes. "[Goths] don't cause us any problems at all. They just dress different," reports Officer Rob Newquist of the San Diego Police Department.

Most Goths just want to be left alone to pursue their interests and have no desire to cause the chaos that people fear. Jennie Dinh, a fifth-grader at Wilson Academy, understands this. "[Gothic] is what they believe in, what they do. It shouldn't be any of our business, unless they're doing things they aren't supposed to."

What's your view: Are Gothic teenagers misguided and lost or simply misunderstood?

Suggested Texts

A huge range of feature article–style texts are available, but they can be hard to collect at the last moment. Our best advice: Plan ahead. Subscribe to a few magazines at the beginning of the school year, and by January or February you should have a collection with enough depth and variety to support a feature article study.

Look beyond just the texts designed for classroom use (these are wonderful, but can feel formulaic if they are all that is available). Be careful in your selections, however. There are some wonderful teen-oriented magazines available at bookstores that can contain great feature articles—*Teen People, Seventeen, Sports Illustrated for Kids,* for example—but many also contain huge numbers of ads in which students can lose themselves for days.

For older students, you may want to bring in magazines and newspapers typically designed for adults: *Newsweek, Time, National Geographic, Scientific American,* and so on. Additionally, great articles can be found in *Esquire, People,* and *Rolling Stone.* But ads and some of the content in these magazines are often inappropriate for classroom use. Clip articles and use them for whole-group or small-group lessons as appropriate.

And don't forget books. Many nonfiction books contain feature article–style writing. These can be a great supplement to your classroom collection.

Feature Articles

The following magazines are specially designed for classroom use. They have no advertisements, and most come in sets of twenty-five to thirty copies.

Grades 3–6

National Geographic Explorer. Tel.: 800-368-2728; <http://magma.national-geographic.com/ngexplorer/>. Published monthly. Each issue has several feature articles. Web site offers good support.

Grades 3–8

Junior Scholastic; Scholastic News. Tel.: 800-560-6816; <http://www.teacher.scholastic.com/scholasticnews/>. Various magazines for different grade levels. Published weekly. Each issue has one or two feature articles.

Grades 3–12

Weekly Reader. Tel.: 800-446-3355; <http://www.weeklyreader.com/>. Various magazines for different grade levels. Published weekly. Each issue has one or two feature articles.

Grades 4–6

Time for Kids. Tel.: 800-777-8600; <http://www.timeforkids.com/>. Published weekly. Center article in each issue is particularly good.

Grades 6–9

Teen Newsweek. Tel.: 800-446-3355; <http://www.teennewsweek.com/>. Published weekly. Similar to *Time for Kids* but for an older audience.

Grades 7–12

New York Times Upfront. Tel.: 800-560-6816; <http://www.teacher.scholastic.com/upfront/>. Published biweekly. Several strong feature articles in each issue. Timely and well written. Great for older audience.

The following magazines are typically designed for individual subscription but are appropriate for classroom use.

Grades 3–6

OWL Magazine. Tel.: 416-340-2700. <http://www.owlkids.com/>.

Ranger Rick. Tel.: 800-822-9919. <http://www.nwf.org/>. Published by the National Wildlife Federation.

Grades 4–8

Muse Magazine. Tel.: 800-821-0115; <http://www.musemag.com/>.
National Geographic for Kids. Tel.: 800-368-2728; <http://magma.national geographic.com/ngforkids/>.

Grades 4–9

Calliope; Cobblestone; Faces; Footsteps; Odyssey. Tel.: 800-821-0115; <http://www.cobblestonepub.com/>.

Grades 6–9

Scientific American Explorations. Tel.: 800-285-5264. <http://www.explorations.org/>.

CHAPTER 4

Editorial

"In a Peaceful Frame of Mind: Patients Demanding Control over Their Medical Care May Not Relinquish It in Their Final Days"

Anna Quindlen

It was the part about reading that got to me. By the time Joan and Chester Nimitz Jr. had decided to die together, their laundry list of physical losses was nearly as long as their rich and fruitful lives. Chester Nimitz, 86, a retired admiral and CEO and the son of the Pacific fleet commander in World War II, was suffering congestive heart failure, constant back pain and stomach problems so severe he'd lost 30 pounds. His wife, 89, who had gone to dental school in her native England but stayed home to raise their three daughters, kept breaking bones because of osteoporosis and needed round-the-clock care. Once she went blind, she could no longer read.

Audio books or no audio books, the very notion of becoming incapable of seeing words on the page gave me a bad case of the shudders, and suggested that the distinction between a life worth living and one worth leaving is probably different for each of us.

Some may fear grinding pain unresponsive to medication. For others it would be the constant losses of physical degeneration or the end of independence, an existence supervised by caregivers. For Joan and Chester Nimitz, who until a few years ago lived a life full of gardening and golfing and reading, it was all of those. "Do not dial 911 in the event we are discovered unconscious but still alive," read a note left behind in their apartment at a retirement facility. It ended, "We wish our friends and relatives to know that we are leaving their company in a peaceful frame of mind."

The greatest advance in health care in our lifetime has not been transplants or new pharmaceuticals. It has been the rise of the informed consumer. Beginning with the natural-childbirth movements and breast-cancer activism of the 1970s, inspired by AIDS patients who refused to take no for an answer, Americans have increasingly demanded more information and more control. People who once took orders from their physicians are now willing only to take advice. They look for information on Web sites, in newspapers and magazines, and in conversations with friends, so that cocktail parties sometimes sound more like hospital waiting rooms than social events.

Why would anyone expect people who have become knowledgeable about cholesterol and PSAs, chemotherapy and MRIs, to suddenly cede control at the end of life? Some medical professionals decried the decision the Nimitzes made, insisting that progress in pain management and advances in modern medicine made such draconian action unnecessary. Perhaps they have never been at the bedside of a dying person being tortured by continuing invasive treatment despite the fact that all hope of recovery is long gone. The truth is that modern medicine, which too often does things because they are possible, not because they are useful, has helped make some of this inevitable.

That is apparent in poll figures that show that two out of every three Americans support the right to euthanasia. It was apparent when the people of Oregon twice approved a statute supporting physician-assisted suicide in the form of a prescription for barbiturates for properly screened terminally ill patients. When that law went into effect in 1997, opponents predicted a bloodbath, vans of the depressed converging on the state in a mass suicide binge. Of course it didn't happen. In three years, 70 people ended their lives after doctors determined they were already near death. But there are still those so-called right-to-life groups fighting the statute, and they've found a friend in John Ashcroft. In the midst of all the other business of his office, the attorney general took time to try to subvert the will of the people by announcing that Oregon doctors would lose their prescription rights if they "participate in an assisted suicide."

His opponents were skeptical when Ashcroft said in the opening statement at his confirmation hearing, "I well understand the role of attorney general is to enforce the law as it is, not as I would have it." Their skepticism was well founded. Ashcroft, a proponent of states' rights, even did a bit of jurisdiction shopping to attack the Oregon law from his federal perch. The editor of Human Events, *a conservative weekly, said on radio that this was entirely proper: "It is the job of the federal government to go in and protect the life of the person whose life is being taken, even if that person wants to commit suicide."*

How unspeakably paternalistic and condescending! How contrary to the American ethos of self-determination and the right to be left alone. Should the Feds have sent marshals in to wrest the pills away from the retired admiral and his well-read and tough-minded wife, united in their desire not to become shadows of their former selves? Chester Nimitz Jr., a man who had become accustomed in the service of his country to taking charge, left a meticulously organized file for his daughters labeled, "WHEN CWN DIES." He ended his life sooner rather than later because he was afraid if he died first of heart disease his wife would not be strong enough to take pills on her own. "That's the one last thing I have to do for your mother," he told one of his daughters. Since the Nimitzes' deaths their daughters have received many letters, filled with rage and grief, from other grown children detailing the indignities their parents suffered during the dying process.

Maybe you believe you could live with the pain, or the immobility, or the incontinence, or the fear, or the loss of literacy. Maybe you wouldn't mind the tubes or the injections or the medications keeping you alive even if you were only days from death, even if you were turned into a medical marionette. But those who can't bear those conditions should be able to use any means to avoid spending their last days or months or even years in a situation they find humiliating and degrading. Some doctors have determined that life ends with something called brain death; perhaps there are those who conclude that it ought to end with life death, the depletion and disappearance of those things that have defined them and given them solace and pleasure. Then, as Chester and Joan Nimitz wrote, "consciously, rationally, deliberately," lights out.

<hr>

Anna Quindlen is a masterful writer. Skimming through this editorial the first time, I found myself nodding along in total agreement. I was horrified at the image of marshals bursting into the private home of a quiet couple to "wrest pills away." The "paternalistic and condescending" words of the editor of *Human Events* left me outraged. And the story of the Nimitzes' suffering was heartbreaking. It was easy to agree with Quindlen's position.

However, during a second reading and discussion with Jessica Lawrence, an eighth-grade teacher with whom I planned to embark on a study of editorial texts, easy agreement gave way to uncomfortable questioning. What about the Nimitzes' family? we wondered. How did they feel about their parents' decision? How do we know that Mrs. Nimitz actually wanted to die, that the decision was entirely hers? Considering the story from other perspectives, and questioning Quindlen's passionate defense of their decision, left us wondering whether the Nimitzes' actions were indeed justifiable, and whether we would make the same choice in similar circumstances.

Digging deeper into the story of the Nimitz family also led us further into the issue of euthanasia itself. What role does religion play in the euthanasia debate? we wondered. Why have so few people taken advantage of Oregon's assisted suicide law? Does allowing doctors to assist with suicides compromise their role as caregivers? Is the view of death as defeat a wrong interpretation of the end of life? How much of this have we brought on ourselves by extending life expectancies and curing diseases?

The more we thought about the issue, the more questions arose. Most were simply left to hang in the air; they didn't require a specific answer; it was the asking itself that prompted thought and understanding. Questioning Quindlen's editorial helped Jessica and me to think through the many considerations surrounding the complex issue of euthanasia, and eventually led us to our own independent conclusions. In the end we both decided that it is not as simple as "Yes, euthanasia should be legal" or "No, euthanasia should not be legal." We found that there are many complex subtleties that need to be considered, both by society and by individuals, when determining when and how to end a life.

Thinking Through the Genre

Editorials reflect the essence of our democratic society. Here is a form of writing that is entirely dedicated to civic discourse, to shaping opinions, changing minds, and effecting change. Certainly, opinions and ideas are present in all forms of text. But it is in editorials that we find arguments and ideas most clearly developed and most ripe for debate. Introducing students to editorials is essential if we want our children to grow up to become thoughtful, participatory members of society. An individual who can read, understand, question, and critique an editorial text is an independent thinker who can be a leader in civic discourse. A writer who can use language to persuade others can influence policy, direct individuals' actions, and re-create the world around him or her. It is only with such thoughtful, literate individuals that our democracy will continue to flourish (Gutmann 1987).

Most children are taught from an early age not to question authority. Everyone from mom and dad to teachers to Scout leaders expects that children will listen and follow directions obediently. And this is good . . . to a point. At some point, we want students to learn to make decisions for themselves, not rashly but thoughtfully. We want them to ask questions, carefully consider alternatives, and choose wisely. Teaching students to read and respond to editorials provides them with a wonderful opportunity to develop these skills. Good editorial readers don't simply accept what is said; they ask questions, carefully consider alternatives, and ultimately determine their own position on the issue.

This thoughtful interaction with editorial text allows readers to better understand their own positions on confusing and controversial issues. As I write this, the United States is in the midst of determining whether or not we should attack Iraq. Personally, I have very mixed feelings on the subject. Part of my indecision comes from realizing that I simply don't have enough information. But even when I read news articles on the subject, I still struggle to understand my response to the facts. In this instance, as in many others, the op-ed pages of the newspaper, the opinion pieces on National Public Radio, and intense discussions with my husband are most helpful to me as I seek to figure out where I stand. Reading or listening to the opinions of others and understanding the thinking behind their positions—

whether I agree or disagree—help me to think through the facts, my own feelings, and the multiple considerations bound up in an issue. And I believe that as a citizen of a democracy and a member of a community it is my responsibility to thoughtfully consider such issues, seek to understand, and then speak out to support, warn against, or question decisions that could affect us all.

Inspiring public debate is indeed the purpose of an editorial. Anna Quindlen (1994) describes her goals as a columnist as follows:

> The standard view of the columnist is of the Voice of God, intoning the last word on any subject: Capital punishment is wrong. Abortion is a woman's right. The point is the conclusion. This seems to me uninteresting, this preaching to the converted, this emphasis on product rather than on process. From the beginning it seemed to me that the point was not to make readers think like me. It was to make them think.

Hence, Quindlen writes about what she passionately believes to be important, subjects close to her heart and issues she wants people to thoughtfully consider. This is true of all great editorial writers; their writing is born out of passion. Dorothy Thompson, who was one of the first female columnists and is still considered one of the best, was often criticized for writing with too much emotion. She did not follow the typical, dry formula that her male colleagues had used for decades, and she was derided as being "too feminine." However, among all the negative comments, one reviewer (Kurth 1990) correctly noted,

> Dorothy Thompson writes fierily. Sometimes she seems to write almost hysterically. . . . She gets mad. She pleads; she denounces. And the result is that where the intellectualized columns of her colleagues fade when pressed between the leaves of a book, these columns still ring.

As a teacher I want students to learn to write as Dorothy Thompson did—fierily. I want them to be able to take their frustrations, joys, and sorrows, recognize the larger issues surrounding their experiences, and craft an editorial that has the power to create change in their communities. To do so, they must learn to balance passion with discipline. They will need to find a way to convince their audience through the use of well-reasoned arguments, clear structure, and strong evidence as well as compelling examples, persuasive language, and at times, raw emotion. Editorial writers must be clinical about their writing without losing their passion for a subject. This is a difficult balance to maintain; it requires a deep understanding of the genre, thorough knowledge about the subject, and thoughtful reflection about one's own position and objectives. Yet, once mastered, these skills have wide application in many aspects of civic life. Everything from persuading a boss to give a raise to leading a petition drive for better community libraries requires this unique blend of passion and discipline. If, in the classroom, we can support students' mastery of these skills, we not only equip them to be successful editorial writers, but we also empower them to be vocal, responsible, and effective members of our democratic society.

Envisioning the Unit

If ever a group of students needed to be empowered, it was this class. Jessica Lawrence's eighth-grade students attended Horace Mann Middle School; it was the lowest-scoring middle school in the district, and they knew it. Despite the fact that they had worked hard in Jessica's class and grown in their ability to read and write (moving up on average a remarkable three grade levels in reading over a six-month period). Although they were comfortable in the classroom, the rest of their world felt out of their control. Most lived below the poverty line, nearly all had parents who were divorced, a large number were immigrants, and few saw school as much more than a race to the finish line: high school graduation. Many had the typical teenage frustrations about parents who are too controlling and teachers who don't listen, but some had problems that ran far deeper than that. LaTisha worried about a friend who was trying to get pregnant at fourteen. (Some students' names have been changed in this chapter to protect privacy.) Jamar worried about his dad returning to beat up his mom. Kristin worried about her mom's increasing use of alcohol. These students had many worries, but they had no idea what to do about any of them: "I'm just a kid, I can't do anything, no one will listen to me, I can't make any decisions."

And then one bright sunny day in April, one of Jessica's students brought a gun to school. He had been picked on by a group of students and had brought the weapon to intimidate them. Thankfully, nothing happened. The weapon was recovered and disciplinary action was taken. But the incident left both Jessica and me rattled. We wondered about the relevance of the editorial study we were about to begin. Did notions of civic discourse and powerful persuasion really matter in the face of a gun in the classroom? Absolutely! we decided. It was precisely because this particular student felt he had no voice that he had brought a weapon to school. He felt alone and powerless, and the only choice he believed he had was to carry a gun. Studying editorials was a way to provide students with other, better choices.

Our work took on a new urgency. Suddenly, this wasn't just about empowerment so that these students could be good adult members of society someday. It was about empowerment so that they would see the possibilities in their lives now. Through editorial reading, we wanted students to see that the issues they felt frustrated or overwhelmed by were not unique to them. Teen pregnancy is an issue that many people are concerned about; many people have opinions about how to address it. Curbing alcohol abuse is a struggle that is debated vociferously. School safety, bullying, child custody issues—all of the things these students were struggling with are societal struggles as well. By reading and discussing editorials we hoped that students would develop their ability to understand and analyze complex issues. We wanted them to be able to think through their own positions, to understand other perspectives, and to find the value in dialogue and debate.

We also wanted students to find their voice. We wanted them to recognize that they can and should have a say in the issues that affect their lives. Recognizing and acting upon the opportunity to participate in civic discourse is what editorial writing is all about. Students needed to see that there is a potential audience out there and to understand how to communicate their ideas to that audience. They needed to know that there is power in using the frustrations and difficulties of their private lives as fuel for public writing: the power to persuade or help others. LaTisha, for example, needed to be able to turn her concern for her friend into an editorial warning young women of the difficulties of teen parenting. Jamar and Anh, both concerned about the abusive situations they witnessed in their lives, needed to find an audience and platform into which to channel their concerns, Anh by writing directly to abuse victims to give them hope in an alternative and to encourage them to seek help, and Jamar by writing to lawmakers, urging stricter penalties for abusers.

Certainly, an editorial study cannot guarantee that a student will not bring a gun to school. But it can empower students to see themselves as participants in a larger discourse, members of society who have a voice and need to use it to effect change in their community. Getting to this understanding, however, would take a lot of salesmanship from Jessica, plenty of opportunity to read, write, and discuss texts, and a solid set of goals that progressively challenged students to think more deeply, analyze more completely, and reflect more thoughtfully.

Teaching the Unit—Reading Workshop

Drugs, school uniforms, teen pregnancy, the death penalty—these were the issues that Jessica's students told us they cared about. So this was where we began. During the first few days of class Jessica brought in editorials about high-interest, highly controversial topics and encouraged students to talk about them. The students were immediately engaged; they loved sharing their opinions and talking

Reading Workshop—Editorial
Goals and Instructional Focus Progression

	Reading Comprehension Study	Accountable Talk Study
	Goal: Students will learn to read, understand, question, and analyze editorial texts in order to develop an improved independent understanding of the issues addressed.	**Goal:** Students will learn to effectively discuss and debate controversial issues with peers in small groups.

Weeks 1–2	**Developing Comprehension—Asking the Essential Questions**
	Students will learn to effectively use a series of guiding questions in order to better understand an author's argument.
	• As you read, ask the following questions:
	  1. What is the issue?
	  2. What is the author's position?
	  3. What are the arguments that support this position?
	  4. How does this editorial change how I feel?
	• Before you read, make predictions, based on your knowledge of the issue, about possible responses.
	• After you read, use these questions to solidify your understanding.
	• Are these questions helpful? Why, or why not?
	
	Developing Comprehension—Decoding the Editorial Structure
	Students will recognize and use common structures and language found in editorials to improve comprehension.
		Developing Appropriate Attitudes and Behaviors for Peer Group Discussions
		Students will learn what is appropriate to say and do before, during, and after a peer debate.
		
		Presenting and Substantiating Your Opinion
		Students will learn to effectively share their ideas aloud.
		• What language is appropriate to use when sharing an opinion?
		• How can you most effectively address your audience?
		• How can you most effectively support your opinion with evidence from the text and/or your experience or prior knowledge?

Weeks 3–4	**Questioning the Text** Students will learn to ask thoughtful and thought-provoking questions of the text and the author. • Ask questions about the small details and the big ideas of the editorial. • Ask questions about things that are said and things that are left unsaid. • Which questions are most helpful to you? Why? • Which questions, if any, do you need to have answered? Where could you find answers to those questions? • What questions are you left with after you have read and analyzed the editorial?	**Persuading Your Peers** Students will learn to persuade others through oral argument. • Listen to your peers' ideas. What are their strengths? weaknesses? Where do you agree? disagree? • How can you persuade your peers to agree with your position? What questions can you ask? What evidence can you use? What comparisons can you make? • Which persuasive techniques are most effective? Why?
Weeks 5–6	**Determining Your Position** Students will reflect privately on their reading, questioning, and debating in order to determine for themselves their opinion of the editorial and their position on the issue. • What is your opinion of the editorial? What do you agree with? disagree with? What is the editorial's greatest strength? greatest weakness? Was the editorial convincing? Why, or why not? • Where do you stand on the issue? What questions do you still have? What additional information do you need to help you determine your own position? • How do your questions help you to determine your opinion of the editorial and your position on the issue? **Evaluating Reading Progress—Self-Reflection and Teacher Evaluation**	**Learning from Your Peers** Students will reflect on their discussions to determine how participating in a debate shaped their understanding of an issue. • What did you think about the issue before the debate began? after? • How did your participation in the debate affect your understanding of the issue? • What did you find most persuasive during the debate? Why? • What did you find least persuasive? Why? **Evaluating Peer Debate—Self-, Class, and Teacher Evaluation**

about "real" stuff in English class. Trouble was, this engagement didn't necessarily bring rigor. Students loved talking about whether there should be uniforms on campus, but they had little substance behind their opinions. The editorials that Jessica provided were quickly skimmed and set aside; students didn't understand their relevance and certainly weren't swayed by their arguments. Discussions quickly degenerated into "should so," "should not" debates reminiscent of a bad sit-com.

At the very beginning of a study, this is okay. Before rigor can be introduced, engagement is essential. But once Jessica had succeeded in capturing students' interest, we needed to add substance to their work. Observing students, we saw that one of the biggest obstacles we faced was the editorial form itself. Persuasive text was unfamiliar to most students, and they simply didn't know how to approach it. Jessica and I decided to address this challenge by teaching students to use a set of "essential questions." These standard, straightforward queries represent the expectations that readers of any editorial have when picking up the text. Introducing these questions to students, and teaching them to look for answers in the text, would provide a scaffold upon which to build basic comprehension of an editorial's meaning.

SAMPLE LESSON: ## Week 1—Reading Workshop

AREA OF STUDY:	**Reading comprehension**
FOCUS:	**Asking essential questions**
TEXT:	**"No Helmet, No Skating?" from *Junior Scholastic***
RESPONSE:	**Reading and commenting on editorial text**

The groans sounded as soon as Jessica put the editorial on the overhead. "We looked at this topic yesterday, Ms. Lawrence. Let's talk about something new." Jessica and I exchanged a smile. We had expected some resistance, and the students did not disappoint. "You're right," Jessica responded. "We did look at this topic yesterday, and in fact I gave you this editorial to read. But, be honest now, how many of you really read and understood it?" A few hands went up, but most students just sheepishly stared at the desk in front of them. "I am thrilled that you are excited about the topics we've been looking at, and delighted that you have opinions about these issues," Jessica said. "But I am concerned that often you can't really explain the reasons for your opinions. And I'm concerned that you aren't really reading and understanding the editorials that we've been looking at. Controversial issues aren't just things to argue about; they are real problems that need to be addressed. In order to do that effectively, you need to understand and listen to both sides of an argument, and part of that is being able to read and understand an editorial. So that's what we are going to do today. We are going to set aside our opinions for a little while in order to focus on what one author is saying in her editorial."

Receiving grudging agreement, Jessica continued. At the front of the room she posted a chart with four essential questions:

Essential Questions for Editorial Readers
1. What is the issue?
2. What is the author's position?
3. What are the arguments that support this position?
4. How does this editorial change how I think about this issue?

"These are the questions I have in my mind when I pick up an editorial," Jessica explained. "They are the guiding questions that help me understand." She talked through each of the questions in turn and then reintroduced the text for the day. The editorial she had chosen was a very short piece from the "Debate" section of *Junior Scholastic*. This magazine provides great introductory editorials that are short, accessible, and topical. This particular text addressed whether young people should legally be required to wear helmets when skating—a hot topic for many of Jessica's students.

"Okay, I'm going to show you how I use these questions to help me understand this particular editorial. While I work, I want you to observe what I'm doing so that you can apply the process later on your own." With students following along on the overhead, Jessica read aloud the "Yes: Helmets Should Be Required" editorial.

Yes: Helmets Should Be Required
People who are dumb enough to skate without a helmet ought to have some sense knocked into them. Unfortunately, those people learn their lessons too late—and we all have to pay for it.

Helmet opponents like to point out that relatively few in-line skaters receive head injuries. But the head injuries that do occur are almost always serious—and sometimes fatal. Furthermore, skaters who do not wear helmets kid themselves that they are making a personal choice. The truth is that their choice affects many others. A massive head injury is not cheap to treat. Taxpayers and insurance companies have to cover the cost of long-term care for people with brain damage.

The best way to cut those costs is to prevent injuries. The best way to prevent the injuries is to make young people, who do the most skating, wear helmets.

As she read, Jessica paused often, thought through what she had just read, and referred to the essential questions. After reading the title, for example, she noted that she could make a guess at both question 1 and 2. Underlining the words *helmets* and *required,* Jessica commented, "These words give me a clue about question 1; this editorial clearly has something to do with requiring helmets." She wrote a 1 in the margin of the transparency and drew arrows to the words that had given her the clue. "And this word *should* tells me that the author's position is in favor of requiring helmets," she continued, underlining *should* and drawing an arrow to a 2 that she wrote in the margin.

Jessica continued in a similar manner through the rest of the editorial, reading, thinking aloud, and taking notes in the margin. When she was finished, she summarized what she had learned. She systematically worked through each of the first three questions, restating the question and then explaining her findings. When she got to question 4, however, she paused. "Now, I haven't yet answered this question. This is one that I have to think through on my own. I can't find that answer in the editorial. So . . . how does this editorial change how I think about this issue? I guess I've always thought that helmets are a good idea, and after learning about the seriousness of the injuries that can result from not wearing a helmet, and about how the rest of us have to pay for this negligence, I think I'm even more convinced that they should be required. I don't like taking choices away from kids, but the damage that could be done by not wearing a helmet seems severe enough that it may be worth it."

Jessica's entire think-aloud had taken just under five minutes. Thanks to a very short text, she was able to keep it quick and to the point. Then it was time for the students to apply the strategy to editorials on their own. To make sure that they were clear on expectations, Jessica reviewed her process with the class: "What did I do to make sense of this editorial?" she asked. Students' responses resulted in the following guidelines:

What to Do When Reading an Editorial
- Think about what you expect before you start reading.
- Take your time. Don't rush.
- Reread to make sure nothing is missed.
- Use the essential questions to help figure out what to look for.
- Think things through in your own words.
- Add answers to the Essential Questions as you read.
- Underline important things in the text.
- Make notes in the margins.
- Use the essential questions to summarize what you find at the end.
- Wait until you are finished and understand the editorial before thinking about your own opinion.

Satisfied that students were ready, Jessica distributed the opposing editorial, "No: Helmets Should Be Optional," and instructed students to read the text and respond to the essential questions on their own.

For the first time that week, students actually read the editorial. As they sought answers to the essential questions, students tried to emulate the behaviors they had observed in Jessica's model. And the resulting jump in comprehension was amazing. When students came back together, they were able to discuss the text itself. They could articulate the author's arguments, and they were able to sustain a discussion about the issue that was much more than the repetitive "should so," "should not" arguments we had heard in previous days. This improvement was evident to the students themselves. "It really helped to have those questions," one commented at the end of the lesson. "They made me know what to look for when I read. When I understand the editorial, it's a lot more interesting."

———————◄○►———————

Throughout the course of the editorial study, the list of essential questions proved tremendously helpful. We used these questions repeatedly, brainstorming possible answers before reading (schema activation), looking for answers during reading (monitoring comprehension), and summarizing our findings after reading (synthesizing understanding).

With questions in mind, students were soon able to breeze through the *Junior Scholastic* editorial and similar short, relatively straightforward editorials. Knowing what to look for kept them focused and gave them direction. However, as editorials became more complex, comprehension faltered. Lack of familiarity with the structure and language of persuasive text caused students to struggle to respond to the essential questions. In order to understand the substance of the text, students needed to understand a bit more about the structure, style, and language of editorials. They needed to know where to look for things such as a position statement, explanation of an issue, or supporting arguments. They needed to understand more about persuasive techniques, to know, for example, that authors often ask rhetorical questions in order to bolster their arguments but that these questions are not intended to be answered by the reader. And they needed to recognize the language that is often used by authors to signal when they are making an argument, denouncing a counterargument, or revealing their position. In the following lesson, Jessica aimed to help students decode the language of editorials by teaching them to recognize these signal words.

SAMPLE LESSON: Week 2—Reading Workshop

| AREA OF STUDY: | **Reading comprehension** |
| FOCUS: | **Decoding the editorial structure** |

TEXT: **"Lighter Loads? Silly Bill Targets Student Backpacks" from *San Diego Union Tribune***

RESPONSE: **Chart showing signal words and their purposes**

Jessica placed a copy of the "Lighter Loads?" editorial on the overhead. The text addressed concern over the amount of weight that students carry in their backpacks, arguing that a bill before the state legislature that would limit the size of textbooks was ridiculous. Instead, the editorial argued, schools ought to bring back lockers, even if transparent ones. The students had previously read and discussed this editorial and were comfortable with its content.

Jessica explained that today they were going to look at the text differently, not looking for answers to essential questions but looking for the words that signal where answers might be found. "There are certain words that authors of persuasive text use a lot when constructing their arguments. They provide a signal for readers, saying 'Pay attention, I'm about to state the position' or 'Look over here, I'm about to explain why the other side is wrong.' If we know what these words are, then it will make reading and understanding editorials easier." Students looked very skeptical. "Let me show you what I mean," Jessica said.

Using an overhead marker, Jessica read through the text, circling words such as *unless, so, however, but.* As she worked, she thought aloud about the significance of the words. For example, in the following sentence, she circled the word *really*: "The blame really resides with California schools, which have been removing lockers for much of the past decade." "The word *really* tells me that the author is now going to tell me his opinion about the problem," Jessica said. "It says, 'Before, I've been telling you about their side, but now I'm going to tell you what I think is the truth.'"

In another paragraph, she circled the phrase *obvious solution* and the words *then* and *and*:

> One obvious solution to the "problem" is transparent lockers. Then, students wouldn't be able to hide drugs or weapons. . . . And they could store their books and other possessions, using them as needed during the school day. And they would still be exposed to a serious-minded curriculum.

"The word *solution* tells me that this is the idea the author thinks is best," Jessica explained "and the fact that he wrote *obvious* tells me he thinks it is much better than any other solution. The word *then* signals that he's going to tell me the reason why his solution is a good one. And the word *and,* which is used twice, tells me that he's going to give me more than one reason why his solution is the right one."

It took only a few paragraphs of modeling for students to catch on, and soon they were sharing their own ideas about signal words in the short editorial. To support their learning, Jessica kept notes of their findings on a two-column chart, recording signal words in the left-hand column and a brief explanation of the purpose of the word in the right-hand one. At the end of the text, the class paused and reflected on the chart that they had made together. "Does this make sense?" Jessica asked. The answer was a resounding "Yes!" After struggling for a week to read and understand editorials, students clearly recognized the value of noting signal words.

To reinforce their understanding, Jessica asked students to take out their editorial folders, review the other editorials that they had read, and look for signal words. "Search out the signal words that we have already talked about. Are they always used the same way? Can you find other words or phrases that are used to signal meaning in an editorial? What are they? What do they signal?" Jessica instructed students to work on their own at first, and then to share their findings with their peers. She passed out sheets of blank chart paper for student teams to record their results. The conversations that ensued were wonderful, especially when students found multiple words that served the same purpose or found the same word used for different purposes. Talking about the words they had found and charting their findings really helped to clarify understanding.

At the end of the period, Jessica collected and posted students' charts (see Figure 4.1). They had developed some amazingly long and thoughtful lists that would prove very supportive for future editorial reading. Debriefing, students unanimously agreed that learning about signal words had been very helpful. So helpful, in fact, that William commented loudly, "How come nobody taught us about this before? This makes sense!"

————◄o►————

Practice, the essential questions, and knowledge of editorial structures and language supported students' ability to read and understand editorial texts. By the end of the second week of the study, students could delve into most of the editorials put in front of them and comprehend the issue and the author's arguments. I should point out, however, that the editorials we used with students were still selected with great care. When Jessica and I looked for editorial texts, our primary concern was content: Would the topic be interesting for students? If we couldn't say yes, the text was set aside. In addition, we considered the difficulty of the language and the level of background knowledge required. Many editorial pieces from daily or weekly publications expect that readers have an ongoing and immediate understanding of an issue from reading the front page or hearing about it on the news. Jessica's eighth-grade students were not exactly newshounds, and while

Figure 4.1 Student's Chart of Signal Words and Their Purposes

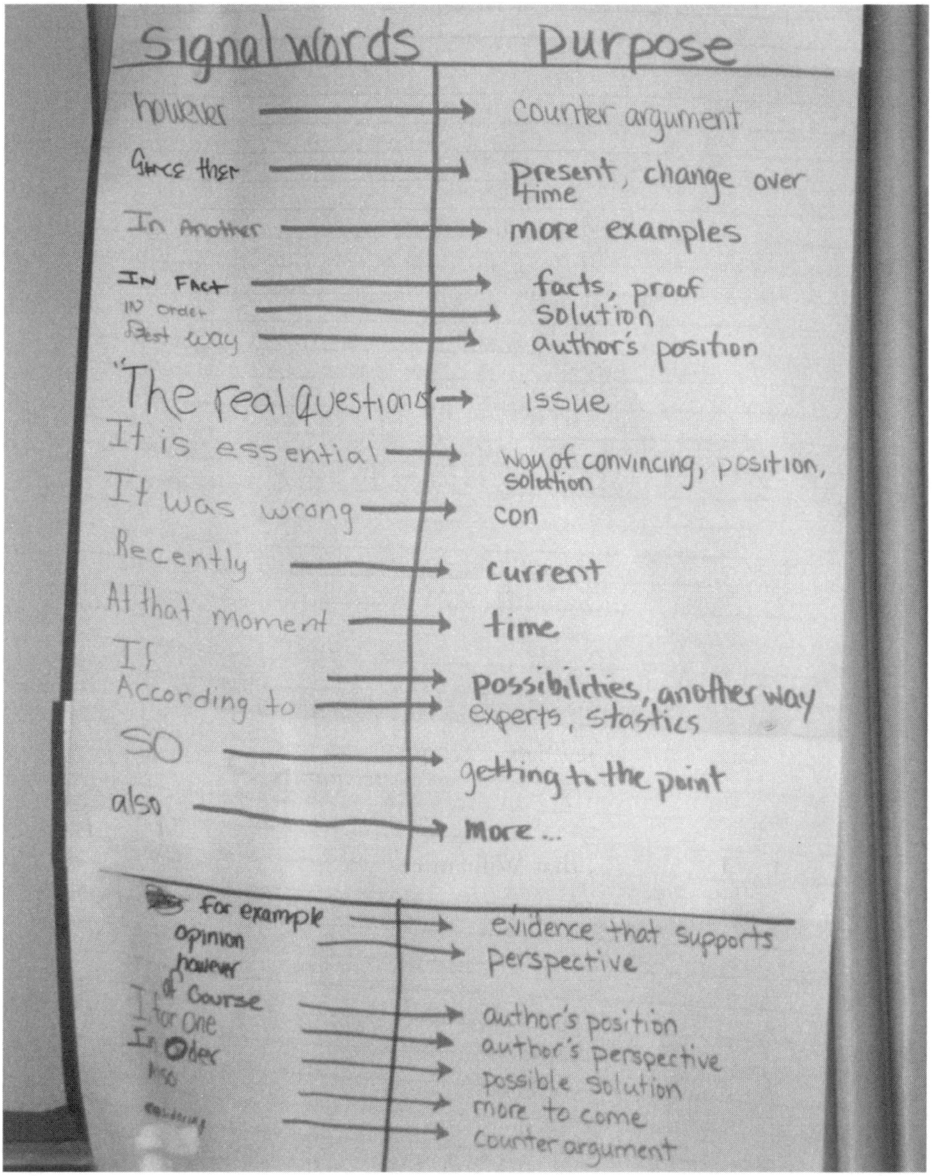

it was reasonable to expect them to infer some information about the issue from the text, it would have been unreasonable to expect that they could read and understand a complex editorial about the Israeli-Palestinian conflict, for example. A final important consideration was whether the text presented editorials on both sides of an issue. These texts (found most often in *New York Times Upfront* and occasionally in the "Debate" section of *USA Today*) were incredibly useful as teaching tools. They allowed us to model or teach a strategy with one side and then to have the students practice that strategy using the text representing the other perspective. In addition, texts that presented two sides really helped to facilitate text analysis and student discussions.

Once students were able to read and understand editorials fairly consistently, we switched gears. Instead of teaching students how to answer questions, we began to encourage students to ask them. Asking questions of the text and the author enables readers to grapple with their individual understandings of the editorial and the issue. Querying the information and ideas used in the editorials provides students with a chance to do more than simply say "I agree" or "I disagree." Questioning allows them to analyze strengths and weaknesses in the author's argument, consider other perspectives, and think through the many considerations that are bound up in a complex issue. After thoroughly questioning and considering an editorials, readers are able to more deliberately refine their own position on an issue.

SAMPLE LESSON: ## Week 3—Reading Workshop

AREA OF STUDY:	**Reading comprehension**
FOCUS:	**Questioning the text**
TEXT:	**"Should Students Do the Grading?" by Kevin Green and Nick Brown, from *New York Times Upfront***
RESPONSE:	**Recording questions in the margins**

"You guys have done a great job finding answers to the essential questions of editorial readers," Jessica said. "Now it is your turn to ask some questions of your own. These authors are expressing their ideas and opinions, and as a reader, you shouldn't just nod your head and agree with everything. It's your responsibility to question what they say. You need to get in there and question their evidence, their ideas, and their arguments. Asking hard questions, not all of which need to be answered, is one great way to figure out the strength of an editorial and determine where you stand on the issue."

Jessica placed a transparency of "Should Students Do the Grading?" on the overhead. This *New York Times Upfront* editorial had been written by students in response to a recent U.S. Supreme Court ruling that allowed teachers to have students grade the quizzes and tests of their peers. The text contained two relatively succinct responses—one supporting the "yes" position and the other the "no" position. This contrast provided a perfect example of why questioning editorials is so important. Jessica planned to use the "yes" editorial to model; then she would allow the students to practice their own questioning on the "no" piece.

After reading the "yes" editorial one time through to ensure basic comprehension, Jessica returned to the text to think more critically about its content. She reread the editorial, stopping every paragraph or so to reflect, ask questions, and record her queries in the margins.

By grading each other's papers and seeing the problems their peers encounter, as well as their own, students double their exposure to the troubles that they may meet on future exams and tests. The basic purpose of school is to learn not just what others have done right, but to learn from what they have done wrong. How better to teach this than to put it directly into the lives of the students?

In response to this paragraph, for example, she asked the following questions:

- How will they be grading the tests? Will they be using a rubric or just marking the answers right and wrong? If they are just recording a score, how does this help them learn what was done wrong?
- Doesn't this risk invading other people's privacy? Do all students want their peers to know what kind of grades they are getting?
- Are there other ways to learn from mistakes? Would self-grading work? How about looking as a class at common mistakes? Is peer grading so much more effective than these methods?

After she had completed rereading and questioning the text, Jessica explained how this process had helped her think differently about the editorial. "After reading it through just one time, I was ready to agree with the author and move on. But now, I am less certain. I don't necessarily disagree with him, but I have some concerns about how student grading would be used, and I wonder if it is really okay in all classrooms." Many students were nodding their heads in agreement. After listening to Jessica's thoughtful questions, they weren't sure where they stood on the issue either.

Together the class reviewed Jessica's process. "What did I do?" Jessica probed. Students noted that she had read the text more than once, had taken her time, pausing to think frequently, and had been willing to question everything. "What kinds of questions did I ask?" Jessica wanted to make sure that students understood the scope of potential questions to ask. Students reviewed her notes on the overhead, shared ideas, and together developed the following list:

Things to Question About an Editorial
- *Sources of information.* "Where did you get this information? Is it reliable?"
- *Author's assumptions.* "How do you know that? Would all people agree?"

- *Alternative possibilities.* "What are other ways that this problem could be addressed?"
- *Possible consequences.* "What will be the consequences if this does/does not happen? Who will benefit? Who will face problems?"
- *Vocabulary.* "What does this word mean?"
- *Things that are confusing.* "This argument is confusing. What are you really saying?"
- *Contradicting evidence.* "What about this other information [not included in the editorial]? How does it fit with the argument?"

Reviewing this list, Jessica stressed that these were general types of questions that provided a good starting place but that should not just be repeated verbatim. "When you are questioning editorials on your own, you need to ask these types of questions, but make them specific to your text. It is helpful to ask questions only if you directly address the specific facts and ideas of that editorial." She also encouraged students not to worry too much about finding answers. "For now, the important thing is asking good questions. We'll worry about whether we need to find answers later."

Then it was the students' turn. Jessica passed out a photocopy of the text that included both the "yes" and "no" positions. She asked students to read the "no" position on their own and answer the first three essential questions. After a few minutes of reading and a quick pair-share to check for understanding, Jessica encouraged students to reread and question the text, recording their questions in the margins of the editorial. The room became very still. Nearly everyone in the class worked hard to reread and think carefully about the questions they had for each argument or piece of evidence in the text. Some simply parroted a few of the more generic questions: "Where did you get this information?" and "What evidence do you have?" But many developed original, thoughtful questions that responded directly to the text itself, especially to the author's opening example about students insulting each other about their grades. "Why doesn't the teacher stop the students from calling out insults? Where was she? Maybe the problem is the teacher?" one student wondered. Another questioned, "If teasing is a problem, why don't students just write the grades on the papers instead of calling them out?"

At the end of class, there was a new sense of control in the room. The editorials no longer held all the authority; students realized they had power, too. "Questioning lets me feel like I'm in control of the editorial," explained Ca'Darius. "It makes me think." However, others weren't so sure. "I like it, but I don't like it," Rosy wavered. "It makes the reading more interesting, but it also makes it harder to form an opinion. I'm left with too many questions."

———————◦———————

It should be noted that the classroom routines of an editorial study look somewhat different from those of most other genre studies. The typical structure of whole-class mini-lesson with a common text, followed by extended workshop time with independently chosen texts, doesn't work so well for an editorial study. To begin with, there simply aren't enough strong, accessible editorials available for students to have a wide range of selection for independent reading. And even if there were, I'm not sure that such an approach would be appropriate. After all, the very nature of the editorial genre makes these texts ripe for public discourse, and in order for this to occur in the classroom, students need to have read common texts. In Jessica's classroom, most days, editorial reading workshop roughly followed this schedule:

Ms. Lawrence's Editorial Reading Workshop Classroom Schedule

10–15 min.	Whole-class mini-lesson (common text)
10–15 min.	Independent strategy application (common text)
10–20 min.	Peer debate (based on common texts)
15–30 min.	Independent reading and individual conferring (student-selected texts, not necessarily from the editorial genre)

At the beginning of the study, when students were first becoming comfortable with the editorial genre, the peer debate time was something of a struggle. Students didn't yet see the subtleties of the issues, and consequently the quality of the discussion was limited. However, as students really began to question the details and ideas of editorial texts, the understandings that they brought with them to the debate improved. They began to state their opinions more thoughtfully and explain their ideas in greater depth. These small-group discussions became much more interesting and engaging.

However, Jessica and I wanted to push students further. We wanted them to do more than just share their opinions; we wanted students to try to persuade their peers to agree with them. The ability to persuade others through oral argument is a powerful skill, one that certainly makes a study of editorial more meaningful and that has widespread application beyond the genre as well. In the following lesson, Jessica introduces students to the art of oral persuasion.

SAMPLE LESSON: Week 4—Reading Workshop

AREA OF STUDY:	**Accountable talk**
FOCUS:	**Persuading your peers**
RESPONSE:	**Small-group discussions**

Jessica gently coaxed Bunthoun up to the front of the room. In listening to his conversations over the past few weeks, she knew that he was her most gifted student in oral argument. Before class had begun, she prepared him: he was to try to convince her that cloning was a bad idea. The class had examined opposing editorials about the issue the day before, and Bunthoun had written a persuasive response in support of the "con" side in his journal. Now, it was his job to try to convince the teacher to agree with him. This challenge was explained to the class, who were told to observe carefully, paying particular attention to the techniques that Bunthoun used: "What kinds of things does he do to convince me?"

Jessica and Bunthoun took seats facing each other. Bunthoun began the discussion by asking Ms. Lawrence what she thought about cloning. She wavered a bit and explained that she wasn't really sure but thought that in general it might have some potential benefits. Bunthoun immediately began questioning her about the details of those benefits: "If you don't know what the benefits are, how do you know it's worth the price?" "What do you think the limits should be?" "How do you know that people would respect the limits?" He provided hypothetical examples to force Ms. Lawrence to consider the practical applications of any cloning policy: "Say that scientists wanted to clone people, who would decide who got cloned?" And he did an excellent job of making the argument personal: "Would you want to be cloned, Ms. Lawrence?" "What if someone stole your DNA and cloned you anyway?" In the end, Ms. Lawrence admitted that she still wanted more information but that she found many of Bunthoun's questions very thought-provoking.

Because the model discussion had been presented as a challenge, the students paid close attention; they really wanted to see if Bunthoun could "take down" Ms. Lawrence. Although this was no WWF match, Bunthoun had done an outstanding job of being persuasive. After listening to him, the class was able to develop a great list of persuasive techniques that could be applied to their own discussions:

Debate Techniques for Persuading Your Opponent
- Ask questions.
- Use evidence from the text.
- Make it personal. Challenge your opponent about what he or she would do if directly affected by the issue.
- Use examples and ideas from your own experience.
- Don't need to state own opinion; can just question opponent's ideas.
- Stay calm.
- Listen carefully to the other person's views.
- Don't give up.
- Be respectful even when you are disagreeing.

Jessica and the class gave Bunthoun a round of applause, and then the rest of the students were invited to apply his techniques in their own debates. After allowing time for students to refamiliarize themselves with the cloning editorials, Jessica rearranged table groupings to make sure that every table had at least one member who supported the "yes" side and one member who supported the "no" side. Then students were instructed to try to convince each other. Twenty minutes later she had to call a halt. For this class, this was a long time to debate. Students felt passionate about the issue, and loved the challenge of trying to convince their peers. The verbal sparring felt like a game, but a game with real stakes. It was simultaneously fun and infuriating to try to get others to come around to your way of thinking. Michelle summed up the feelings of many when she said, "I liked this, but it was also really frustrating, because when we started, I knew what I thought, but then they asked me all these questions, and now I'm just not sure."

—◄○►—

Students were becoming confused, and we counted this a good thing. We wanted students to recognize that the world is not uniformly filled with starkly contrasting, absolute opinions. While there are always a few people at opposite ends of the opinion spectrum, the majority of us are somewhere in the gray area in the middle, believing that capital punishment, for example, may be appropriate in some cases, but wanting to see it used sparingly.

Teaching students to question and debate editorial texts supported their ability to grapple with the complexities of controversial issues. During the final weeks of the editorial study, we built on students' growing abilities by teaching them to question not just the editorial but also the issues surrounding the text, to consider what was not said as well as what was said. Together the class thought about what to do with questions once they were asked, recognizing those that required an immediate response (usually questions related to vocabulary or background information), those that might make interesting research for later, and those that could be allowed to remain unanswered. And they considered where answers to questions might be found: in research materials, in the text itself, or most frequently, in their own hearts and minds. Students discovered that ultimately they were the ones who had to make decisions about the most vexing of questions. Are the benefits of increased security worth the loss of some personal privacy? Should we limit people's right to free speech if what they say might hurt a person or group?

Throughout this time, Jessica supported students' growth by providing rich editorial texts, models of questioning, and lots of time for student-to-student debate. She also encouraged students to follow their public questioning and debating with private decision making. Good citizens ask questions, listen to many differing opinions, recognize the complexity of issues, and ultimately determine their opinions for themselves. We wanted students to become independent thinkers by following a similar practice. So, as the study drew to a close, Jessica increasingly encouraged students to make use of reading response journals to respond to the text and to the issues, to determine for themselves where they stood and why.

The response of one student to a *Teen Ink* editorial follows:

Response to "Book Banning"
Rosy
This editorial is very powerful. The author uses great persuasive language and powerful quotes to make us believe that book banning is bad. He says things like, "Book banning will bring about a new Dark Ages," and compares the things that we see on TV to the things people are scared of in books.

As an author myself, I agree that the idea of banning books is bad. I don't like the idea that someone would prevent me from reading what I want to just because they might think it is too scary or whatever. I like what the editorial says about how reading about things in books helps people to figure things out in real life. I think that's very true.

But when I ask myself, "Are there any books worth banning?" then I think that the answer is yes. Books that spread lies about people or teach hate of a particular group should be banned. So should books that teach people how to build nuclear bombs. The editorial never mentions these things. The closest it comes is when it says, "Imagine if we weren't allowed to read *A Farewell to Arms, Of Mice and Men,* or even *Fahrenheit 451*? What morals, knowledge, and history would we be missing?" I have never read those books, so I don't know what I might be missing, but I do know that some books it might make sense to ban. The author says that "reading is an essential part of gaining knowledge," but what if the book you read is full of hate and lies? I don't think that reading that kind of book would help me to gain knowledge.

In general, I agree with this editorial. I think that people should be able to write and read what they want. But I also think that there should be limits. I don't want the government or my teacher telling me what I can and cannot read, but I also don't want someone to be able to print lies about me that will hurt me. The author has a very one-sided view of the issue of book banning, but I think that it is more complicated.

Teaching the Unit—Writing Workshop

Editorial writers must feel passionately about their topic. For most of Jessica's students, the idea of being passionate about writing was a new concept.

Writing Workshop—Editorial
Goals and Instructional Focus Progression

	Text Structure Study	Writing Process Study
	Goal: Students will recognize and learn to use the structure and techniques of editorial text. Students will learn to choose structure and techniques appropriate to their issue and their audience.	**Goal:** Students will learn to build on their passion for an issue to craft a well-organized and persuasive editorial.
Weeks 1–2	**Defining an Editorial** Students will construct a clear and exacting definition of an editorial. • What are the defining characteristics of an editorial? What must an editorial have? What may an editorial have? • What is the purpose of an editorial? • For whom is an editorial written? Why is audience so important to editorial text?	**Finding Your Passion** Students will consider the controversial issues and questions about which they are most passionate in order to select an editorial topic. **Collecting Ideas and Information** Students will use their own experiences, those of acquaintances, and (easily accessible) texts and Web sites to gather information related to their editorial topic.
Weeks 3–4	**Understanding the Structure of an Editorial** Students will recognize and learn to use the structural elements of an editorial. • What is the author's goal for each section or paragraph of an editorial? What purpose does it serve? • How do the various elements of the text work together to support the author's position? • Are all of the elements essential in every editorial? Why, or why not? How do authors make their structure fit their issue and audience? **Crafting Argumentative Text** Students will analyze and learn to use the techniques appropriate to argumentative text. Among the techniques to be explored are the following: • Building transitions • Integrating facts, statistics, and quotations • Using comparisons • Introducing anecdotes • Introducing and refuting the opposing point of view	**Organizing Information and Ideas** Students will organize their information and ideas in a manner appropriate to their topic and audience. • Who is your audience? What information and ideas will be most persuasive to your audience? Why? • How can those pieces of information and ideas be best organized? Which elements of the organizational structure should be used? Why? **Outlining and Drafting** Students will outline their editorial and then draft it in a manner that incorporates appropriate argumentative text elements.
Weeks 5–6	**Persuading Your Audience** Students will recognize and learn to use persuasive techniques and language in order to more effectively appeal to their audience. • What language and techniques do authors use to appeal to their audience? • How do the language and techniques used complement the issue and audience addressed? • Which techniques would be most effective with your editorial topic and audience? Why? How can these be effectively integrated into your text?	**Review and Revision** Students will learn to put themselves in the position of their audience in order to reread and revise their editorial. • What parts of your editorial are most convincing? least convincing? • Are there additional arguments or evidence that should be included? • Is your language and structure accessible? Is it persuasive? • How could the editorial be strengthened? **Evaluating the Writing** • Establish a set of evaluation criteria • Measure your final published piece against established criteria • Reflect on learning

Although they may have been interested in topics before, this was unfamiliar territory. To inspire students, Jessica surrounded them with information about controversial issues. Nonfiction texts filled the room. Editorials that had been read and marked up during reading workshop were posted prominently. Lists of controversial issues were drawn up. Student discussions about potential topics were encouraged. Jessica modeled her process of finding her own passion. And lots of student reflection was encouraged through journal writing and one-to-one conferring.

As we neared the end of that first week of writing workshop, every student had found at least one potential topic about which he or she felt passionately, ranging from teen pregnancy to fur coats to euthanasia to domestic violence to racial profiling. However, despite their passion for these topics, many students were at a loss as to how to approach their topics in their writing. Derrick, for example, knew that he wanted to write about teen drug use. But when I questioned him about his editorial plans, his repeated answer was, "I don't know." He didn't know what aspect of drug use he wanted to address; he didn't know if he wanted to punish users or send them to treatment programs. He wasn't sure whether drug education should be taught in school or if the medicinal use of marijuana was appropriate. The more I asked, the more frustrated Derrick became: "I just want to say that drug use is bad, okay?"

Well, no, it's not okay. For an editorial to be effective, it needs to have a specific goal addressing a specific issue and targeting a specific audience. It was not enough for Derrick's editorial to simply say that drug use is bad. He needed to address a controversial question within the larger topic. He needed to convince a specific group of people of a position related to drug use. Many students were exhibiting problems similar to Derrick's, so Jessica and I decided to teach a lesson in which students would learn to reframe their issues as controversial questions. Our hope was that by asking questions, rather than simply making statements, students would better understand the controversial and persuasive nature of editorials, and that they would find specific issues within their larger topics that could be appropriately addressed through their writing.

SAMPLE LESSON: Week 1—Writing Workshop

AREA OF STUDY:	**Writing process**
FOCUS:	**Finding your passion**
RESPONSE:	**Development of controversial questions related to individual topics**

"So you know that my topic is nutrition, right?" Jessica asked. Students nodded. Jessica had modeled her topic selection earlier in the week. "But I can't just write an editorial saying that nutrition is important. Pretty much everybody knows that nutrition is important, even if they don't always eat well. I have to find a more controversial question to address. I've been doing some thinking, and here's what I've come up with so far." At the front of the room Jessica posted a list of five questions:

- Should cafeterias serve more nutritious lunches?
- Should students be taught about nutrition in school?
- Should junk food be taxed?
- Should there be classes for parents about nutrition?
- Should they sell junk food on campus?

She read through the list with the students, explaining a bit about each question, and thinking aloud about whether responding to that question would make for a good editorial. Then she asked students for their suggestions. Some offered great ideas, and Jessica added their questions to the list: "Should more choices be available at lunch?" "Should fast food restaurants offer healthier options?" "Should gym be required?"

Others offered questions that didn't work well for Jessica's purpose. Fact-based and research-oriented questions, such as "What kinds of food are good for you?" were politely set aside. Jessica explained that these questions weren't really appropriate for an editorial to address; they were more about information than persuasion. Her explanations of which questions were appropriate and which weren't helped students develop a list of questions for the nutrition topic and, more important, provided them with an understanding of the types of questions that editorials typically address.

To make certain that this understanding was strong, Jessica reviewed the process explicitly. "What kinds of questions are appropriate for editorials to address?" she asked. She charted students' responses, creating a guide for them to use as they developed questions related to their own editorial topics:

Questions That Can Spark an Editorial
- Have more than one reasonable answer
- Often begin with *should*
- Focus on smaller issues within the larger topic

Jessica then issued a challenge: Ask eight questions about your topic that meet these criteria. Students groaned. "Why do we need to ask eight, Ms. Lawrence? We're only going to write one editorial; can't we just ask one question?" Jessica responded that sometimes the best ideas are not the first ideas and that she wanted them to have a chance to consider multiple issues when they were shaping their editorials. They grudgingly agreed and went to work.

It took a bit of time and some prompting from Jessica and myself, but students were able to generate some great lists. Derrick, for example, had questions ranging from "Should drug users be sent to jail? to "Should schools give drug tests to students?" As they developed questions that caught their attention, excitement grew. By framing their topics as questions, students were beginning to see the purpose for their writing.

————◂◦▸————

To determine which question to respond to in their editorial, we asked students to consider several factors: What issue do you feel most passionately about? What issue is most familiar or accessible? Will you be able to reach your intended audience? These questions were designed to balance the practical and the idealistic nature of writing an editorial. We absolutely wanted students to respond to an issue that they felt strongly about; without passion, the work would simply be an exercise that would quickly be forgotten. At the same time, we needed students to work on an issue that was familiar and accessible. They would need to be able to gather evidence and arguments to support their position, and we didn't have the time or the resources to pursue an extended research study. Finally, we asked students to consider their audience. Since editorials are intended to persuade, it is essential that they be able to reach the people who need to be persuaded. We talked with students about possible ways to publish their work—in a community newsletter, the school paper, or through a letter addressed to a targeted audience—and asked them to consider whether one or more of these methods would allow them to reach their intended audience.

After issues had been selected and students' positions determined, we got into the nitty-gritty of editorial writing: gathering arguments and evidence. Initially we told students to write down any ideas they could think of. The class brainstormed potential supporting arguments and thought about counterarguments. They considered the various types of evidence that could be included: personal anecdote, hypothetical example, facts, statistics, and so on. And they searched through their own experiences as well as a few books and Internet sites to find evidence to support their position. Near the end of the second week, most students had quite a list of ideas. And that was great. But we didn't want every idea to be thrown randomly into the editorial. Students needed to be more selective, choosing the most persuasive arguments and the best evidence. In the following lesson, Jessica begins to teach that process by showing students how to use their knowledge of their audience to choose their arguments.

Week 2—Writing Workshop

AREA OF STUDY: **Writing process**
FOCUS: **Organizing information and ideas**
RESPONSE: **Audience profile, and argument and evidence selection for student editorials**

"Should junk food be sold on campus?" Jessica wrote her focus question at the top of a piece of chart paper. Previously she had determined her position—that soda and snack machines should be removed from campus—and her target audience, parents of students enrolled in the school. But today she wanted to model the process of looking more closely at the intended audience and using audience information to determine the arguments and evidence that she would include in her editorial.

"So, my audience is your parents," Jessica began, thinking aloud. "What do I know about your parents?" On the chart paper, Jessica listed what she knew about her intended audience: they care about their kids, they want their children to be successful in school, many work, often money is tight, some struggle with their own health problems, and so on. Despite the occasional giggle or snort of disagreement, students generally agreed with Ms. Lawrence's description.

Jessica then taped up a previously developed chart that showed potential arguments and evidence that supported her position. Students were familiar with the chart, and many had similar lists in their notebooks related to their research and brainstorming for their own topics. "There are lots of ideas and pieces of information here," Jessica observed. "Too many for one editorial. It was important to gather together all of these potential arguments and evidence so that I really understood the issue and felt firm in my position. But now it is time to choose which arguments and which evidence will be most convincing for my readers.

"For example," she continued, "this argument about cost. Since I know that money is tight in many households, I think that would be a really strong argument to use to convince parents. If I show how much students spend on soda and junk food each month, I think that parents would be really convinced. The money that kids ask for really adds up and could make a difference in parents' ability to buy clothes, food, and other essentials." Jessica used a marker to put an orange star next to this argument and the evidence to support it. Then she continued through her list, talking about each idea or piece of information and explaining why it would or would not appeal to her audience. After completing her first pass through the list, she made a second sweep, limiting her selection to the three strongest arguments.

Once the decisions were made, Jessica reviewed her process with the students. Together, they went through her steps to develop a list of guidelines that could apply to students' own work:

Choosing Arguments and Evidence

- *Describe your audience.* General description of who they are and what they are like.
- *Consider their position on the issue.* What do they already know? How do they feel about it?
- *Review your arguments and evidence.* Which would appeal to the audience? Why? Which would not appeal? Why not?
- *Choose the best arguments and evidence.* Which are the most convincing? Why?

Then students were sent to work on their own writing. This process was a challenge because it forced them to recognize shortcomings in their work thus far. Some realized that they didn't know enough about their target audience or that they needed to define their audience more narrowly. Some had difficulty because they simply had too few arguments and too little evidence, making tailoring difficult, while others had so many ideas listed that they had trouble choosing. However, despite these difficulties, the lesson was one that students found very helpful. Focusing on their audience forced students to pull together the work and research they had done thus far and to consider how it might be shaped into a strong editorial. My favorite comment came from a student who reluctantly eliminated her favorite argument after realizing it didn't address her intended audience: "That's the argument that makes the most sense to me, but I am not the audience, and I have to find things that make sense to them."

————◀◦▶————

Getting students organized is always a challenge. But it is an even greater challenge when the organizing structure that they'll need to use is unfamiliar. Therefore, before we even began to work on organizing students' editorials, we set out to help students develop an in-depth understanding of the structure of editorial text.

It would have been simple to hand students a predeveloped outline of an editorial and tell them to use it to begin organizing their own, but it wouldn't have been very helpful. Students didn't need a graphic organizer with unfamiliar terms such as "position statement," "argument," and "counterargument." What they needed was an understanding of how these structural elements work. They needed to see what these things looked like and how they could be used to support an author's purpose. By analyzing how other authors crafted and used structural elements, students would have a better understanding of how they themselves might craft and use those elements in their own editorials.

SAMPLE LESSON: ## Week 3—Writing Workshop

AREA OF STUDY:	**Text structure**
FOCUS:	**Understanding the structure of an editorial**
TEXTS:	**"Should Teens Be Tried as Adults?" by Julia Kay and Rocio Nieves, from** *New York Times Upfront*; **various other texts**
RESPONSE:	**Small-group analysis of published editorial**

On the overhead Jessica placed a transparency of the "yes" response to "Should Teens Be Tried as Adults?" This text was straightforward in its organization and structure. Students had previously read and questioned the editorial as readers; now they would return to it as writers.

Together the class read through the editorial, pausing at the end of each section to consider its purpose. "What is the author's goal here?" Jessica repeatedly asked. "What is the purpose of this paragraph?" It took a few moments for students to shift their thinking from that of readers analyzing the content to that of writers analyzing the structure. But Jessica persisted, modeling potential responses and supplying students with language appropriate to the task. For example, when a student explained, "The author is explaining how she feels about the issue," Jessica responded, "Yes, she's stating her *position.*" She then drew a box around that section of the text and wrote "Position" at the top.

Jessica drew boxes around all sections of the text, each delineating a particular structural element of the editorial. When the analysis was done, the class had identified and labeled five separate components: position, supporting argument 1, supporting argument 2, counterargument, and conclusion. Then came a bit of magic. Jessica had previously laid a blank transparency on top of the one with the editorial text. When students were finished analyzing "Should Students Be Tried as Adults?" she pulled the text transparency off the overhead, leaving a blank version of the outline on the screen. (Okay, so it's not magic, but the kids thought it was pretty cool.)

"This is one way," Jessica explained, referring to the boxed outline on the screen, "that an editorial text can be organized. I could use this structure to organize my own editorial, filling in my position statement and arguments in appropriate boxes. But this isn't the only organizing structure that is possible. Other editorials may not include all these things; they may be in a different order, or they may include other structural elements that aren't listed here. Your job now is to do some analysis of your own."

She organized students into groups of three and distributed to each group clean copies of two previously read editorials. The students then worked together to repeat the process that their teacher had modeled on the overhead: reading a section, considering its purpose, boxing, and labeling each piece of text accordingly. As students worked, they debated where to draw the lines, haggling over the purpose of each paragraph and sometimes the sentences within the paragraph. Jessica and I moved in and out of groups, introducing questions to push students to consider the text further. "Why do you think the author of that text chose to put the counterargument before the argument?" "Why do you think that author left off a narrative and jumped straight into the position?" "How many arguments did this author use? Is that enough?"

By the time we called students back together, the class was able to identify eight different structural components that could be found in editorial texts. More important, students could explain the purpose behind each element.

Editorial Structure
- *Introduction.* Builds reader interest in the topic.
- *Background information.* Provides general information about the issue.
- *Position.* States the author's position on the issue.
- *Argument 1.* Explains one reason why the author's position is correct.
- *Argument 2.* Explains a second reason why the author's position is correct.
- *Argument 3.* Explains a third reason why the author's position is correct.
- *Counterargument.* Explains why the other side is wrong.
- *Conclusion.* Restates opinion; gives reader a mandate.

"Which elements do you think are absolutely necessary?" Jessica asked. Students agreed that editorials absolutely needed to have a position and at least one argument, although as one student pointed out, "If that's all there is, then it's not going to be very convincing." Jessica smiled. "Okay, then, how do authors decide which of the other elements to include?" Student response: "It depends." They explained that it depended on the audience, the strength of the arguments, and the availability of the evidence. Often they were able to point to specific text examples, explaining, for instance, that the authors of "Should Teens Be Tried as Adults?" didn't need to provide any background information because "everybody already knows about that issue."

In the end, students decided that there was no one best way to organize an editorial. There were standard components of an editorial text, a clear structure from which all authors seemed to pull elements. But the elements that were used and the manner in which they were organized were necessarily determined according to the purpose of the individual author.

How to insert thoughtfully chosen arguments into a clear editorial structure seems like it should be obvious, but it is not. Many students struggled to find the best way to organize their editorials. In some cases, these struggles represented problems of understanding, and for these students, Jessica and I stepped in to help. But more often students struggled because they saw multiple possibilities and weren't sure which one was best. "If I put my position first, then it makes a really strong statement," explained one student, "but that may turn some people off. Maybe I should start with an example." "Do you think I should use two supporting arguments or three?" asked another student. "My third argument isn't as strong, but it might help convince a few people." These were healthy struggles, and we encouraged students to talk to each other, experiment in their outlines, and weigh the effect of their choices on their audience.

After observing their thoughtful outlining, Jessica and I looked forward to receiving the first round of student drafts. Our enthusiasm dimmed, however, when we saw their work. A few had completely ignored their outlines. The results were disastrous: disorganized information, unsupported ideas, and redundant arguments. These students were sent back to find their outlines and try again. On the other hand, many of the drafts from students who had used their outlines also fell flat. They did a much better job of organizing ideas and following a clear structure, but many followed their outlines too closely. The pieces were all there, but they weren't developed. Students had failed to explain the relationships between their ideas. There was no clear connection between the author's position (typically stated right up-front) and the subsequent paragraphs detailing what should have been supporting arguments and evidence. The text read like a series of choppy, disconnected paragraphs. Writing conferences revealed that, in their heads, students understood the connections that were inherent in their work but that they didn't know how to make those connections explicit to the reader. Therefore, we decided to teach a lesson on transitions.

SAMPLE LESSON: ## Week 4—Writing Workshop

AREA OF STUDY:	**Text structure**
FOCUS:	**Crafting transitions in nonfiction text**
RESPONSE:	**Revision of individual writing**

Jessica began with a straightforward example. "Let's say you want to persuade your mom to let you stay out past your curfew. Which of the following two requests would be more effective in convincing her? 'I always return home on time. I want to stay out later this time' or 'Since I have always returned home on time in the past, I can be trusted to stay out a little later this time.'" Students unanimously chose the second one. Why? "It explains it more." "It tells you why being on time before is important." "It sounds less like whining." "My mom would like it better."

Jessica agreed with all these explanations but wanted to push students to understand further. "When you are trying to persuade someone of something," she explained, "you have to make it very clear how your *argument* supports your *position*. That is what the second request does. It shows how the argument—you've always been on time in the past—supports the position—you should get to stay out later this time. The connection between these two ideas is called a transition. The first request doesn't have a transition and neither, I'm sorry to say, do many of your editorials. Many of you have great ideas and great evidence, but you aren't connecting them all to your main position. Now, you may think that the connection is self-evident, but you can't assume that your audience will just figure it out. You have to make the connections obvious. So today we are going to work on building transitions."

On the overhead she placed a pared-down version of a student's editorial:

Position: People should not buy fur clothing.
Argument 1: The animals are treated poorly.
Argument 2: Many animals are killed.
Argument 3: There are lots of fur substitutes.

"We're not going to worry about the evidence for now," Jessica said. "I just want you to think about the first sentence or two of each paragraph. How can we get from this (the position) to this (the argument)? For example, if I just say, 'The animals are treated poorly,' does that convince you it's a bad idea to buy fur? No! So, as an author, I need to think, how can I show the relationship between buying fur and the poor treatment of animals? Any ideas?" A few students volunteered ideas. Jessica listened and then combined their suggestions into the following: "If you buy fur, then you are contributing to the poor treatment of animals." "Great," Jessica enthused. "Now, if I were writing this editorial, I would go on to describe the awful conditions of the housing, the poor diet, the lack of freedom, the smell—all the gross and gruesome stuff about how these animals are treated. And because we've made the connection right at the beginning between the people who buy the fur and the treatment of the animals, we've made it really clear that all the information relates back to my central position: people should not buy fur clothing."

The class repeated the process to build a transition for the second argument. The result: "In order for you to wear that lovely fur coat, many animals had to lose their lives." Again, Jessica praised the utility of the transition: "This is good. It allows the author to go on to describe just how many animals have to lose their lives to make a coat, jacket, hat, or other item. And it makes it clear that the person who buys the fur is responsible for all of those deaths."

By now students were catching on to this transition idea. So, for the third argument, Jessica changed pace a bit. Rather than having students share their initial ideas, she challenged them to write down sample transitions in their writing notebooks. This gave students a chance to try building a transition or two for themselves. We got a terrific range of ideas. Everything from the simple "People should not buy fur because there are lots of fur substitutes available" to the more original "Unlike in the old days, there are lots of alternatives to fur today. There is no need to kill animals in order to get a warm coat."

After a few minutes of experimentation, Jessica called the students back together and encouraged them to share their ideas. As they did, she charted, underlining the words and phrases that could be used with any issue as a way of establishing connections between a position and arguments. The result:

Transition Sentence Starters
- People shouldn't buy fur *because* . . .
- *Another reason* people shouldn't buy fur is . . .
- *If* people buy fur, *then* . . .
- *When* people buy fur, *it causes* . . .
- *It is a problem* when people buy fur *because* . . .
- *One result* of people's buying fur is . . .
- *An example of the problems* that buying fur causes is . . .
- *Since* . . . , people do not need to buy fur.

This list provided students with a strong selection of possible transitions to apply to their own writing. And that was, of course, the next step. Students were asked to go back and reread their work. "Look for the transitions in your work," Jessica instructed. "If they are there, highlight them. If not, figure out a way to make a transition between your position and your arguments. Get creative. You don't need to stick to our list of transition sentence starters. But each paragraph must begin with some sort of transition that connects your argument to your position."

Working with editorials that were in various stages of completion was much more challenging than simply writing from a basic outline. Despite Jessica's clear instructions, many students struggled to find a way to integrate transitions into their writing. The list of transition sentence starters proved very helpful for many. Others were able to develop great original transitions on their own. But quite a few needed direct one-on-one help through a writing conference. They knew what they were supposed to do, but they couldn't quite figure out how to make it happen in their own writing. However, once the transitions clicked, many students were amazed at how readily the rest of their argument flowed. Several wrote whole new paragraphs, because, as William explained, "Once I got the transition worked out, the rest of it just came. It was easy."

————◄○►————

A lesson on transitions, demonstrations of how to use evidence, and lots of individual writing conferences helped to clear up confusing, choppy editorials. By the fifth week of the study, nearly everyone had a well-organized and substantiated draft of an argumentative essay. However, when trying to convince an audience, more is needed than organization and substantiation. It is necessary to really grab readers, to shock and surprise, to appeal to their emotions, drill ideas into their heads, and leave them feeling energized for action. Students (and teachers) had been so preoccupied with getting their editorials to be clear that they had often failed to communicate their passion to their audience.

By analyzing favorite published editorials, students recognized the following persuasive techniques as possible ways to communicate passion through text:

Persuasive Techniques That May Be Used in Editorials
- Powerful introductions
- Repetition
- Rhetorical questions
- Appeals to emotion
- Strong conclusions
- Tone
- Comparison
- Hypothetical situations ("Imagine if . . .")
- Testimonials (first-person experiences)
- Strong language
- Attacks on the other side

There were too many techniques here for Jessica to teach each one. And doing so was not necessary. Many students were able to glean an understanding of appropriate techniques from model editorials and apply them on their own. However, some techniques were so important, and their application so universal that Jessica decided everyone would benefit from more in-depth analysis. In the following lesson, she leads students through an analysis of the effective use of introductions.

SAMPLE LESSON: Week 5—Writing Workshop

AREA OF STUDY:	**Text structure**
FOCUS:	**Crafting introductions in persuasive writing**
TEXTS:	**Various**
RESPONSE:	**Analysis charts; independent revision**

One copy of a chart for analyzing editorial introductions was distributed to each pair of students (see Figure 4.2). Their task, the students were informed, was to review the editorials in their folders and analyze the introductions. "Like so many things about editorials," Jessica explained, "there is no one set formula for what makes a great introduction. Great introductions can be funny, aggressive, or thought-provoking. It all depends on the author's purpose. Your job today is to consider what kinds of introductions are possible and what purposes they serve. You'll analyze published editorials first and then use the ideas you've learned to work on creating a great introduction for your own editorial."

Students set to work. With their partner they considered the match between the audience and the introduction of each editorial. They spent time describing the kinds of introductions they encountered, using phrases such as "sad story" and "what if? example" to describe a narrative testimonial and a hypothetical situation. Jessica and I smiled at some of their descriptions but didn't try to correct their terminology; their phrases made sense to them and were often more descriptive than ours. Students also considered the audience (not always easy to define in a nationally published editorial) and thought about whether the introduction would appeal to its intended readers. More than one group quickly decided that the introduction to "Brand-Name Schools" didn't work. The introduction reads, "Imagine going to a school where the uniforms are made by Nike, the cafeteria food comes from Pizza Hut, and the math lessons involve adding and subtracting M&M's, then eating the answer." The editorial was trying to argue that advertising in schools is a problem, but students didn't think that the introduction sounded too problematic. In fact, most thought that this sounded better than the reality of their own school. If this editorial was trying to appeal to kids, the students decided, it didn't work.

Students found two different editorials where the introduction was quite literally an introduction—of the author. One of these, students decided, didn't work. The author of "It's Time to Pay the Price" began his editorial as follows: "I am an eighth-grade student at Fowlerville Middle School, and I am upset over the way our teachers are being treated." Students decided that this statement was boring and didn't really add any value to his argument. After all, "There are lots of eighth-grade students; why should we pay attention to him?"

Figure 4.2 Chart for Analyzing Editorial Introductions

Title of the Editorial	Description of the Introduction	Intended Audience	How Does the Introduction Appeal to the Audience?	Does This Introduction Work? Why, or Why Not?
Example: *"Should Students Do the Grading?— No"*	*A story about a realistic situation related to the editorial*	*Teenagers*	*It is trying to appeal to the emotions of the audience by showing them the horrors that might occur if students are allowed to grade papers.*	*Not really. The story doesn't seem believable. It makes the reader question the credibility of the author.*

On the other hand, students heartily approved of the introduction to an editorial arguing against racial profiling. In the "no" response to "Is Racial Profiling Justified?" the author writes,

> As a Palestinian-American, born in Jerusalem and raised in the suburbs of Washington, D.C., I have experienced racial profiling each time I return to my birthplace. Arriving at Tel Aviv's airport as a young Arab male, I am assumed to be a threat. I am routinely interrogated; five times, I have been strip-searched. These remain the most dehumanizing events of my life.

This introduction, students decided was very valuable because it showed that the author was in a unique position to know about the issue.

After twenty minutes of analysis, Jessica called, "Time." Students discussed their findings, sharing favorite or least favorite introductions and explaining why those introductions did or did not work. Then Jessica challenged them to think back to their own editorials: "Which type of introduction would work best for your purpose and your audience?" Students were encouraged to review their analysis notes, use the published texts as examples, and most important, consider their purpose. They were also urged to be creative: "Try out several different introductions. See which one works best. Don't be afraid to ask your peers for their feedback; sometimes it helps when someone else takes a look."

The very individual nature of crafting an introduction meant that student success varied tremendously. A few students ignored introductions entirely and simply leaped right into their position statement. Some produced utilitarian introductions that were functional but didn't prove overly persuasive. Others, however, drew inspiration from the samples they had analyzed and produced incredibly persuasive introductions that very much fit their purpose. Jamar, for example, used a shocking piece about a 911 call made by Nicole Brown Simpson to introduce his editorial about domestic abuse. Ramon, on the other hand, began his appeal to the school board with direct confrontation: "You want to prevent school violence, improve student achievement, and help students from low-income families to fit in. All of these are great goals. But, your solution, school uniforms, isn't working."

————◄○►————

The final days of the editorial study were spent working to polish students' editorials. Although there were the occasional whole-class lessons that focused on elements of grammar or revision, most of the work took place working with small groups or individuals, according to need. It would have been easy to get caught up in the mechanics of student work as a final deadline approached, but Jessica was smart; she made certain that the focus stayed right where it should be—on passion. As students worked to improve their use of persuasive techniques, solidify their arguments, and clean up their structure, Jessica repeatedly queried, "Are you showing your passion?" By keeping the focus on passion even as the study concluded, she ensured that students really owned and cared about their work.

In the end, there was a final flurry of self- and peer-assessment using the student-developed rubric and last-minute revisions, and then the editorials were gone, literally. Editorials are written for a purpose and need to be published with a purpose as well. Certainly, we kept copies for the class, but the originals were sent away to the school newspaper, the *San Diego Union Tribune,* the school board, the parent and staff newsletter, and even a few national publications. When this idea was initially discussed, students were intimidated by the concept of distributing their work so publicly, but the idea grew on them (and also served as a great motivator). By the time it came to addressing envelopes and drawing up a cover letter, students were in a state of nervous anticipation. For the majority, this was the first time they saw themselves as potential agents of change, realizing that they had power to make a difference, not some day, but now. Putting those letters in the mail was perhaps the most powerful lesson of the entire study.

Evaluating Student Progress . . .

This was an intense study. The nature and content of editorials meant that every day we were grappling with heavy issues and big questions. In both reading and writing students were being asked to think and reflect, read and analyze. The pressure was on, and every now and then the class needed a break to "kick back" and recharge their batteries. But an interesting shift occurred midway through the study. The pressure source changed from being the teacher and the texts to being the students themselves. As they became aware of their power as readers to form their own opinions and as writers to persuade others, students began to put pressure on themselves. The students became the ones who pushed themselves to really take apart a text, develop strong arguments that would appeal their audience, ask hard questions that got to the heart of an issue, and infuse passion into their writing. Students became the owners of the study.

. . . in Reading Workshop

This was a very different class than the one that had begun this study six week earlier. Students were confident in their abilities, thoughtful in their opinions, and reflective about their process. Jessica and I delighted in listening to them describe their thoughts with phrases like, "I thought his argument was a little weak here because . . . ," "She has some great ideas, but doesn't address a central question . . . ," "The evidence is very convincing because. . . ." These were phrases that would never have come out of their mouths before the study began, and now they tossed them out without even noticing. We had fun participating in the discussions; students worked hard to persuade others of their position, and a couple of times I found myself changing my own mind about issues. By the final weeks of the study, students craved substantive texts and articulate editorials. They were no longer content with *Junior Scholastic*'s three-paragraph editorials; they wanted the real thing. Ramon explained, "I like the editorials that are more controversial, not just the little ones about teen issues. The real editorials have more to question, more to think about. They help me form a good opinion."

Of course, there were still struggles. Some students continued to have difficulty getting to the big questions on an issue; a few steadfastly refused to be vocal participants in discussions; and there remained many texts that were simply too difficult, either in reading level or content information, for the majority of students to handle. However, in attitude and process, these students had come a long way.

. . . in Writing Workshop

Jessica's students repeatedly proved that passion can carry you a long way in editorial writing. The diversity of their topics, arguments, and styles was astounding, with each editorial reflecting the true passion of the writer. Their use of persuasive language and techniques revealed both an understanding of craft and a remarkably strong desire to persuade their readers. They had clearly come to understand that they have a potential audience and that their words have power. Even among students who still struggled with structure or mechanics, their passion for their content shone through. This was particularly true of Malcolm. For weeks he appeared to do nothing except distract other students. I was amazed when, in the final week of the study, he handed me a typed copy of his editorial. I was blown away when I read it. His writing, directed at men who abuse their wives, was very raw but very powerful. He made wonderful use of his own experiences as a child to argue that women and their families should not be made to suffer. Although there were a few gaps in his argument and some structural difficulties, it was clear that Malcolm had been paying attention throughout the study. He had absorbed it all and used what he thought was most appropriate in order to communicate an idea about which he cared deeply. We might quibble with his grammar or encourage the use of an outline next time, but Malcolm had captured the essence of an editorial. When I asked him what had made him decide to write it, he commented, "I just thought maybe if I wrote about it, I could help somebody else. I dunno, I guess I was hoping I could change something."

Here are samples of editorials that students created.

A Warning for Teens
LaTisha D., Grade 8

Jill is a fifteen-year-old teenage mom. She is struggling with her five-month-old baby, Jacob. Despite his promises that he would stay with her, her boyfriend is no longer in the picture. Every morning she wakes up at around 4:30 A.M. to his cry. On this morning she has a test at 8:30 A.M. She wants to do well, to succeed for the sake of her son, but she worries that she will fail. "I can't get no sleep." Why not? "Because I gotta wake up to a hollering baby," Jill cries. "I just can't take it. It's too hard." She picks up the baby and holds him in her arms, rocking him back and forth. He continues to holler. She plays with him, he still continues to cry. She checks his temperature to make sure that he isn't running a fever. Then she realizes that he's hungry. She furiously looks through cabinets for formula. She finally finds the formula can, but it is almost empty. She runs to her room and pulls out her last five dollars. Jacob is on the bed hollering his little heart out. Jill looks at him. "Okay baby, Mommy's gonna buy some milk for you. Okay?"

Jill's story is an example of the problems that many teenage parents will experience. Teens get pregnant every day. Some pregnancies are mistakes, but many are intentional. Some girls believe that having a baby will provide them with someone to love, and someone who will love them back. They think that getting pregnant will guarantee that the father will stick around. And they think that everything will be okay because welfare will help take care of them. But that is not the case. Teens who have babies often end up alone, unhappy, and living in poverty without anything to offer their children.

Becoming a parent is a huge responsibility that completely changes your life. Most teens aren't emotionally ready to have a child. Babysitting can be fun for a while but parenthood is all day, every day. You have to be responsible to feed the baby every few hours, change the poopy diapers, console them when they cry, and nurture their development. This is your job all the time—you can't just leave the baby when you're tired or need a break. You can't go out on dates or with friends. Friends may come by at first to "help out," but gradually they'll drift away because you are not available to do the stuff you used to do. Some friends may no longer be allowed to come around because their parents are afraid they'll follow in your footsteps. And the baby won't replace your friends. The baby needs you to be their parent, not their playmate.

Wouldn't it be embarrassing for your friends to be graduating from high school while you are a ninth-grade dropout? It is hard to stay in school when you have a child. You have to find child care for the baby, and that can be expensive. Even when you are at home, it is hard to concentrate on your work and your baby at the same time. As a result many teen moms drop out. This may seem attractive if you don't like school. But you need an education. Education is the key to success. You need an education to accomplish your dreams. If you have a good education, you can have more job opportunities and you'll get further in life. By waiting to have kids until after you've completed your education, you'll provide a better life for yourself and for them.

Will you be able to provide for your baby? Babies may be small but they are expensive. Diapers, cars seats, clothes, toys, formula, and child care all cost a lot of money. Many teens think that they can support their baby with a minimum wage job, but minimum wage will barely even cover the cost of child care. Welfare payments are often small and parents and the baby's father may be unwilling to help. Even if you are able to provide for the baby, you'd have to give up the things that you like to buy like CDs, designer clothes, trips, and even favorite foods.

Are you ready to take on the full responsibility of raising a child? Are you willing to give up your freedom and future opportunities? When you really look at the full burden of raising a child, I think that you'll decide that it is better to wait. If you are smart, you will keep your legs closed and your pants up. Not having a baby while you're young is the smartest thing that you can do.

An Open Letter to the Board

Spring 2002

Dear Board of Education:

You want to prevent school violence, improve student achievement, and help students from low-income families to fit in. All of these are great goals. But, your solution, school uniforms, isn't working.

School officials believe that uniforms can protect students from gangs and violence. Certain gangs wear certain colors. Schools have uniforms to prevent them from wearing those colors. But students still sag (pulling their pants down) to show that they are gang-related or bring their colors to school on a bandanna. Even if they are required to wear navy blue and white, gang members still find a way to show their colors and violence still occurs. According to Officer Woods, the police officer in charge of our school, "Horace Mann Middle School has more crimes than Crawford High School." This means that Crawford, a high school with no uniform policy, has less violence than a middle school that has a strict uniform policy in place. Both of these schools serve the same population. If uniforms aren't preventing crimes and violence, why have them?

Also, school officials support the idea that uniforms make students pay more attention, in other words, make them more productive. At Long Beach School District, in California, many believe that uniforms have changed students around. But the truth is it is not uniforms that improved the students. At the same time that the uniform policy was put into place, teachers developed a stronger discipline policy and the district began cooperating with the police. It was more teachers disciplining their students more harshly and more patrol officers who did the job of improving student achievement. They're the ones who deserve the credit for all that has changed in the Long Beach District, not uniforms. At Mann, we have a uniform policy, but the teachers and police have not enforced a strict discipline policy, and our test scores have not gone up. If uniforms aren't improving student achievement, why have them?

An additional reason why officials claim that uniforms are needed is to help students from low-income families to fit in. However, these students' families often don't have the resources to buy uniforms. The students are forced to wear hand-me-downs, which make them stand out even more. Some students who don't want to wear hand-me-downs attend school in normal clothes, breaking the uniform policy. And that only makes things worse. Students get in trouble for breaking the rules and staff members have to go through the hassle of writing a referral, negative notes, phone calls home, lectures for students, and sometimes even suspensions. This takes a lot of time away from class, all because a student's low-income status prevents him or her from wearing the right clothes required for school. If uniforms aren't helping low-income students to fit in, why have them?

Uniforms are not only ineffective, but they are also just a waste of money and time. They don't prevent violence. They don't help improve student achievement. They don't help students from low-income families. I strongly encourage you to end the uniform policy once and for all.

Sincerely,

Ramon P.

Grade 8

Suggested Texts

Editorials that are accessible for fourth- to tenth-grade readers are hard to find. The following are a few sources that Jessica and I found helpful. Of course, editorials change constantly, depending upon what is in the news. Thus, an editorial that works beautifully one year may be a flop the next (although there are some issues that, unfortunately, seem to be timeless, such as skateboarding on campus and school uniforms). When choosing editorials, be sure to choose texts that are at an appropriate reading level and are of high interest to the students, especially at the beginning of the study. Your local newspaper may also be a good source, but beware that too frequently editorials in daily papers build on previous editorials or news stories and require background knowledge that students may not possess.

Editorials
Grades 3–6
Junior Scholastic. Tel.: 800-560-6816; <http://www.teacher.scholastic.com /scholasticnews/>. Most accessible of the editorial collections. Each editorial provides background information and pro and con viewpoints, which are good starting points but not substantive enough to serve on their own.

Write Time for Kids. Tel.: 800-662-4321; <http://www.teachercreated.com /writetime/>. Materials drawn from magazines like *Time for Kids* are published in kits for appropriate grade levels (grades 2–8). Each kit includes a "Persuasive" section with some strong editorial samples.

Grades 6–10 (Young Adult)
New York Times Upfront. Tel.: 800-560-6816; <http://www.teacher.scholastic .com/upfront/>. Published biweekly. Each issue includes an editorial

question with pro and cons. Some editorials by high school students, some by experts. Timely and well written.

Newsweek's "My Turn" column. Tel.: 800-632-1040; <http://msnbc.com/>; <http://school.newsweek.com/>. Written by people from all walks of life, these op-ed pieces make great sample texts.

Teen Ink. Tel.: 617-964-6800; <http://TeenInk.com/>. Monthly publication written by and for teenagers. Good diversity of topics and styles. Web site contains more than 900 editorials. Great place to submit student editorials.

USA Today. <http://www.usatoday.com/>. Most accessible of the daily newspapers. Written at a fourth-to-fifth-grade reading level. Editorials are often short and to the point.

Write Time for Kids. Tel.: 800-662-4321; <http://www.teachercreated.com /writetime/>. Materials drawn from magazines like *Time for Kids* are published in kits for appropriate grade levels (grades 2–8). Each kit includes a "Persuasive" section with some strong editorial samples.

CHAPTER 5

Short Story

"The Flowers"

Alice Walker

It seemed to Myop as she skipped lightly from hen house to pigpen to smokehouse that the days had never been as beautiful as these. The air held a keenness that made her nose twitch. The harvesting of the corn and cotton, peanuts and squash, made each day a golden surprise that caused excited little tremors to run up her jaws.

Myop carried a short, knobby stick. She struck out at random at chickens she liked, and worked out the beat of a song on the fence around the pigpen. She felt light and good in the warm sun. She was ten, and nothing existed for her but her song, the stick clutched in her dark brown hand, and the tat-de-ta-ta-ta of accompaniment.

Turning her back on the rusty boards of her family's sharecropper cabin, Myop walked along the fence till it ran into the stream made by the spring. Around the spring, where the family got drinking water, silver ferns and wildflowers grew. Along the shallow banks pigs rooted. Myop watched the tiny white bubbles disrupt the thin black scale of soil and the water that silently rose and slid away down the stream.

She had explored the woods behind the house many times. Often, in late autumn, her mother took her to gather nuts among the fallen leaves. Today she made her own path, bouncing this way and that way, vaguely keeping an eye out for snakes. She found, in addition to various common but pretty ferns and leaves, an armful of strange blue flowers with velvety ridges and a sweetsuds bush full of the brown fragrant buds.

By twelve o'clock, her arms laden with sprigs of her findings, she was a mile or more from home. She had often been as far as this before, but the strangeness of the land made it not as pleasant as her usual haunts. It seemed gloomy in the little cove in which she found herself. The air was damp, the silence close and deep.

Myop began to circle back to the house, back to the peacefulness of the morning. It was then she stepped smack into his eyes. Her heel became lodged in the broken ridge between brow and nose, and she reached down quickly, unafraid, to free herself. It was only when she saw his naked grin that she gave a little yelp of surprise.

He had been a tall man. From feet to neck covered a long space. His head lay beside him. When she pushed back the leaves and layers of earth and debris Myop saw that he'd had large white teeth, all of them cracked or broken, long fingers, and very big bones. All his clothes had rotted away except for some threads of blue denim from his overalls. The buckles of the overalls had turned green.

Myop gazed around the spot with interest. Very near where she'd stepped into the head was a wild pink rose. As she picked it to add to her bundle she noticed a raised mound, a ring, around the rose's root. It was the rotted remains of a noose, a bit of shredding plowline, now blending benignly into the soil. Around an overhanging limb of a great spreading oak clung another piece. Frayed, rotted, bleached, and frazzled— barely there—but spinning restlessly in the breeze. Myop laid down her flowers.

And the summer was over.

———◄○►———

Shock. That's what I felt the first time I read this story. In this short, exquisite piece, Walker has managed to bring together the repugnance of one of our history's most shameful times with the innocence of childhood. The result, for me, was shock. But when I brought this story along to a meeting with Donna Bates, a sixth-grade teacher at Wilson Academy, she posed a challenge that led me to appreciate the full horror of the story. In the middle of our discussion, she said simply, "Imagine how that little girl felt." This was spoken as an instruction; it was not rhetorical; it was not followed by any tsk, tsk, tsking, it was a quiet command. "Imagine how that little girl felt." And so I did.

It took me a few minutes to be able to imagine the little girl herself, to know her enough to understand her reality. I had to go back and reread the images that Walker had painted: Myop as a free spirit dancing around the farmyard, the light playing on her face and joy radiating from her being; Myop wandering through the woods, thoughtful and observant as she gathers flowers; Myop after she has stepped into a skull; a little girl who keeps her wits about her and seeks to investigate. This was a complex child. As I considered these images, Myop came alive in my imagination, and I found myself ready to follow Donna's instruction. I could imagine Myop's horror as the realization dawns that the hatred she'd only heard her parents whisper about has come into her life. I could feel the childlike sense of security and simplicity drain away. And I could understand the sadness that pervaded her spirit, seeping down into her bones and stealing away her ability to find joy in the warm sun, the beating of a stick, and a bunch of freshly gathered flowers.

Donna's challenge had led me from shock to horror, and I wasn't sure that I liked it. As we talked, I realized that previously I had been seeing the story from a distance, able to recognize its characters, historical relevance, and potential value to a classroom of students but never really interacting with the text itself. Donna's command transported me into the text and allowed me to experience the full horror of that day. And once I had felt Myop's horror, it was hard to forget. I couldn't simply put that sensation on the shelf and catalog it. Instead I saw it in the faces on television of wives and children who lost husbands and fathers on September 11. I saw it in the eyes of students who had lost siblings to urban violence, lost parents to jail, or escaped a civil war. I'd seen these faces before, but a good text will change the way the reader understands the world, and Walker's text did that for me. It took me outside my own reality and allowed me, for a moment, an insight into the horror that can be visited upon the innocent.

Thinking Through the Genre

> There is no frigate like a Book
> To take us lands away . . .
> *Emily Dickinson*

A good story transports the reader. We lose ourselves in the printed word and travel away from the crowded airplane, bustling dentist's office, or tedious faculty meeting. We find ourselves instead in a new reality, one that may be imaginary but that feels very real. As a child, Anna Quindlen was an avid reader. In her essay *How Reading Changed My Life*, she describes her foray into a favorite, *A Tale of Two Cities:*

> Like so many of the other books I read, it never seemed to me like a book, but like a place I had lived in, had visited and would visit again, just as all the people in them, every blessed one—Anne of Green Gables, Heidi, Jay Gatsby, Elizabeth Bennett, Scarlett O'Hara, Dill and Scout, Miss Marple, and Hercule Poirot—were more real than the real people I knew. My home was in that pleasant place outside Philadelphia, but I really lived somewhere else. I lived within the covers of books and those books were more real to me than any other thing in my life.

Few of us have the opportunity to truly experience different worlds; we are much too bound to our own reality. But by living between the covers of books, we can temporarily suspend our own reality in order to experience that of another. Hazel Rochman, a South African author, explains the power in this opportunity, saying, "Reading makes immigrants of us all. It takes us away from home, but, most important, it finds homes for us everywhere."

Experiencing other realities through reading enriches our lives. It helps us to understand the other people we encounter in our lives; it helps us to understand our own reality and perhaps to imagine a new reality for our futures. As readers, we are often able to know more about the characters in stories than we are about close friends and associates. We can see inside the head of a character and experience her reality in a way that few real people are willing to take the time and the risk to allow us. Yet being inside that character's head often helps us to understand and feel compassion for the real people in our lives.

It may seem axiomatic to those of us who love reading so much that we became English teachers that while reading a great book one lives within the story. But this is not axiomatic for all. Many students who enter our classrooms see reading as a chore. They see the characters on the page as caricatures rather than potentially real people and the story itself as distant and strange. Too many students think of literature as "just a story," something shallow and imaginary that can be easily dismissed, something that leaves no footprint on their lives.

As a teacher of English, I believe that it is my job to help my students love books. I want them to know the wonder and the power of literature. I want them to be able to lose themselves in a story, to live between the covers of a book. Many students need to be taught to engage this intensely with literature. They will need to be shown how to "go inside [a character's] head and heart, [to] use his or her thoughts and feelings as a prism for living in the story" (Atwell 1998). They need to learn how to use all the clues on the page—spoken words, description, actions, and reactions—to envision a multidimensional character. They need to learn how to set aside their reality, their judgments and assumptions, and to step into the reality of the character. They need to learn how to see the story through the eyes of the character, to understand the conflicts, the context, the relationships between characters, and the themes explored in the text. And (just in case you were thinking this might be easy) all of this needs to be done in a manner that brings students closer to the literature and teaches them to love it.

In reading workshop I have found that short stories provide a wonderful opportunity for teaching students to engage intensely with literature while simultaneously nurturing their love for great stories. Like novels, well-written short stories provide rich characters, fascinating conflicts, thoughtful and thought-provoking themes. However, because they are short, they are often more focused on a single main character and a single conflict, ideal for nurturing student engagement. Short stories engage the reader immediately. Readers are forced to rapidly develop a sense of the characters so that their perspectives can be understood. As a practical matter, short stories provide us, as teachers, with wonderfully varied tools that can be read and reread multiple times for multiple purposes and that need not be committed to for weeks on end (unlike a novel). And, of course, reading short stories provides a necessary bridge to writing short stories.

Fiction writers experience the omnipotence of inventing new worlds. Authors create entirely new people and experiences, and in doing so come to intimately know other realities. The novelist Joyce Carol Oates (2001) writes, "I believe that any form of art is a species of exploration and transgression. To write is to invade another's space." When authors invent a new reality, they must put themselves totally and completely into that world. They must see the landscape through their characters' eyes, experience the stresses and comforts of relationships between characters, know intimately each event that will appear in the story as well as a thousand different influencing events that won't. Oates continues, "By the time I come to type out my writing formally, I've envisioned it repeatedly. I've never thought of writing as the mere arrangement of words on the page but as the attempted embodiment of a vision: a complex of emotions, raw experience."

Teaching students to write as Oates describes is to provide them with a powerful experience. Such a craft is not just about plot lines and dialogue; it is a complex, highly cerebral exploration. It is a meld between imagination and reality in which students are free to imagine any possibility but must understand the logic intertwined within such possibilities. Student authors must call upon their knowledge of human relationships, individual emotions, and societal norms in the real world and adapt this framework to their imagined world, shaping their characters, the relationships and conflicts between characters, in such a way that the story is believable because it holds true to its internal logic. They must then go further to craft their story in a way that will communicate this imagined, logical reality to their readers in a fresh, immediate, and engaging manner.

From an academic perspective, story writing expands students' creativity, logic, and mastery of language—all valuable pursuits in any classroom. But as Bomer (1995) points out, story writing is also a democratic exercise in breaking down stereotypes and building understanding:

> If they can imagine the world through the eyes of someone who is not themselves in constructing a story, there's a chance they may be a little less likely to see other human beings as objects or stereotypes. For that reason, I do not see fiction writing as frilly or unrigorous playtime but rather as a hard rehearsal of valuable habits of mind.

Envisioning the Unit

Like most students who had been through five or six years of schooling, Donna's sixth-grade students knew and could identify the elements of story: characters, plot, conflict, setting, and theme. However, few really understood these elements or their importance. Students could identify the characters' names and physical characteristics but had difficulty understanding a character's perspective. Students could point toward the major outward conflict and resolution in the story but didn't see the inner struggles within characters that frequently went unresolved. Similarly, themes could be identified only at a most superficial level. Students had a few stock "theme-sounding" phrases that they had picked up somewhere, but they were lost when asked to explain their ideas in any depth.

Throughout the fall and the early part of the winter Donna immersed her students in great juvenile and young adult literature. They spent many hours reading independently and together explored a few much-treasured books, including Babbitt's *Tuck Everlasting*, Gantos's *Joey Pigza Swallowed the Key*, and Sachar's *Holes*. These common texts took students deeper into the experience of living in the book. Listening to their teacher read aloud, thinking through teacher-posed questions together, and responding regularly in their journals allowed students to more thoroughly understand the worlds within these texts. But many were unable to transfer such an experience to their independent reading. On their own, texts still seemed distant and hard to reach. Donna had led them through the doors and into the worlds explored in the common texts; on their own, the gates to fictional worlds remained locked.

Because the worlds of fiction remained so distant for most, the idea of writing a short story of their own seemed totally unapproachable. When we initially brought the idea up, students universally declared that it was too hard, with one student moaning, "You mean we would have to make everything up? We couldn't borrow any of the characters? That's not fair."

It seemed that most of Donna's students were too well grounded in their own reality—they were stuck. These sixth-graders were mostly from low-income families, and they attended a quintessentially urban school. Within the school, they were considered high achievers; most of them were reading at or near grade level, were academically motivated, and had performed well in previous years of schooling. Many of them were first- or second-generation immigrants, and nearly all would be the first in their families to attend college. Support at home varied; some families remained intact while others were splintered. Nearly all the students were entering the stage of adolescence in which they were questioning their parents, the rules, and authority figures in general. They were casting a more critical eye on the world around them and wondering about their own futures.

Both academically and developmentally it was a good time to engage these students in a short story study. Reading short stories would provide an ideal platform for teaching them the mechanisms by which they could engage more thoroughly in literature. Writing short stories would empower them to imagine new realities, an exercise that would encourage complex thinking, support strong narrative writing, and potentially lead them to imagine new realities for their own futures. As Donna and I pondered the specific goals for the study, we kept in mind both the academic and developmental imperatives that guided us toward the study. Yes, we wanted students to live within the pages of a book, we wanted them to be able to create great stories, but we wanted these things for a reason. Ultimately, we wanted students to be able to see, understand, and imagine realities beyond their own.

Teaching the Unit—Reading Workshop

Characters are at the heart of stories. As a reader, it is essential to understand the characters in order to fully appreciate stories. It is through characters that we enter into stories, exploring their internal reality, understanding the themes, conflicts, and resolutions that are represented. However, our initial assessment of Donna's students revealed that their perception of characters was typically very superficial. They saw them as flat, one-dimensional figures incapable of complex emotions or substantive change. This understanding needed to change. In her first lesson, Donna teaches students to pay close attention to text in order to thoughtfully infer information about the characters.

SAMPLE LESSON: ## Week 1—Reading Workshop

AREA OF STUDY:	**Reading comprehension**
FOCUS:	**Describing a character**
TEXT:	**"Slower Than the Rest," by Cynthia Rylant, from *Every Living Thing***
RESPONSE:	**Margin notes and text underlining**

Donna began with a read-aloud. We had selected "Slower Than the Rest," a wonderful story by Cynthia Rylant, as our first text. It tells the story of Leo, a boy who has been labeled "slow" by his classmates, teachers, and parents. He has few friends and little self-confidence. But when he finds a turtle, he finds a friend. His love for his pet allows him the confidence and the motivation to make an outstanding school presentation about the dangers of forest fires. His presentation is publicly lauded and with the acclaim comes newfound happiness. The story ends, "That night, alone in his room, holding Charlie on his shoulder, Leo felt proud. And for the first time in a long time, Leo felt *fast*." The story has one clear central character, wonderful descriptions, and, in Leo, a boy who should not have been pigeonholed as "slow." Not only did this story provide wonderful opportunities for student readers to develop a character portrait, but it also had an important mes-

Reading Workshop—Short Story
Goals and Instructional Focus Progression

	Reading Comprehension Study	Accountable Talk Study
	Goal: Students will learn to immerse themselves in a story in order to analyze and later evaluate the characters, conflicts, and events of the text.	**Goal:** Students will learn to engage in meaningful small-group discussions about short stories.
Weeks 1–2	**Describing the Characters** Students will learn to use text clues to develop a description of the characters in a short story. • What does the text tell us directly about the characters? • What can we infer about the characters based on what they say, do, and think? • Justify your inferences with text evidence. **Questioning the Characters** Students will learn to ask thoughtful questions in an effort to better understand the characters in the text. • What questions do you want to ask the characters in the text? Why? What is the purpose of each question?	**Establishing Student Story Discussion Groups** Students will learn what is appropriate to say and do before, during, and after a story discussion group. • Establishing a group and selecting a story • Preparing for the discussion • Gathering the group in an appropriate environment • Starting a discussion • Using appropriate behavior during a discussion
Weeks 3–4	**Understanding the Character's Perspective** Students will learn to step into the character's shoes in order to consider potential responses to their questions from the character's perspective. • Put yourself in your character's shoes. How would your character respond to the questions asked? • Support your response. What text evidence do you have that supports your understanding of your character's point of view? **Reflecting on the Character's Conversation** Students will learn to reflect on their conversations to thoughtfully analyze the characters and their role in the text. • Describe your character as you now understand him or her. Consider his or her actions, motivations, interactions, conflicts, reactions, strengths, and weaknesses. • Explain how talking to your character helped to shape your understanding of the story.	**Sharing Ideas and Insights About a Story** Students will learn appropriate ways of sharing their own reading observations with peers. • Sharing ideas about the text • Sharing insights about your process • Referencing the text when appropriate **Responding to Peers** Students will listen and respond to peers in a manner that invites further discussion and greater understanding of the text. • Questioning the speaker to better understand his/her ideas • Requesting evidence • Sharing your own thoughts on the topic • Pointing out supporting or contradictory evidence • Asking further questions
Weeks 5–6	**Evaluating the Story** Students will learn to thoughtfully assess the value of a short story. • What are the strengths of the story? weaknesses? • Is the story internally consistent? Do the characters make sense? Are their actions and reactions reasonable? • What do you value about this story? • Would you recommend this story to other readers? Why, or why not? **Evaluating Reading Progress—Self-Reflection and Teacher Evaluation**	**Working Together to Reflect on a Text** Students will learn to work together to analyze the perspectives of the characters and value of the story more thoughtfully. • What have we learned about the characters and their perspectives? • What do we value about this story? • Would we recommend this story? Why, or why not? **Evaluating the Discussion—Self-, Class, and Teacher Evaluation**

sage about the necessity of seeing individuals as complex, multifaceted beings—an echo of our purpose for the lesson.

Students listened attentively. They had been with Donna for several months now and enjoyed hearing stories told in her rich and animated voice. And they were ready with quick responses when the story was over and Ms. Bates asked her first question. "Tell me about Leo," Donna requested. Hands shot up. "He's a boy," said one student. Half the hands went down. "He has a turtle," explained another. The other half of the hands went down. "Anything else?" Donna prompted. The students were silent. A few looked at each other and shrugged. "We answered the question," the shrug seemed to suggest. "What more does she want?"

We wanted a lot more. "You are right," Donna confirmed. "He is a boy and he does have a turtle. But there's a lot more to Leo than that. The characters in stories are like real people; they have likes and dislikes, strengths and weaknesses, relationships and expectations. Now, stories typically don't come right out and tell us all about these things. We have to figure out what a character is like based on what they say and think and do in the story. Let's look a bit more closely at Leo's story, and I'll show you what I mean."

On the overhead she placed a transparency of the first page of "Slower Than the Rest":

> Leo was the first one to spot the turtle, so he was the one who got to keep it. They had all been in the car, driving up Tyler Mountain to church, when Leo shouted, "There's a turtle!" and everyone's head jerked with the stop.
>
> Leo's father grumbled something about turtle soup, but Leo's mother was sympathetic toward turtles, so Leo was allowed to pick it up off the highway and bring it home. Both his little sisters squealed when the animal stuck its ugly head out to look at them, and they thought its claws horrifying, but Leo loved it from the start. He named it Charlie.
>
> The dogs at Leo's house had always belonged more to Leo's father than to anyone else, and the cat thought she belonged to no one but herself, so Leo was grateful for a pet of his own. He settled Charlie in a cardboard box, threw in some lettuce and radishes, and declared himself a happy boy.

Donna slowly reread this section of the text. At the end she paused. "One thing I can infer about Leo based on what I just read," she said, "is that he is kind-hearted. I can tell that because right at the beginning, when they are driving up the hill, he shouted, 'There's a turtle.'" Donna underlined that portion of the text. "Now, the fact that he shouts it, instead of simply saying it or just ignoring the turtle, tells me that he is really concerned about the turtle and wants to take care of it. That makes me think that he's kind-hearted." Donna recorded "kind-hearted" in the margin of the transparency adjacent to the underlined text.

She continued, modeling a second observation about Leo. "Another thing that I can infer about Leo is that he's not very close to his dad. It says that his father, 'grumbled something about turtle soup' when Leo wanted to stop to pick up the turtle. Later, in the third paragraph, it says, 'The dogs at Leo's house had always belonged more to Leo's father than to anyone else.' From those two sentences, it sounds like Leo and his dad are interested in different things, like they are not very close." Again, Donna underlined the sentences that she had read from the text and then recorded "distant from dad" in the margin of the transparency.

Then she turned back to her students to explain her process. "What I've just done here is to infer things about Leo based on what he has said or thought or done. I've looked at what it says in the text and then thought to myself, 'What does this tell me about Leo?' I want you to give it a try now. What do you see in the text that helps you understand Leo? Does he say or do or think something that helps you to understand who he is?" The hands took much longer to appear this time, but gradually students began to volunteer. One explained that she thought Leo was lonely because the text said he was "grateful for a pet of his own." Another explained that she thought he was close to his mom, because his mom was willing to stop the car and let him bring the turtle home. A third described Leo as "easily satisfied," because he "declared himself a happy boy" after placing his turtle in a cardboard box with a little bit of food. As students volunteered, Donna prompted them to explain (1) what they could infer about Leo, (2) what in the text led them to that inference, and (3) how the text evidence supported their inference. Only when she was satisfied with students' responses to these three crucial considerations did she record the observation on the overhead and underline the appropriate text evidence.

Once students had thoroughly picked apart this section of text, Donna decided they were ready for a bit more independence. She passed out a copy of the story to each student and instructed, "Read Leo's story on your own. As you read, pay close attention to what he says, does, and thinks. Pause every few paragraphs to consider what you can infer about Leo based on what you have just read. Underline pieces of text that lead you to make inferences about Leo, and record your inference in the margins."

Students scattered back to desks and comfortable chairs. For the next twenty minutes they combed through the text, carefully identifying aspects of Leo's personality and relationships that they had completely missed during the first reading. Donna and I were available to help those students who struggled, but most were able to readily apply the strategy that had been modeled for them.

When students came back together, Donna reiterated the prompt with which she had begun the period: "Tell me about Leo." This time the response was considerably greater. I charted while Donna directed the discussion. The result: three pieces of chart paper filled with more than thirty different observations!

◄◦►

Donna and I spent the better part of the next week reinforcing this lesson. Students practiced in small groups and on their own. They tried to infer descriptions about characters in more sophisticated texts and longer stories. And they worked to construct thoughtful character profiles in their reading response journals. By the beginning of the second week of the study, all students were able to recognize and articulately describe the individuals who populated their stories. However . . .

There is a significant difference between recognizing and understanding. Although students could recognize the strengths and weaknesses, positive and negative traits, interior and exterior descriptions of characters, many still struggled to understand those characters and their unique perspectives. It was hard to separate students' own personalities and judgments from the story. It was hard to believe that if the character did things differently than they, the readers, might have done, that there could be a good reason. Despite their obvious growth, students still saw characters in stories as fictional beings who didn't necessarily need to follow any pattern of logic or growth. Just as they had accepted that Little Red Riding Hood didn't immediately recognize that the wolf was not her grandmother, students readily accepted that if "Slower Than the Rest" said that Leo was slow, then he must be slow. They didn't feel the need to dig deeper for any kind of explanation.

Conferring first with students, and then with each other, Donna and I decided that we needed to teach students to engage more fully with these stories, and that the vehicle through which we would encourage this engagement was questioning. When we ask questions, it is because we are seeking to understand that which we do not fully comprehend. Teaching students to ask questions about a story would enable them to explore the reality of the text, to ask, "Why do the characters interact in a particular way?" "What motivated that response?" "What will be the repercussions of an event?"

We knew from earlier experience with students and questions, that simply asking, "What questions do you have?" often failed to elicit thoughtful responses. So we decided to try something a bit different: teach students to ask questions directly of the characters in the text. And then later, when it came time to consider answers, we would ask them to step into the role of a character and consider what he or she might say back. This interior conversation between a reader and a character would not only enliven the story and bring the characters to life, but would also support students' understanding of characters and their perspectives in a way that simply describing text elements or responding to standard teacher prompts could not. Donna introduced the first part of this strategy in the following lesson.

SAMPLE LESSON: ## Week 2—Reading Workshop

AREA OF STUDY:	**Reading comprehension**
FOCUS:	**Questioning a character**
TEXT:	**"An Education," by Marie G. Lee, from *But That's Another Story*, edited by Sandy Asher**
RESPONSE:	**Class chart of types of questions; margin notes**

Donna called her students up to the front of the classroom. They crowded close to her, pulling their chairs with them. They brought no paper or pens this time. Their job would be to observe only, but each knew that they would be held responsible for their observations. "Today we are going to try something a little different," Donna began. A few students rolled their eyes, others looked skeptical. Donna continued, "You've done a good job developing complex portraits of characters as you read. Today, you are going to take those portraits off the canvas and talk to them as if they were real people. Good readers interact with the characters in their stories. We have a running commentary that goes on in our head; sometimes we give advice, sometimes we try to offer a warning, and always we question. We question characters in order to find out what's happening in their world, to understand their reality. Now, talking to your character may sound a little crazy, but I think that if you give it a try, you'll find that it helps you understand a story better, and it also makes reading more fun."

Donna placed a transparency of the first page of "An Education" on the overhead. The text, by Marie G. Lee, is a dramatic short story about a young woman's encounter with prejudice during her high school graduation ceremony. Helen had always known that her Korean heritage was a source of derision among some of her classmates, but she had consistently followed her parents' example and pretended that there was nothing wrong, that she was just another American. But during her graduation, a racist epithet is hissed across the stage at her, causing both Helen and her family to confront the reality of what it means to be Korean and American. It is a story that invites questions—well suited to our purposes. Students had read and enjoyed the story earlier in the week. Now we were returning to it in order to introduce this new strategy.

Donna began to reread the text with her students. Every now and then she would pause and "talk" with her character. For example, after reading the description of an argument between Helen and her parents about learning Korean, Donna reread a line from the text: "'If I'm Korean,' she had once said to her parents, 'then why won't you teach me to read and write Korean?'" Donna stopped and looked up at the class. "Right here, after this section, I would like to ask Helen, 'Why is it important to you to learn Korean?' I'd like to ask that because it doesn't seem like it would be very useful in her daily life at school and her parents never speak in Korean, so I'm curious as to why she is interested." Donna recorded the question in the margin of the overhead. Then she continued, "A little later, after her parents have refused her request, it says, 'She didn't argue with her parents but she wanted to know more . . . they made it seem like being Korean was something to be ashamed of.' That makes me sad when I read it, and I want to ask her, 'Do you really believe that? Why do you feel that way? Why don't you talk to your parents and tell them how you feel?'" Again, Donna recorded her questions in the margin.

Then she asked the students, "What about you? What would you like to ask Helen?" Several students wondered why Helen's parents behaved as they did. Others wanted to know if she'd ever talked to other Korean Americans who felt the same way. A few had comments rather than questions. "I want to tell her that she should not be ashamed of her heritage," said one student. "She should be proud of who she is." Donna smiled at the student's demonstration of support but asked her to rephrase her thoughts as a question. "I appreciate your viewpoint, and I agree with it. But your views may not apply to Helen's reality. That's why we are asking questions, to try to understand her reality and have it make sense."

Together the class read two additional sections of the story. After each section, Donna would pause and ask students to share their questions. They were required to explain what piece of the text had prompted the question, and instructed to phrase the question directly to Helen. Donna listened carefully, helped students adjust their questions if necessary, and recorded their thoughts in the margins of the overhead.

Once she was confident that most students understood when and how to question the character, Donna prepared to release students to work on their own. But before letting them go, she took the time to ensure that they were clear on what type of questions to ask. "Look back at the questions we've asked so far," Donna instructed. "What do you notice about the types of questions that we've been asking? We haven't, for example, asked Helen questions about the color of her shoes or what the weather is like. What have we asked about?" Students' responses:

Questioning a Character
I can ask questions about . . .
- The events in the story

- Why the character does certain things (character motivations)
- Why the character doesn't do certain things
- Character reactions
- Character relationships
- The history behind things that are going on
- Predictions about what will happen later

Satisfied with this list, Donna sent students off to apply the strategy on their own. They were told to read the remainder of "An Education" and record their questions in the margins. As they worked, Donna and I made our way around the classroom, glancing at student notes and conferring one-on-one. In general, we were impressed with the quality of the questions and the sensitivity students were showing Helen. I complimented one student on a particularly insightful question and asked how she had thought of it. "Well," she responded, "at first I didn't think I had any questions, but when Ms. Bates told us to talk to Helen directly, I started thinking about what I would tell her if she was my friend. If she was real, that's what I'd want to know, so that's what I asked."

———◄◦►———

A few days of practice were needed to help students develop the ability to consistently ask insightful questions of their characters, but soon they were ready to start thinking about answers. Now it was time for them to leave the world they knew to step inside the story and understand its internal reality. We knew it would be a challenge for students to put themselves into someone else's place. But we thought they were ready to try it. In the following lesson, Donna uses "An Education," which at this point had become an oft-referenced "touchstone" text, to introduce the other side of the conversation.

SAMPLE LESSON: ## Week 3—Reading Workshop

AREA OF STUDY:	**Reading comprehension**
FOCUS:	**Understanding a character's perspective**
TEXT:	**"An Education," by Marie G. Lee, from *But That's Another Story*, edited by Sandy Asher**
RESPONSE:	**Reading response journal entries**

"What do you mean, the characters are going to talk back?" James asked incredulously. "They aren't real, they can't talk back." Donna and I smiled over the students' heads. This response represented the very reason we were embarking on this challenge. "You're right, James," Donna explained. "The characters aren't real, but the authors who created them tried to make them as realistic as possible. And, as readers, we can really understand the story only if we think about it from their perspective. You have all asked lots of questions from your perspective. Now you need to think about how to respond to those questions from the perspective of the characters." James and his peers remained suspicious, but Donna continued.

On the overhead she placed the first page from the story, "An Education." It still had the notes from the mini-lesson a few days earlier. Today Donna would use those notes, her questions to Helen, as response prompts. She quickly reread part of the text to refresh students' memories and then paused when she reached one of her first recorded questions. "Remember here, I wanted to ask Helen, 'Do you really believe that?' after she said that she almost felt like being Korean was something to be ashamed of. Now, thinking about it from her perspective, I imagine that she might say something like, 'I know that I shouldn't be ashamed, but that's a lot easier to know in your head than feel in your heart. My parents always pretended that being Korean-American didn't make any difference; they won't talk to me about our heritage. How can I be proud of something that I don't know anything about?'"

Donna continued, "I think that she might say something like that because of some of the other things that she has said or done. For example, here it says that a lot of her friends tease her about her Asian looks, and 'she didn't feel smart, she just felt Korean and didn't know if it was a good feeling.' A few paragraphs earlier, when they are talking about learning Korean, her mom says, 'You're American. . . . You don't need to waste your time on that old stuff.' I really get the impression that she feels torn. She wants to know what it means to be Korean-American but she isn't getting any support from her parents, and she's getting a lot of negative input from her friends. I think her response to my question would show a lot of frustration."

Donna checked to see if students understood her response and then moved to the next question. As before, she repeated the question, explained that she was thinking about it from Helen's perspective, and then thoughtfully incorporated evidence from the text into her reply. As Donna modeled, students visibly relaxed. Having the characters talk back sounded weird, but the practice wasn't nearly as strange as they had feared. After modeling several responses, Donna began to encourage student participation, asking students what they thought Helen might respond to the questions, and why. Students were told to think about what they knew about Helen's character and to include evidence from the text when responding. Though not perfect, their ideas were remarkably thoughtful. It was fascinating to listen to them respond to questions that they themselves had wondered about a few days before. Occasionally, students would disagree, prompting more careful, text-based justification for the responses.

About half of the way through the text, Donna determined that the students were ready to try responding to questions on their own. Students were told to independently review their copies of the text: "First, reread the text to reacquaint yourself with Helen and the story. Then review the questions that you asked during our earlier lesson. Choose the three questions that are most interesting. Write those questions in your journal. After each question, write a response from Helen's perspective. Be thoughtful in your responses, make sure that you are speaking as Helen, and explain your point of view clearly. Be sure to consider evidence from the text when crafting your response. Ms. Lattimer and I will be checking in with you if need help."

The students got to work. Reviewing the text was easy. Selecting questions was easy. But responding proved more of a challenge. Many students found that putting themselves into Helen's shoes required a more thoughtful understanding of the text than they had previously developed, prompting them to go back and read for specific details. Others quickly wrote answers down but, when asked to justify their response, found that they weren't able to do so and therefore needed to go back and think more carefully. Despite a few early frustrations, by the end of the period most had begun to adjust their thinking. "It was actually kinda fun," admitted Frances, "and it made me think about the story in a new way. When I thought from the character's perspective, the ending made a lot more sense."

◄○►

Over the next few days, students grew more confident and competent in their ability to think through the character's perspective. As this happened, Donna and I reduced our reliance on students' use of reading response journals. We wanted students to learn to carry on a conversation with their characters in their heads, to constantly consider, while reading, questions from their own perspective and potential responses from the characters' point of view. During weeks 3 and 4, as students developed their internal conversations with characters, Donna and I spent considerable time conferring one-on-one with students about their work and listening in on their small-group discussions.

Throughout the unit, students had been meeting once or twice a week in groups of three or four to discuss a story that all members of the group had read. Donna and I had found that encouraging students to discuss texts in small groups was a wonderful way to reinforce their learning. After a whole-class lesson, many students were not prepared to apply new skills and strategies to reading texts on their own. But keeping the entire class together in the same text for an extended period of time felt too regimented and allowed struggling students to hide behind the strengths of their peers. Small-group discussion opportunities provided a nice bridge as we gradually released responsibility to the students.

At this point in our study, when students came together to discuss a story, they were encouraged to share their conversations. However, too often their sharing became a dry litany of "I asked," "The character responded," "I asked," "The character responded," and so on. It was ironic, but somehow teaching students to have a conversation with the characters in their stories diminished their ability to have a conversation with their peers. We decided to address this disturbing trend with a lesson focused specifically on accountable talk—teaching students to challenge one another, to hold peers responsible for their ideas.

SAMPLE LESSON: ## Week 4—Reading Workshop

AREA OF STUDY:	**Accountable talk**
FOCUS:	**Responding to peers**
TEXT:	**"The Mechanical Mind," by Gary Soto, from *Local News***
RESPONSE:	**Observation notes; small-group discussions and reflections**

Our discussion sounded as if it were being read from a very stilted script. The students sat surrounding us as Donna and I modeled a text discussion. They immediately recognized the dry tone of our talk; it sounded like something each of them had participated in during previous small-group literature discussions. One student would share, stating what the text said, what I said to the character, and what the character might say back. Repeat, Repeat, Repeat.

Students shifted uncomfortably in their chairs as Donna and I took turns sharing with, but never responding to, one another. After working our way through four or five cycles of "sharing," Donna turned to her students. "What do you think? Is this a good conversation?" A bit sheepishly, students admitted that it was not. "Okay, we're going to try it again," said Donna. "But this time, instead of just stating our own ideas, we're going to respond to each other. For example, we may ask each other questions or challenge each other's ideas. I want you to notice what we do differently. Afterward we'll talk about how those differences affect the quality of the conversation."

Donna turned back to face me, and we began our conversation again. It started out in a manner very similar to the previous attempt. Donna described a question she wanted to ask Philip Quintana in Gary Soto's very funny short story "The Mechanical Mind": "On page 114, when it says that he 'got it into his head that he would look inside the telephone hanging on the wall,' I wanted to ask, 'Are you sure that's a good idea?'" In our previous conversation, Donna would simply have moved on to her next comment, but this time I interrupted.

"Why would you want to ask him that?" I wondered. Donna paused and thought for a moment. "Well, because I don't think it is such a good idea," she said. "I think phones are probably pretty complicated, and it would be easy to break. But I don't want to hurt his feelings by just telling him that it's a bad idea, so I'm phrasing it as a question to kind of break it to him gently." "That makes sense," I agreed. "I'd ask pretty much the same thing. What do you think that he would say back?" Donna responded, "I think he'd probably tell me that it was fine and that I shouldn't worry. He seems so full of confidence at this point that nothing is going to stop him." "I agree," I said. "But I wonder how much of that confidence is just bluster. After he took off the plastic cover, on page 115, it says that 'he strummed his fingers on the bunched strands of red and yellow wires, then put his ear to the receiver.' If he really believed he had a mechanical mind, it seems like he'd have taken the wires apart. I wonder if he's just having a good time experimenting and showing off for his sister. What do you think? Do you think he really believes that he has a mechanical mind?"

Our conversation went along this way for several minutes. Donna and I came back to the original "script" two or three times, sharing a text reference and a question that she or I had formed as we were reading. But each time, instead of just letting the comment stand, the listener queried and probed, asking why a particular question was asked of a character, what response might be expected from that character, and insisting on justification for the response. These simple questions led to some thoughtful debates over Philip's motivations, his expectations, and his relationship with his sister.

When we wrapped it up, students were unanimous in deciding that this conversation had been a lot more interesting. "Good," Donna said. "It was supposed to be." Then she asked them to explain the differences. "You guys didn't just listen to what the other one said," one student noted. "Yeah," another chimed in. "You were always asking questions and putting in your own ideas." "It was like you were making people defend what they were saying," observed a third. Donna agreed with this general assessment but pressed students to be more detailed in their observations. She knew that having specific expectations would help students when their turn came to talk about the text. The students' findings:

Good Listeners Respond to a Speaker's Comments
- *Ask why.* "Why do you believe that?"
- *Request evidence.* "Where do you see that in the text?"
- *Share your own ideas about the* same *topic.* "Here's what I thought about that."
- *Point out contradictory evidence.* "If that's true, then how do you explain . . . ?"
- *Point out supporting evidence.* "I agree. Here's why."
- *Ask a new question based on the comment.* "I hadn't considered that before. That makes me wonder . . ."

With these response prompts posted prominently at the front of the room, students were sent off to their own literature discussion groups to engage in more in-depth conversations. For now, they were all to discuss "The Mechanical Mind." We had read it together recently, so it was fresh in students' minds, and Donna and I had intentionally introduced some ideas from the piece but left a lot of potential discussion points untouched. Students had an easy familiarity with the text that would allow them to focus on developing the conversation skills rather than worrying about the particulars of the text.

As Donna and I wandered around the classroom, we observed much more engaging discussions. Students were leaning forward and focusing on one another as they spoke, a behavior that they had been taught before but that now appeared more genuine. At first, some of the discussions felt stilted, with students stating the response prompts in a mock serious tone. But as they became more engaged in the story itself, the mocking disappeared and they truly began to discuss the characters—their motivations, their growth, their strengths, and their weaknesses. After fifteen minutes, Donna interrupted their discussions to call students back together, noting that this was the first time that all conversations had been sustained for so long. "That's because it was more interesting," one student explained. Her peers nodded their agreement, with another chiming in, "I liked this a lot better because it made me feel good about what I had to say. When they asked questions, it was like what I said mattered." Such a belief is crucial, not only to a good discussion but to developing a sustainable interest in reading and understanding literature.

———◄o►———

During the final weeks of the short story reading workshop study, we pushed students to further engage with short stories by focusing on two additional learning objectives.

Reflecting on Character Conversations   Students had done a good job learning to thoughtfully question characters and to respond in the character's voice. This strategy had taken them into the story and engaged them with the text in a meaningful and substantive manner. Through their conversations students had considered character actions, motivations, interactions, conflicts, reactions, strengths, and weaknesses. However, these considerations were often made without conscious recognition. During reading conferences Donna and I found that many students had developed very thoughtful analyses of their characters without even realizing it. As the study drew to a close, we wanted to make sure that students were aware of, and could articulate, these analyses.

To meet this objective, we began requiring students to reflect on their character conversations. In class discussions and reading response journals, students were asked to respond to two key prompts: "Describe your character as you now understand him or her." "Explain how talking to your character helped to shape your understanding." The resulting reflections were rich with thoughtful understanding and evidence of successful work that had been done during the study. Teaching students to go into the story to understand its internal reality meant that when they later extracted themselves from the text, they came away with a much more insightful understanding of the characters and the story. An example of one student's reading response follows:

Response to "The Inside Ballerina," by Carol Coven Grannick
Julius M., Grade 6
"The Inside Ballerina" is the name of this story, but it is also a description of the main character. Sara dances differently inside her mind than she does outside in her ballet class because she is afraid that people will laugh at her. She is bigger than the other girls, and some of them are mean to her.

    The first time I read this story I didn't really think about Sara's perspective. I just thought that she should get over it and not be embarrassed or anything. There are lots of big people, and it's nothing to be ashamed of. But when I tried to put myself in her place, I understood more about why she felt like she had to hide. There was a big difference between what she thought the rest of the world wanted from her and what she felt she had to offer. Inside herself she felt beauty and energy. She knew that she was a dancer. But when she looked around, she realized that she didn't fit the image that other people had of dancers. Her friends made fun of her, and her mom put her on a diet. Even when people were nice, it was like they were saying that she was a good person but they weren't letting her be what she really wanted to be. She felt trapped and uncomfortable in her own body.

    I think that it must be really, really hard to feel like you want to be something but not be able to be that thing because something you can't control stands in the way. I understand why Sara kept her true desires inside herself. She didn't want to risk sharing something so personal because if people laughed about it, then it would really hurt because it was so important to her. So she just kept everything inside as a defense. I bet there are lots of other people who feel the same way and that is really sad, because if they never risk sharing their dreams, then they will never achieve them.

Evaluating the Short Story In the end, we asked students to form judgments. What was the value of this short story? This question had been saved until the end intentionally. If it had been asked earlier, students would have been quick to simply praise or reject stories without taking the time to truly engage with the literature. But now it was appropriate to ask students to become more clinical in their thinking. Among the questions that we asked them to consider: "What are the strengths or weaknesses of the story?" "Is the story internally consistent? Do the characters make sense? Are their actions and reactions reasonable?" "What do you value about this story?" "Would you recommend this story to other readers? Why, or why not?"

Although evaluating the story required a shift in mind-set for students, it built upon all the work undertaken previously in this study. The intensity with which students had engaged with stories enabled them to assess the value of a text more thoughtfully. Before the study started, most would have been able to pass only superficial value judgments: I like (or didn't like) the story because it was funny, sad, had lots of action, etc. Now they were able to much more readily appreciate the subtleties and ironies in text, to recognize a story's strengths and weaknesses, and to find value in the experience of living, if only for a moment, in another reality.

The work on evaluating a short story led directly into the class's response to literature study, in which students wrote reviews of short stories (see Chapter 7).

Teaching the Unit—Writing Workshop

Great short stories depend upon great characters. But developing such a character out of thin air can be a challenge. At the very mention of the term *character,* most of Donna's students immediately thought of Superman, Mickey Mouse, and Bugs Bunny—popular caricatures that are flat, one-dimensional, and unrealistic. Although these characters serve their medium well, such caricatures would have been inappropriate for the short stories we wanted students to produce. Instead, we wanted students to imagine thoughtful, multidimensional, realistic characters who could interact and struggle with realistic conflicts.

The first step toward developing such complex characters was to immerse students in their reading. Reading short stories, understanding and interacting with characters as a reader, provided students with a gut-level sense of what a character should look like. However, a "sense," while a good barometer for assessing published stories and rereading and assessing your own work, is a difficult starting point when budding authors are attempting to develop a character of their own for what may be the first time. We needed more concrete expectations of the qualities that make up a believable character. For example, we wanted students to know that a believable character has both positives and negatives, strengths and weaknesses, specific quirks and funny obsessions, a history of who he or she is, and a community within which he or she exists.

Writing Workshop—Short Story
Goals and Instructional Focus Progression

	Text Structure Study	Writing Process Study
	Goal: Students will learn to use the elements of a narrative to craft an engaging and realistic short story.	**Goal:** Students will develop an original story involving unique characters and conflicts.
Weeks 1–2	**Defining a Short Story** Students develop a definition of a short story • What are examples of short stories? nonexamples? • What elements must a short story have? not have? Why? **Character Analysis** Students will analyze characters to determine the necessary qualities of credible and engaging characters. • Analyze a favorite story. What are the qualities of the characters that make them believable? not believable? • Compare analyses. What qualities should a believable character have? not have?	**Planning—Developing a Character** Students will use the determined qualities of "believable" characters to imagine unique, complex characters of their own. • Does this character have both positive and negative qualities? • Will you be able to understand this character's point of view? • Determine the character's relationships.
Weeks 3–4	**Conflict Analysis** Students will analyze conflicts to better understand the size and scope of conflicts appropriate to short stories. • Analyze a favorite story. What is the central conflict in the story? How is it introduced? resolved? • Compare analyses. What are the qualities of conflicts used successfully in short stories? **Plot Analysis** Students will analyze plots to better understand the means of organizing and telling a story. • Analyze a favorite story. How is the plot sequenced? How does the author show the movement of time? • Compare analyses. What sequencing structures and time movement devices are most successful? Why? **Style Analysis** Students will analyze styles to better understand how authors use language to breathe life into stories. • Analyze a favorite story. How are characters revealed? How is perspective shown? What tone or voice is used? • Compare analyses. What language and stylistic techniques are most successful? Why?	**Planning—Defining the Conflict** Students will narrowly define the conflict for their story and consider it from the perspective of their character. • What conflicts does your character have control over? • Which conflict is most appropriate for your story? Why? **Sequencing and Drafting the Story** Students will develop a rough sequencing outline for use in their drafting. **Shaping the Story—Revealing Character** Students will make choices about how to best reveal the characters and their perspectives. • How can you best show experiences from your character's point of view? • How can you best balance dialogue, description, internal thoughts, and actions? • Do you want to use first or third person narration? Why? • What tone do you want to use? Why?
Weeks 5–6	**Engaging the Audience** Students will analyze the beginnings and endings used by authors to engage their audiences. • What stories have beginnings and/or endings that you find most compelling? Why? • How do the beginnings and endings used support the characters, plot, and style of the story?	**Editing—Keeping the Story Focused** Students will reread, cut, add, and revise in order to keep the story focused. • What is essential to developing the conflict and the character's perspective? • What can be cut? **Evaluating the Writing** • Establish a set of evaluation criteria • Measure your final published piece against established criteria • Reflect on learning

Donna's class spent the first several days of the short story writing workshop considering favorite characters from stories and novels. What made them favorite characters? Were they believable? Why, or why not? Then, as explained in the following lesson, Donna took students through the process of developing a character together, highlighting important considerations and providing a series of prompts that they would later be able to apply on their own. (Note: This lesson draws heavily on ideas described by Bomer in the "Fiction" chapter of *Time for Meaning*.)

SAMPLE LESSON: # Week 1—Writing Workshop

AREA OF STUDY:	**Writing process**
FOCUS:	**Imagining and developing a character**
RESPONSE:	**Class character development; individual character development**

"We've spent the past few days looking at other characters in published stories. You've told me who your favorites are, and why. You've considered which characters are most believable and what makes them believable. Today it is your turn. You now get to imagine a character. We'll try this together first, and then you'll try it on your own. Ready?" Students looked a bit shocked. Analyzing other characters was one thing; inventing a character from scratch seemed overwhelming.

"Let's start with a name. Names tell us a lot about our character's identity. What shall we name this character?" Several students volunteered name suggestions. Donna grabbed one of the first she heard and wrote it down on the chart paper at the front of the room. Her goal here was to teach students the process of creating a character, so she didn't spend a lot of time worrying about gathering class approval of the name or any other characteristic.

"Timmy. Our character's name is Timmy. Now, tell me about Timmy. Is he a boy? How old is he? What else do I know about him?" Together students brainstormed ideas. Timmy quickly became a twelve-year-old boy with dark hair and brown eyes. He was a skateboarder who was in sixth grade. As they worked, Donna frequently paused to explain why she accepted or didn't accept student suggestions for Timmy's character. "I think that it would be fascinating to read a story about a 92-year-old great-grandfather named Timmy," she cautioned at one point, "but I don't think any of us are prepared to write that story. I am not a 92-year-old great-grandfather and neither are you. Now, we don't have to or necessarily want to be exactly like our characters, but we will need to be close enough to our characters to really be able to get inside their heads, understand their actions, their reactions, the conflicts in their lives, their relationships with others, and their emotions. A 92-year-old great-grandfather is not close enough to my experience or the experience of anyone that I know well, so I would have trouble understanding and really living his perspective in a story. Let's stick with the twelve-year-old suggestion. It's a lot closer to our experience."

The class continued with their creative process. In response to Donna's questions about Timmy's loves and his family, students decided that he was loved by all his family and friends, that he was a great boy to hang around with, and that he was understanding and nice to everybody. When Donna asked about Timmy's fears and needs, students explained that he was afraid of losing a family member because he needs them all. Donna let this little love fest continue for a while. Then she stopped the students. "Read back over what you have so far. Does this person sound believable? To me, this sounds kind of like a glossy, picture-perfect boy. I don't know many people like that. Most people that I know are not so perfect. They have faults and problems, they make mistakes, and they have people who don't like them very much. Take a minute, think about Timmy, and then tell me about the Timmy behind the picture-perfect facade."

Gradually, students broadened their description of Timmy. Turns out that he is afraid of losing a family member because his parents are in the middle of a divorce. That he is friendly to everybody and makes everyone laugh, but that only his best friend, Mike, knows how much pain he is in because his dad has left. And that he likes to skate because it is the only time when he can forget about trying to tell jokes and making everybody else happy, he can just skate. Thanks to Donna's careful questioning and students' creative responses, within fifteen minutes a thoughtful portrait of a realistic Timmy emerged.

It was time to shift the creative responsibility to the students themselves. Nearly every student now had ideas about where to begin. Having watched Timmy emerge, they were energized by the possibilities, and many had ideas that they now wanted to transfer to their own characters. But before releasing students to "go create," Donna was careful to review the process with them. Together they noted some of the general questions that Donna had asked during Timmy's creation:

Character Qualities to Consider
- Name?
- Age? Grade?
- Gender: male or female?
- Parents? Siblings?
- Things he/she likes? dislikes?
- Places where he/she is happy? scared?
- Things he/she is good at? not so good at?
- Relationships with parents? siblings? grandparents?
- Friends? Who are they? What are they like?
- Enemies? People he/she is scared of or intimidated by?

- Things about him/her that people make fun of?
- Fears? Worries?
- Things that make him/her feel proud? embarrassed?
- Favorite memories? Favorite objects?

Donna cautioned that this list should be considered a starting point: "You don't need to consider every one of the qualities on this chart. Use this as a place to generate ideas, and see where your imagination takes you. Don't be afraid of making it perfect. You can always cross out, rearrange, or reinvent later." She also reminded them of her two earlier warnings: "Be sure that you keep your character close to you, someone that you will really be able to understand." "Be sure that your character has weaknesses as well as strengths. He or she shouldn't be too perfect or too miserable. We want realistic characters, not soap opera stars."

With these instructions, students set off to probe their own imaginations. Some were able to immediately develop highly original characters. Others were more simplistic in their character development. They went straight through the list of character qualities, responding to each with straightforward, two- or three-word phrases. Over and over, Donna and I asked questions to these students to prompt further thought. "You wrote down that your character loves chocolate. Why? What kind of chocolate does he like? Has his love for chocolate ever gotten him into trouble?" "Your character loves school. How come? What are the best and worst parts about school for your character? Why?" These questions prompted students to be more detailed in their imaginings, and through these details, more interesting and believable characters began to emerge.

◄○►

Donna's class spent over a week just focusing on character development. It took time for students to move away from developing bright, shiny caricatures and toward creating complex, realistic individuals. Students developed relationship webs and life histories for their characters. They fleshed out the "stress points" in their characters' lives and wrote a typical "day in the life" agenda. And they repeatedly shared, revised, and revisited the characters to make them more believable, more interesting, and more alive. All this work would provide our student authors with a better understanding of the characters that they were creating, and this would in turn help them to create richer, more believable stories.

However, stories need more than just great characters. They need those characters to be involved in a realistic and engaging conflict, something that will challenge the character's relationships, morals, or worldview. And just as we couldn't choose characters for our students, we couldn't choose their conflicts. Students had to raise conflicts out of the lives of their characters. In the following lesson, Donna uses the class's character, Timmy, to model the process of imagining conflicts appropriate to the characters that have been created.

SAMPLE LESSON: ## Week 2—Writing Workshop

AREA OF STUDY:	**Writing process**
FOCUS:	**Imagining a character in a "what if" situation**
RESPONSE:	**List of "what if" situations for characters**

"Stories are built around great characters," Donna began. "But the characters aren't just talked about in isolation. They are involved in some sort of conflict. What makes a story interesting is the manner in which characters approach, react to, and resolve conflicts. You've done a great job developing some wonderful characters; now it is time to put them in the middle of some reasonable conflicts and see what happens." Students nodded approvingly. They'd enjoyed creating characters, but in recent days had been growing restless and were ready to move to the next step.

At the front of the room, Donna posted a chart that listed the "stress points" the class had identified for Timmy during an earlier lesson. These stress points were based on the important relationships, pressures, and expectations—positive and negative—in Timmy's life. Each student had developed a similar list for his or her own character. Today Donna would ask students to build on these lists to identify a potential conflict for their stories: "Every day there are lots of little conflicts in each of our lives: whether to buy lunch or bring it from home . . . a sibling who is rude . . . forgotten homework. Most of these conflicts are minor, and we get over them fairly quickly. However, if the conflict relates directly to something that is important or stressful to us, then it is much more difficult to resolve. These are the interesting conflicts that can make great stories.

"For example," Donna continued, "in Timmy's case, one of his stress points is his relationship with Mike. He and Mike are best friends, and he has trusted Mike with a lot of secrets. We know that Timmy doesn't have a lot of close friends and that he really relies on Mike's friendship, especially now that his parents are going through a divorce. What would happen if Mike betrayed Timmy's trust? What would happen if Mike told one of Timmy's secrets? Or if Mike found a new friend and Timmy was left out? Exploring these possibilities might lead to an interesting story. Maybe Timmy would decide that he was so mad at Mike that he would demand all his stuff back, or maybe he'd even go take it back. Or maybe . . ."

Donna continued to talk through possibilities for Timmy's potential conflicts. As she worked, she made notes on the Stress Points chart, adding a column entitled What If? In this second column she wrote down hypothetical situations that could develop from the stress points. Initially, she created these possibilities, but soon the students were chiming in with ideas of their own. The result:

Finding Potential Story Conflicts

Stress Points	*What if . . .*
Timmy depends on Mike to be his best friend.	. . . Mike tells one of Timmy's secrets?
	. . . Mike finds a new friend, and Timmy is left out?
Timmy and his father rarely see each other since his dad moved out.	. . . his dad missed an important skating competition?
	. . . Timmy confronts his dad with his anger about his divorce?
	. . . his dad got custody?
	. . . his dad and mom got back together, and his dad moved back in?
Timmy loves to skate and is very good at it. He takes a lot of pride in his ability. He is considering competing.	. . . Timmy and Mike end up competing against each other?
	. . . Timmy breaks the rules and gets caught skating on school property?
Timmy struggles with his schoolwork. Mom wants him to get good grades.	. . . his mom threatens to take away his skates until he does better in school?
	. . . he cheats on a test in order to bring up his grades?
	. . . he gets caught for cheating?

"Many of these could be great possibilities for story starters," Donna remarked, looking over the list that the class had created. She then prepared students to take responsibility for imagining their own conflict possibilities: "Take your list of stress points. For each, think through the 'what if's. Imagine situations in which that stress could become a conflict. Record your ideas in your writer's notebook. Don't worry about finding the 'right' conflict right away. Instead, focus on exploring possibilities. We'll worry about figuring out the 'right' conflicts later."

As students worked, Donna and I made the rounds, offering suggestions and further possibilities. To the student who had an extensive but not very specific list of possibilities: "I like your idea here about 'What if she brings home a failing report card?' How about we push that one step further? What if she brings home a failing report card and then tries to change the grades before her dad finds out? Does that fit with her personality?" To the student who was struggling to come up with ideas: "One of your stress points is about the relationship between your character and his older brother. What kinds of things might cause conflict in that relationship? What if the younger brother got selected over the older one for a foot-ball team? What if the older brother snitched to mom and dad? What else?" And to students who were able to come up with a strong list of possibilities: "Which one is most interesting to you? Why? Try having a conversation with your character about that conflict, just as we do in reading workshop. Ask questions, put your-self in your character's place, and answer back. See where the conflict goes."

———◄○►———

During the creative writing process, it is a challenge to achieve an appropriate bal-ance between creativity and discipline. Donna and I wanted students to be creative with their characters and their conflicts, and we wanted to allow them the time to explore possibilities. However, we also recognized that students would eventually need to limit the scope of their stories to something relatively small and manage-able. In a short story, only a handful of characters should be involved, the conflict should be resolvable, and the time period that is addressed should be fairly short. It might have been tempting, therefore, to forgo the nearly two weeks that Donna's class spent imagining possibilities, in order to jump straight to the selec-tion of characters and conflicts. But experience had taught us that allowing stu-dents time to develop their characters and their characters' lives is crucial. Without that time, characters can be flat, conflicts unimportant, and stories uninteresting. It was only when students showed evidence that they really understood the lives of their characters through their characters' eyes that we moved to shaping the story itself.

In the following lesson, I model for students the process of reviewing a con-versation with a character to find a small piece appropriate for the focus of a short story. We had been encouraging students to have similar conversations for several days, an activity that proved to be tremendously helpful in getting to the details of a character's life and helping students to see the unique qualities of the charac-ter's voice, experience, and point of view. This strategy, a transfer from reading workshop, illuminated many story possibilities for every student. Now each stu-dent needed to choose the most appropriate focus for a character and a story.

SAMPLE LESSON: Week 3—Writing Workshop

AREA OF STUDY:	**Writing process**
FOCUS:	**Planning the story**
RESPONSE:	**Selection and explanation of focus conflict for story**

On the overhead I placed a copy of a portion of one of my conversations with Timmy:

Conversation with a Character

Ms. L.   What are you mad about?

Timmy   I'm mad because Mike embarrassed me. He's known me for so long, and I've trusted him with lots of stuff, but now he's found some new friends, and he just blew me off today. We were supposed to go skateboarding after school, and he just took off with somebody else. I was left standing there like a dork. It was just totally uncool.

Ms. L.   So what did you do about it?

Timmy   At first I didn't do anything. I just went to the skate park and hung around by myself. But I was so mad that I kept falling, and that made me even madder. The madder I got, the more I wanted to hurt Mike.

Ms. L.   I hope that you didn't beat him up.

Timmy   Nah. I don't fight. I wanted to hurt him, like, get back at him. I wanted to make him feel bad the way that he had made me feel bad.

Ms. L.   That seems kind of mean.

Timmy   Well, now I guess it does, but then I felt like it was only fair. After all, he made me look like a dork. Anyway, I went to his house and snuck in through the back window, the way we always get in when Mike loses his keys (which he does a lot; he can be kind of a dork, too).

Ms. L.   Weren't you afraid of getting caught? What if Mike was there?

Timmy   He wasn't; I checked it out. I knew what I wanted to do. I wanted to get back my rabbit foot.

Ms. L.   Your what?

Timmy   Yeah, I know it seems kind of stupid now, but when I was little and our parents were getting a divorce, my sister gave me a rabbit foot for luck. She had one, too, and she said that it would help us both stay lucky. I gave mine to Mike a couple of months ago when he broke his ankle and was feeling really bummed. But now he's fine and obviously doesn't need it anymore; after all, he has new friends. He doesn't need me anymore, and he doesn't need my rabbit foot.

Ms. L.   Don't you think you are being a little judgmental? After all, he didn't say he didn't need you. He just went off with other friends. Maybe he didn't even remember that you were supposed to go to the skate park.

Timmy   Well, that's what he says, too. I don't know if I believe him, though. I mean, we always go to the skate park after school. It's not the kind of thing that you just forget.

Ms. L.   So, did you get the rabbit foot back?

Timmy   Actually, no. I was all charged up and ready to grab it, but when I got into his room, I just couldn't do it. I wimped out.

This conversation mirrored many of the conversations that students had engaged in with their characters. It explored some interesting conflicts and thought through the character's perspective, but it rambled. This was as it should be during the exploration of conflict possibilities, but now that we were moving into story creation, both the students and I needed to pick a small piece of a conversation to write about. After reading through my conversation with the kids, I explained my thinking: "This is a conversation with lots of story possibilities, but there's too much here to make into a single short story. As a writer, it is my job to choose a particular conflict to focus on during my story, a conflict that will be interesting for me to write about and my readers to read about. Here are the criteria that I use when choosing the best conflict for my story."

Ms. Lattimer's Criteria for Choosing Focus Conflict

- The conflict needs to be resolvable. The conflict needs to have some resolution at the end of the story. Within my conversation I have lots of conflicts that can be resolved, but some would be difficult to resolve within the scope of a short story. For example, Timmy has broken into someone's house. If he got caught, he could be charged with breaking and entering. That would involve the police, the courts, parents, and so on. That conflict is just too big to be resolved in a short story. I need to choose a conflict with fewer characters and a shorter time span.
- My character needs to have some control over the conflict. I don't want everything to *happen to* my character. I want him to have some control over the choices that shape the situation. In my conversation with Timmy, he's mentioned several conflicts that he does have control over—for example, deciding whether to take back his rabbit foot. However, there are also situations that he can't really control, such as when Mike and his friends decide to leave him. Timmy has no influence over that decision. A story that was just about how sad he was wouldn't be very interesting.
- The conflict has to be interesting to me. If I find it an interesting conflict to explore, then I'll be able to write a better story. If it is boring to me, then the story will be boring to my audience.

"Given those criteria," I continued, addressing the students, "the best conflict for my short story is the conflict within Timmy when he is in Mike's room deciding whether to take the rabbit foot back. First, it's a small choice that he has to make. It has potentially big consequences, but the decision can be made and resolved during the story. Second, it's completely within Timmy's control. He's motivated by angry feelings from other stuff, but the decision about the rabbit's foot is his. Third, I like the idea of exploring the moral issues here. When does one wrong deserve another? And what makes people change their minds, even when they are really hurt and angry? So, for my short story, I would choose to start when Timmy is breaking into the house, when he is very sad and angry and hurt and determined to take back his rabbit's foot. And I would end the story when he leaves the house without the rabbit's foot."

I paused and placed a premade transparency about my decision on the overhead. It categorized the explanations I had just thought through with the students: choice of conflict for story, explanation of why conflict was chosen, and starting and ending places.

"Now it's your turn," I instructed the students. "Review the conversations you've had with your characters. Find conflicts within your conversations that fit the three criteria that we just discussed: the conflict is resolvable, the character has some control, and the conflict interests you. Choose the best one. Then record your decision using the format provided. Take your time. Don't worry about finishing; worry about choosing the conflict that will make the best story."

The model seemed simple enough, but students discovered that when they returned to their own stories, it was hard to find a focus conflict. They had all invested a lot of time, energy, and creativity in developing characters and situations. Now the idea of focusing in on just a small piece required letting other things go—a struggle for most budding writers. Donna and I spent a great deal of time on this day and subsequent days encouraging individual students to "get smaller" by asking them specific questions, reviewing their conversations to find particular pieces that seemed promising, and suggesting possibilities of how a story might develop. This individual attention, combined with a clear set of expectations, paid off. Instead of writing about the divorce of her character's parents, Frances decided to write about the character's decision to tell his mom about his dad's affair. Rather than recording the long and sordid story of a feud between two cousins, Edith chose a single incident, the breaking of a crystal elephant, and decided to write about how difficult it was for the cousins to confess the accident to their parents. Once students were able to find a small and manageable conflict, excitement began to build toward crafting a publishable story.

———◦———

After students had found appropriate and engaging conflicts, we quickly moved into the process of planning and drafting stories. Students analyzed the sequencing in some of their favorite stories, plotted out their own story line, considered the advantages of first- versus third-person narrative, and then tentatively began crafting their text. Donna and I were wary of giving too many directions about the specifics of writing too soon. Overwhelming students with instruction about style, technique, and voice can paralyze beginning writers into indecision. Instead of having students make all their decisions up-front, we provided them with published models, suggested that they build from the energy and immediacy of their character conversations, and allowed them room to experiment. The majority of our lessons and conferences about narrative techniques came in response to what we observed in students' work. The following is an example of one such lesson. We found that many students, as they began their drafts, did a great job using dialogue, action, and details to tell the story, but few showed their character's perspective on the events that they were describing. This lesson sought to address that need, teaching students to recognize the importance of showing perspective and then providing them with the tools to revise their own drafts appropriately.

SAMPLE LESSON: **Week 4—Writing Workshop**

AREA OF STUDY:	**Text structure**
FOCUS:	**Revealing a character's perspective**
TEXT:	**"An Education," by Marie G. Lee, from *But That's Another Story*, edited by Sandy Asher**
RESPONSE:	**Highlighting and revision of individual drafts to reveal a character's perspective**

"Authors reveal their characters' perspectives in a variety of ways," Donna began, "through their words, their actions, and their thoughts. In your writing, one of the things you need to work on is revealing the perspective of your character. I know that many of you have been trying to do this, but it is hard to accomplish when you are first beginning to write. When I first try to write a story, I often concentrate so much on what is happening that I have trouble remembering to show how my character feels about and reacts to those events. So, today we're going to work on incorporating the character's perspective into what we have already written, first by looking at how another author approaches this challenge and then by revising our own work."

On a sheet of chart paper at the front of the room, Donna had written an excerpt from "An Education." Thanks to repeated use in reading workshop, the story was very familiar to students, and they were quickly able to recognize its source and to remember the context. Donna instructed students to reread the excerpt and look for specific places where the author shows the character's perspective. They read, they pair-shared, and then they shared their findings: "The part where it says, 'Her feet froze,' because she was the one who felt that they were frozen. Anyone else might have just said that she stopped, but to her it was like the moment was frozen in time because it was so horrible." "The word *briskly* when it says that she 'stepped briskly into the light,' because it shows that she was really focused on moving and getting her diploma, she was excited and moving fast." "The whole part where it says, 'She had no idea how long she'd been petrified like that. Seconds? Minutes? Years? Now, what were her parents going to think?' Those are all her thoughts, and they really show what she is thinking inside." As the students spoke, Donna underlined their findings:

> "Helen Kim," Mr. Maki said, finally. Helen stepped <u>briskly</u> into the light of the stage amidst the sounds of clapping for the person who'd gone ahead of her.
>
> "Chink!" hissed a voice from the line of kids.
>
> <u>Her feet froze.</u> She looked into the dark audience, <u>but there was no one there to help her.</u>
>
> "Karen Lang," said Mr. Maki, and <u>by some miracle,</u> Helen's feet lifted and started to move again. <u>She had no idea how long she'd been petrified like that. Seconds? Minutes? Years? Now, what were her parents going to think?</u>
>
> "Congratulations," Mr. Oleson said, handing her a diploma. <u>As if in a fuzzy dream,</u> Helen shook his hand, smiled, and <u>calmly</u> walked off the stage.

"Is it important to include Helen's perspective?" Donna wondered aloud. "Let's see how the story would change if those pieces were not included." She reread the excerpt without the underlined sentences. In response, students agreed that the piece was still understandable but less interesting. "It's hard to get into it," explained one student, "because it's harder to understand what it's like without Helen's perspective."

"Okay, then," Donna agreed. "Using your writer's eyes, tell me what you notice about how the author, Marie G. Lee, included Helen's perspective. What kinds of techniques did she use, and where did she use them?" The students' observations:

Ways to Show a Character's Perspective
- Use strong verbs. "Her feet froze" instead of "Her feet stopped."
- Use descriptive adjectives and adverbs. "She stepped briskly."
- Use similes and metaphors. "As if in a fuzzy dream."
- Describe what the character saw. "She looked into the dark audience, but there was no one there to help her."
- Share the character's thoughts. "She had no idea how long she'd been petrified like that. Seconds? Minutes? Years? Now, what were her parents going to think?"
- Show the character's perspective throughout the story. Don't keep it to just one part.

Donna had instructed the students to bring their draft paragraphs with them to the front of the room. She passed out highlighters and told them to do to their own stories what the class had done together to "An Education": "Go through your story and highlight the places that reveal your character's perspective." For a few moments, the room was practically silent. Then, as students completed their analysis and reflected on their work, we could hear small whispers of realization. Students had discovered that too often their character's perspectives didn't come through.

Donna reviewed the results with the whole class, asking "What did you discover about your work?" "What could you do to improve your story?" "All of my highlighting was at the end," one student commented. "I told about how my character felt then, but I didn't really show it anyplace else. I think that maybe I should try to include some more descriptive words earlier." "I wasn't about to highlight anything," another admitted. "I'm going to look back at my conversation with my character from when I was planning to see if there are some thoughts that he used then that I could include now."

The time that Donna spent with the students highlighting and reviewing their findings proved invaluable. It made visible to students their use (or lack of use) of a key writing strategy, and helped them figure out how to revise their work in a concrete and collaborative fashion. When students returned to their writing desks, nearly everyone was able to make substantive revisions that helped to reveal their characters' perspectives.

◄○►

Weeks 4, 5, and 6 were spent rereading, revising, and improving students' stories. Donna and I regularly collected and commented on drafts. We spent many hours conferring with students. We directed them toward examples of published stories that used styles and techniques we thought would be helpful for them to consider: "You have a bit of a sarcastic edge to your story. I like that. Take a look at 'The Mechanical Mind,' by Gary Soto. He uses a sarcastic tone, also. Look at how he develops that tone throughout the story, and consider which of his techniques you might want to apply to your own story." We encouraged students to share story ideas with their peers: "Marissa was having a similar problem explaining the relationships between her characters. Go talk to her about how she solved it." And we taught quick craft lessons that addressed areas of concern that were fairly universal. For example, one of the trends we noticed was the proliferation of the word *then,* as in "And then they went to the movies . . . And then she said . . . And then I said. . . ." Students needed a more effective way to move time. The following lesson was designed to address that need.

SAMPLE LESSON: ## Week 5—Writing Workshop

AREA OF STUDY:	**Text structure**
FOCUS:	**Moving through time**
TEXTS:	**Various**
RESPONSE:	**Lists of time-moving techniques and phrases; revision of individual short stories**

Students were given a time limit, a team assignment, and a specific task. They had twenty minutes to work with a group of three peers to review the stories in their collection folders and identify as many ways as possible to move time. "It could be forward or backward. It could be a word, a phrase, or a text feature," Donna instructed. "Get creative and look for possibilities!"

Thanks to a time limit and the challenge of friendly competition, students got right to work. Each group gathered their ideas into a list, and soon the room buzzed with possibilities. Donna and I poked our heads into the groups' work at times, but for the most part, we left them to work on their own.

Twenty-five minutes later (we had allowed an extra five minutes after students had begged), Donna called, "Time," and students gathered to share their finds. Among the possibilities that they identified:

Ways to Move Time

Forward

- "The next day/week/month/year . . ."
- "Suddenly . . . ," "all of a sudden . . ."
- "It happened so quickly/slowly . . ."
- "After that . . ."
- "Still," "continued"
- "When . . ."
- "Later . . ."
- "Then . . ."
- "It was only a few days later when . . ."
- "At three o'clock . . ."

Backward

- "It didn't used to be . . ."
- "It hadn't always been . . ."
- "Before . . ."
- "Back when . . ."
- "Last week/month/year . . ."

- "The day before . . ."
- "Earlier . . ."

Parallel
- "At the same time . . ."
- "In another place . . ."
- "Meanwhile . . . ," "while all this was going on . . ."

Text Features
- Section breaks
- Flashbacks or flash-forwards in italics
- Headings for different times
- Dates and times

"Now, how shall we use this information?" Donna queried. By now, students had had plenty of practice with the idea of learning narrative craft by analyzing published text and then applying that learning to their own work. Donna had articulated and explained the instructions many times. Now it was the students' turn to demonstrate not only what they knew about ways to move time but also what they knew about the process of learning and growing as writers.

"We should apply it to our own stories," regurgitated one student mechanically. "Okay," Donna agreed, "but how? What exactly are we going to do?" "We should look for places where we have time moving in our own stories and see if we do it well," a student suggested. "We should look for places where we say 'and then' and see if we can find a better way of explaining the order of what happens," another student explained. "I want to look more at my flashbacks," chimed in a third student. "Before I just had them as short memories, but I like the idea of expanding them some more and using paragraph breaks and italics. That would make it seem real professional."

Donna encouraged students in their individual and collective plans and sent them off to work. As they edited, we were impressed with the range of applications that they used in their own work. Some just crossed out a few words and added a few new phrases. Others rewrote whole sections based on what they had discovered. But each was able to articulate the reasons behind their choices. And most were able to point to specific texts that they were using as guides for their own work, an important indicator of growth in the process of becoming reflective, resourceful writers.

———◦———

Each time I walked into the room during the final days of the short story writing workshop, I could sense the nervous excitement. Students scrambled to put the final touches on their work, improving their spelling and grammar, adding a bit more detail here and a bit more dialogue there, getting up the nerve to cut a section that they loved but that just didn't work with their story, finding the perfect title, and changing the tone to add just the right edge to the story. Students had worked hard during the study, and collectively the class had learned a great deal. But in every sense, the stories belonged to their individual authors. The characters, the plots, the conflicts were unique creations. And as the final deadline approached, each student grappled with his or her story's needs. Donna and I continued to confer, we encouraged students to get feedback from peers, and we made certain that charts and resources from the study were posted so as to be easily accessible. However, it was the students themselves who decided what to work on within their stories and how to do it. The lessons that we had investigated together had taught students not only about crafting a short story but also about the process of analyzing and assessing text. Now, they were much more independent, able to reread their own work, assess what needed to be done, and find the resources they needed to help them do it.

Evaluating Student Progress . . .

By the time the short story study grew to a close, there were multiple realities going on in the classroom. While reading, students were often lost in the worlds of their books. While writing, students were often lost in the worlds of their imaginations. At times, Donna and I found it difficult to pull students out of their stories and their characters long enough to hold their attention in the reality of the classroom, but this was a hardship we were only too glad to put up with.

We did manage to hold their attention long enough to assess their work and progress. Donna introduced reflection prompts for students in both reading and writing. She interviewed students individually about their growth, asking them to bring evidence to the interview that exhibited their progress. Students assessed themselves on rubrics that they had helped to develop, and peers read stories to provide an additional level of feedback and assessment. At first, all this work elicited groans from students who had thought they would be finished when they turned in that final story. But as they reflected, students were thrilled to realize how much they had grown, and each was able to identify areas to work on for future growth.

. . . in Reading Workshop

When Donna and I initially thought about teaching students to talk to their characters, we expected it to be a small part of the unit. But it turned out to be a substantial, significant component. Developing a running dialogue with characters as they read helped students to truly understand and value the perspectives of the characters in their stories.

At exit interviews at the end of the year, nearly every student described having "conversations with my characters" as the strategy that helped them grow as readers the most. And students applied this strategy to nearly every text they read. Observing students during free-choice reading, we would see them occasionally stare off into space and move their lips silently. Their facial expressions made it clear that they were in deep conversation mode; they were trying to understand a particular event, emotion, or reaction from the perspective of the character. We are still finding notes with snatches of conversations written on them in independent reading books that students had taken home. Toward the end of the study I walked into class one day and found Richard with his eyes closed and his book facedown on the desk. His explanation: "I was reflecting on my conversation, Ms. Lattimer, trying to figure out the story from the character's perspective." Given what I knew of this child, I might not have believed him except for the fact that he immediately launched into a thoughtful monologue about the interaction between the events in the text and the character's point of view.

Certainly, there is plenty of room for Donna's students to continue to grow as short story readers. They would be among the first to admit that they don't necessarily understand all the complexities of every character and that they can't always fully appreciate a character's perspective. However, I would argue that this admission itself represents tremendous progress. It reveals a recognition of the complexity of characters, a willingness to actively engage with a text, and an openness to the possibility of accepting multiple interpretations of stories. What Donna and I had hoped for more than the mastery of any particular skill or text was a shift in attitude—that students would recognize that stories can be more than entertaining escapes from one's own reality, that they offer tremendous opportunities for growth in understanding the realities of others. This goal was largely achieved.

Here are some student reflections on how studying short stories helped them:

> Now I think more about characters and understand them and the story better. I can understand why the characters do what they do. I understand more about the meaning of the story, why the author wrote the story, and what he wanted me to know and learn from it.
> —*Daniel M.*

Before I didn't think stories had much purpose to them. I only read them because I had to. But now I have learned so much. I know that from stories we can learn about people and problems and how the world is.
—*Angie D.*

Now I have a purpose for reading. It has made me slow down and really think about the story. It makes the stories stick with me. I remember the characters and think about their perspectives even after I've stopped reading.
—*Willie W.*

. . . in Writing Workshop

After the last revisions had been made, the celebratory cake eaten, and the students dismissed, Donna and I settled in to read the stories. Having acted as students' editors for so many weeks now, we found it hard initially to set aside the urge to circle a misspelled word or to make yet another suggestion about how to improve a particular section. But now was not the time for that. Now was the time to look back at our original goals, as represented in the scoring rubric we had made with the class, and assess students' growth. Were these short stories strong? Did they create believable, engaging characters? Did the conflicts and character interactions ring true? Was the perspective of the character shown to the reader? Was the story itself compelling?

As we read, Donna and I were relieved to find that, for the most part, the answer to these questions was yes. Certainly, problems still existed: endings were a bit too abrupt (and often overly optimistic), characters' points of view didn't come through as strongly as they could have, a few conflicts were still too big for the scope of a short story. But when we considered how far students had come, we were pleased. Every student had turned in a story, and every story was truly a piece of realistic fiction. Gone were the caricatures of bright, shiny people that had initially populated students' imaginations; they had been replaced by solid, believable characters. Gone were the mind-numbingly large conflicts; they had been replaced by concerns that the characters could negotiate. And negotiate they did. While reading, we could see and understand the characters' perspectives, their struggles to make decisions, their joys and frustrations at the reactions of others. More than once, I found myself lost in a student's story. Although flaws still existed in their writing, students had succeeded in imagining and communicating a new reality. As short story writers, they were well on their way.

Here are some samples of the short stories that students wrote.

Miracles Happen
Erika G., Grade 6

Nikki paced back and forth outside her dad's bedroom. *Should I?* she wondered. *Dad hasn't really had time for me in a long time. Should I even bother to ask?* In one hand she held the invitation for the father and daughter picnic celebration. With the other she was scratching her head. Back and forth. Back and forth.

Finally she got up the courage to ask. She reached for the doorknob, but decided that was a bit intrusive. So she knocked first. "Come in," said her dad in a tired voice. When she went in the first thing she noticed was all the paperwork he was filling out and the crumpled paper all over the floor.

"Hey, Nik, what do you want?" he asked without looking up.

God. Please make him say yes, she thought.

"Well, I was wondering if you could go to this father and daughter picnic celebration with me." She took the invitation out of her pocket and slid it onto his desk in slow motion. She took her time to savor this breathtaking moment that was still full of hope.

He picked up the invitation and examined it very carefully. He ran his hand over the golden print on the front. "Nikki Scanfort and Jeffery Scanfort," he read under his breath. He looked up at her with a smile that filled her with hope. "When?" he asked.

She smiled back, looking into his eyes with a real smile. So often in the past she'd had to force a smile after being rejected. But he'd actually asked when. Maybe there was hope.

"It says on the back," she replied, holding her breath.

When he turned it over and saw the date, his smile faded right away. June 30, 2002.

"Oh, I'm sorry, Nikki, but I can't go. I have court that day." He turned quickly back to his papers to get away from the hurt on her face.

"Okay, Dad, but if you change your mind . . ." her voice trailed off. She left quickly, feeling crushed.

Nikki left for the picnic early. She wanted to get a head start. The sun was bright and she enjoyed its warmth. She stood gazing at the little kids on the swings. She wished she was one of them. She closed her eyes to try to blink away the tears. It wasn't fair that her dad never had time for her. It just wasn't fair that all of her friends had their parents everywhere they went looking after them and her dad was always busy doing this and that.

She looked away from the playground, trying to block the hurt out of her mind. Her mouth dropped open. Was that her dad? *No, it couldn't be. He's at court,* she told herself, not daring to hope again. She blinked and looked again. She felt a knot in her stomach as confusion, anger, doubt, and joy rushed through her. It was her dad.

She ran in his direction, screaming, "Dad! Dad!"

"Nikki," he called and broke into a run. She was running, too, and when they met she jumped into his arms. For the first time in a long time she was able to say those magic words, "I love you," and really mean them.

"I love you, too, honey," he whispered back. And this time she believed him.

I Need to Tell

Priscilla N., Grade 6

"You could not believe what happened, Jennifer," Kim squealed into the phone. "He told on me. Now I'm grounded for two weeks. That is so not fair. I mean, he promised he wouldn't tell."

"Well, guess what?" Jennifer asked angrily back.

"What?" asked Kim.

"Your parents called and told my parents so now I'm grounded for two weeks, too."

"Let's get back at him," suggested Kim, fuming.

"Okay, I'm in. I gotta go, see you tomorrow."

"Okay, bye."

The next day was Monday. Kim and Jennifer met early in the morning to plot their revenge. After school, when everyone was out, Kim and Jennifer went to Andy's locker and wrote something on it.

"Kim, hurry up, your mom is waiting," said Jennifer in a worried and frustrated voice.

"Okay, okay," replied Kim.

When Kim was finished writing, Jennifer read, "ANDY IS A STUPID BOY."

They ran off feeling smug and satisfied. Revenge was delicious.

Everyone laughed as they passed by Andy's locker on Tuesday morning. Andy felt really embarrassed. As she watched her brother's humiliation, Kim began to feel guilty. But she was still too mad at him to admit that she was the one who had written it on his locker.

"Jennifer."

"What?"

"I kind of feel sorry for Andy. I mean, he just told on us. We didn't get embarrassed or anything, right?"

"Yeah, but we got grounded for two weeks."

"Yeah, but . . ."

"But what? Now just finish your lunch and go to class. And stop worrying. Okay?"

"Okay," said Kim sadly. The whole day at school, Kim felt like her soul was somewhere else. She didn't talk, eat, or do anything that day. All she did was walk to class, sit down, and pretend to listen to what her teacher was saying.

By Wednesday, things were going a little better. Andy's locker had been cleaned and people stopped laughing at him. But Kim still felt bad. She felt like something was stuck in her body like a sad feeling. She couldn't even walk by Andy. She turned and ducked when she saw him coming. She had moments of happiness, but then she would remember and quickly become sad again.

Every day when she passed by his locker, she would ask herself should she tell Andy what she had done. She wanted to, but she didn't have the courage.

It was a Friday, two weeks later, when Kim finally decided that she was sick and tired of being a liar. She was sitting at the lunch table surrounded by her friends but feeling all alone. She and Jennifer didn't really talk anymore. Her friends ignored her because they said she wasn't any fun. And she was too ashamed to hang out with her brother, the one person she always used to be able to go to. "I need to tell Andy what I did," she thought to herself. Immediately she started to feel better. "Yeah, that's right! That's exactly what I'm going to do," Kim said proudly to herself.

"Hi, Andy," said Kim nervously.

"Hi, Sis," Andy replied.

"Uh, Andy, there is something I have to tell you," said Kim, struggling. There was a long pause.

"Well, what is it?" Andy asked.

"Andy, I was the one who wrote that you were stupid on your locker," Kim spit it out as fast as she could.

"You?"

"Yes." Kim looked down at her shoes. This was hard. "I'm really sorry. I know it was wrong now. I haven't felt right since I did it. Will you please forgive me?"

"I can't believe you! Do you know how much I was embarrassed? All my friends were laughing at me!" Andy closed his locker with a loud bang and stomped off.

After that, Andy wouldn't talk to Kim for about a month. Jennifer was mad at her, too. But despite their anger, Kim felt relieved. She was released from her sadness and got her soul back. She was able to be happy again.

Suggested Texts

Finding short stories that are appropriate in length (many short stories are substantially longer than a mini-lesson will allow), interest, and reading level can be a challenge. Fortunately, there are multiple sources. Some of Donna's and my favorites follow. Additionally, trade books and even those heavy literature textbooks stored away in classroom cupboards and the back shelves of the school library can reveal hidden treasures.

Short Stories
Grades 3–6
Cricket Magazine. Ages 9+. Tel.: 800-827-0227; <http://www.cricketmag
    .com/>.
Cynthia Rylant, *Every Living Thing*
Gary Soto, *Local News; Petty Crimes*
Stone Soup. 800-447-4569; <http://www.stonesoup.com/>.

Grades 6–10 (Young Adult)
Sandy Asher, ed., *But That's Another Story*
Cicada Magazine. Ages 14+. 800-827-0227; <http://www.cicadamag
    .com/>.
Maxine Clair, *Rattlebone*
Chris Crutcher, *Athletic Shorts*
Bruce Emra, ed., *Coming of Age: Short Stories About Youth and Adolescence*
Mary Frosch, ed., *Coming of Age in America: A Multicultural Anthology*
Don Gallo, *Thirteen; Connections; No Easy Answers; Join In*
James Howe, ed., *The Color of Absence: 12 Stories About Loss and Hope*
David Levithan, ed., *You Are Here, This Is Now: Poems, Stories, Essays and Art
    from the Best Young Writers and Artists in America*
Anne Mazer, ed., *America Street: A Multicultural Anthology of Stories; A Walk
    in My World: International Short Stories About Youth*
Walter Dean Myers, *145th Street*
Teen Ink. Tel.: 617-964-6800; <http://TeenInk.com/fiction/>.

Grades 10+ (Adult)
Ron Hansen and Jim Shepard, eds., *You've Got to Read This: Contemporary
    American Writers Introduce Stories That Held Them in Awe*
Robert Shapard and James Thomas, eds., *Sudden Fiction: American Short-
    Short Stories*

CHAPTER 6

Fairy Tale

From "Snow"

Francesca Lia Block

When she was born her mother was so young, still a girl herself, didn't know what to do with her. She screamed and screamed—the child. Her mother sat crying in the garden. The gardener came by to dig up the soil. It was winter. The child was frost-colored. The gardener stood before the cold winter sun, blocking the light with his broad shoulders. The mother looked like a broken rosebush.

Take her please, the mother cried. The gardener sat beside her. She was shaking. The child would not stop screaming. When the mother put her in his arms, the child was quiet.

Take her, the mother said. I can't keep her. She will devour me.

The child wrapped her tiny fingers around the gardener's large brown thumb. She stared up at him with her eyes like black rose petals in her snowy face. He said to the mother, Are you sure? And she stood up and ran into the house, sobbing. Are you sure are you sure? She was sure. Take it away, she prayed, it will devour me.

The gardener wrapped the child in a clean towel and put her in his truck and drove her west to the canyon. There was no way he could keep her himself, was there? (He imagined her growing up, long and slim, those lips and eyes.) No, but he knew who could.

The seven brothers lived in a house they had built in the side of the canyon among the trees. They had built it without chopping down one tree, so it was an odd-shaped house with towers and twisting hallways and jagged staircases. It looked like part of the canyon itself, as if it had sprung up there. It smelled of woodsmoke and leaves. From the highest point you could see the sea lilting and shining in the distance.

This was where the gardener brought the child. He knew these men from work they had all done together on a house by the ocean. He was fascinated by the way they worked. They made the gardener feel slow and awkward and much too tall. Also, lonely.

Bear answered the door. Like all the brothers he had a fine, handsome face, burnished skin, huge brown eyes that regarded everyone as if they were the beloved. He was slightly heavier than the others and his hair was soft, thick, close cropped. He shook the gardener's hand and welcomed him inside, politely avoiding the bundle in the gardener's arms until the gardener said, I don't know where to take her.

Bear brought him into the kitchen where Fox, Tiger, and Buck were eating their lunch of vegetable stew and rice, baked apples and blueberry gingerbread. They asked the gardener to join them. When Bear told them why he was there, they allowed themselves to turn their benevolent gazes to the child in his arms. She stared back at them and the gardeners heard an unmistakable burbling coo coming from her mouth.

Buck held her in his muscular arms. She nestled against him and closed her eyes—dark lash tassels. Buck looked down his fine, sculpted nose at her and whispered, Where does she come from?

The gardener told him, From the valley, her mother can't take care of her. He said he was afraid she would be hurt if he left her there. The mother wasn't well. The brothers gathered around. They knew that she was the love they had been seeking in every face forever before this. Bear said, We will keep her. And the gardener knew he had done the right thing bringing her here. The other brothers, Otter, Lynx, and Ram, came home that evening. They also loved her right away, as if they had been waiting forever for her to come. They named her Snow and gave her everything they had. . . .

The gardener went to her and held her hand. It felt like it would slip away, it was so thin and light; it felt boneless. The gardener said he was going to take her away with him, help her get better. Why was he hesitating? He wanted to look at her like this, for a while. He wanted this stillness. She was completely his, now, in a way she would never be again. His silent, perfect bride . . . He brushed the dark, damp strands of hair off her smooth forehead. He leaned close to her, breathing her like one would inhale a bouquet. He looked at her lips, half parted as if waiting for him. He wanted to possess.

But when he touched her with his mouth and her eyes opened she did not see him there. She called for the men, the seven brothers. She wanted them. More than gardeners or mothers. She wanted them the way she needed the earth and the flowers and the sky and the sea from her tower room and food and sleep and warmth and light and nights by the fire and poetry and the stories of going out into the world and almost being destroyed by it and returning to find comfort in the real meaning of freak. And I am a freak, she thought, happily. I am meant to stay here forever. I am loved.

She pushed the gardener away and called for them. In her sleep she had seen love. It was poisoning. It was possessing. Devouring. Or it was seven pairs of boots climbing up the stairs to find her.

◇

I found a great collection of fairy tales!" Cheryl exclaimed. Cheryl Hibbeln and I had begun planning for our work with fairy tales, and we were both on the lookout for resources. She had come across Francesca Lia Block's *The Rose and the Beast* almost by accident and was thrilled with the rich language and mature themes of the tales. This text would provide some great samples for our unit of study with her struggling tenth-grade students. Cheryl was particularly excited about the tale "Snow." We had already talked about the possibility of teaching students to explore themes and interpret authors' messages in reading workshop, and this story had a message to which she believed students could really relate. "My boys in particular are always talking about how girls come and go but their 'brothers' are always there for them and really 'watch their backs.' I think this text really gets to that . . . about the importance and endurance of family love, and the true meaning of love."

We sat down to look more closely at the text, to spend some time thinking about how the author conveyed her message and how we could best use the text in the context of our study. But as we examined the tale together, Cheryl and I began to find more complex themes than a first reading had indicated. Certainly, love is a central theme in the text: the sources and qualities of love are starkly contrasted between the cold and distant image of the mother, the dark and lustful portrayal of the gardener, and the warm, earthy descriptions of the brothers. Snow's eventual decision to stay with the brothers rather than leave to pursue a life with the gardener is indeed a powerful statement about the strength of unconditional love.

However, as we talked, other pieces of the text began to tug at us. The use of the word *devour;* the sensual terms in which the gardener describes Snow, both as a baby and as a young woman; the interest Snow shows in the lecherous gardener. These pieces made us uncomfortable and prevented easy categorization of the tale as being a statement about the power of unconditional love. Right from the beginning, it is clear that Snow is attracted in some way to the gardener. As an infant she screams in the arms of her mother—a woman who dehumanizes her as an "it" rather than regarding her as a baby girl—but quiets when held by the gardener. In his possessing love she is silent, pliable, and willing. Even though she eventually chooses to stay with the kind and generous brothers, why is it that she was ever attracted to the gardener? Was Block indicating that we are naturally attracted to that which is dangerous? that women instinctively respond to the domineering power of men? And what about the mother? Why was she willing to give her baby over to such a man? Why was she so afraid of being devoured? Does Block want us to believe that women are in competition for the attraction of men? Or was she indicating that women who rely on such men are weak and tragic?

There were no definitive answers to our questions. Each time we looked back to find evidence to support one idea, we came away with further insights about the themes and messages in the text. After nearly an hour of intense debate, Cheryl pushed the text away and commented, "I'm not sure I like this story anymore. Here I thought it was a nice straightforward little tale about love, and now there's all this. And some of these ideas I'm really uncomfortable with." She sighed. "But I will say that I'm really impressed with Francesca Lia Block. She is clearly a thinker and has a lot to say. Now I want to go back and think further about some of her other stories. There is probably much more to them than I realized."

Thinking Through the Genre

Tales of wonder have been around for centuries. With their dramatic characters, action-filled plots, and fantastic situations, these stories have long had the power to hold their audiences spellbound. However, the stories we know best today, those fantasies trapped on Disney celluloid, are far different from the original tales passed down by oral tradition. Years ago fairy tales were much darker, more brooding. They were stories told by adults and intended for adult audiences. Sleeping Beauty wasn't awakened by the prince but by two suckling infants conceived while she lay sleeping. Cinderella didn't have the help of a sweetly plump fairy godmother but had to better her situation using her own cunning and anger (Datlow and Windling 1993). It was only when society changed that the stories changed. Those older tales were told by commoners, peasants living difficult lives, to express hope in the face of oppression: "If Cinderella, a lowly kitchen maid, could improve her life, then perhaps we can, too."

In Victorian times the darker stories faded away. Fairy tales became the property of the middle classes, those who were happy with their lives and wanted to maintain the status quo. Writers, Hans Christian Andersen most prominent among them, cleaned up the tales and, as J. R. R. Tolkien described it, "banished them to the nursery." Fairy tales were infused with the Protestant values of hard work, humility, honesty, and obedience. They were told to children to instill in them similar virtues. No longer was Cinderella cunning and angry; it was her sweetness and obedience that won her the ultimate reward, the love of the prince.

In the introduction to his authoritative text *Spells of Enchantment: The Wondrous Fairy Tales of Western Culture*, Jack Zipes explains that this evolution is no surprise. In all societies throughout history, the stories that are told reflect the values of the teller and the needs of the audience. He writes,

> The nature and meaning of folk tales have depended on the stage of development of a tribe, community, or society. Oral tales have served to stabilize, conserve, or challenge the common beliefs, laws, values, and norms of a

group. The ideology expressed in wonder tales always stemmed from the position that a narrator assumed with regard to the developments in his or her community, and the narrative plot and changes made in a tale depended on the sense of wonder or awe that the narrator wanted to evoke. In other words, the sense of wonder in the tale and the intended emotion sought by the narrator are ideological.

We all adapt stories to fit our purpose and audience. Whether telling a ghost story around the campfire or weaving an elaborate fishing yarn, the details we choose to include, the way characters are portrayed, and the events that we emphasize vary depending on our needs at the time. Why? Because stories have meaning. Every story, from biblical parables to science fiction allegories to the pulp fiction available on supermarket shelves, carries meaning. Stories have the power to shape readers' conscious and unconscious understanding of themselves and the world around them. This is why Hitler burned books, why *Catcher in the Rye* is still banned from some library shelves, and why authoritarian regimes around the world lock up novelists as political dissidents. Stories have the power to communicate meaning and values.

Introducing fairy tales into the classroom enables students, particularly struggling students, to recognize and use the power of story. Ultimately, we want students to recognize meaning in all narrative text. But many students are not prepared to discuss the symbolism of the green light at the end of Daisy's dock or consider the manner in which Jay Gatsby is portrayed. Realistic fiction, with its complex characters and densely packed story lines, is often too tightly wound for students to unravel in order to find meaning. Fairy tales, on the other hand, are much simpler. They have stock characters who never change. Plots are straightforward. Language is direct. Symbols are clear. And conflicts are always resolved neatly. Students are able much more readily to recognize the themes explored and the messages communicated in these simple texts. They are less bound by the literal and can see the abstract. They can develop strategies for recognizing themes and interpreting the message of the author. These analytical skills are essential for any story, and once learned through a study of fairy tales, they can be applied to a much larger range of narrative texts.

Engaging students in the process of planning and writing fairy tales similarly expands their ability to think abstractly about narrative text. Retelling a familiar tale requires that students experiment with the manipulation of stock characters and conflicts. A witch can change from bad to good. A prince may no longer want to marry the princess. And then what happens? Students discover that changing one element of a story necessarily changes others. If the witch is good, then she is no longer going to want to eat Hansel and Gretel. Why then does she have them in her house? Asking such questions and proposing potential solutions provides students with remarkable insights about how the elements of story interact. Through this experimentation they learn how to shape their characters and conflicts in order to create stories, both fairy tales and other types of narrative text, that suit their purpose.

A study of fairy tales is not just a means to an end. Fairy tales are an absolutely legitimate form of narrative text, and there are many excellent reasons to read, analyze, and create them. However, a study of fairy tales can have value beyond the scope of the genre itself. Through such a study students can learn to understand and use the power of story.

Envisioning the Unit

Cheryl Hibbeln's tenth-grade students were a tough bunch. They had been grouped together in a "blueprint" English class at Kearny High School because they had all tested below or significantly below grade level in their reading ability. Needless to say, they didn't like the distinction. In addition to having academic difficulties, the majority lived in poverty, about one-third had special needs, and quite a few were involved in gangs. Cheryl had succeeded in creating a safe space for them in her classroom. Although reluctant to come to school, many students enjoyed coming to English class. She had gotten them into books. They loved stories by Beatrice Sparks, Dave Pelzer, Walter Dean Myers, and Sharon Draper. Many could sit for more than half an hour (an eternity for a reluctant reader) and immerse themselves in a high-interest text.

But despite their progress, Cheryl was concerned that she wasn't doing enough. "Next year, these kids are going to be mainstreamed," she explained to me. "They are going to leave the nice, safe little cocoon that they have this year. I've been in those classes, and I know what is expected. They'll need to be able to read and discuss as a whole class novels at a deeper level. They'll need to be able to recognize the themes in text, interpret an author's message, find evidence to support their ideas, and defend their thinking process in discussions and in writing. Right now, they are totally unprepared for that. I need to get them ready."

Her concerns were legitimate. When I met them in January, the students were very literal readers and writers. When asked why they thought an author had portrayed a character in a certain way or had chosen to discuss a particular event in the text, students looked at us as if we were from another planet. "Because that's the way that it happened," they explained. To their minds, a story was a story. There was no craft, no manipulation of characters and events; it just was the way it was. This inability to consider narrative texts more abstractly limited students.

They were unprepared for the analytical nature of eleventh-grade literature classes as well as for the newly instituted California High School Exit Exam. More important, they were not getting to fully experience the power of literature.

Cheryl and I set out to design a study that would move students from the literal to the abstract. Our goal was to develop strategies through which students could find and create meaning in narrative text. Our vehicle—fairy tales. When initially suggested, the idea seemed almost comical; these kids were a long way from the nursery. However, studying this genre with this group of students offered multiple benefits. The texts are accessible. In reading workshop, students would be able to analyze plots, characters, conflicts, themes, and messages relatively easily. The stories are familiar. In writing workshop, students would be able to experiment with the elements of story and learn how those elements can be manipulated to create meaning. And, believe it or not, the tales are engaging. Fairy tales don't just belong in the nursery anymore; Roald Dahl, Jane Yolen, and Francesca Lia Block are among the authors who have created wonderful retold versions of fairy tales that are appropriate for much older students. These short, funny, slightly racy, and occasionally violent tales would engage even our most cynical tenth-graders. Moreover, the availability of a range of different texts—from traditional picture books to fairy tale adaptations for young adults to original fantasy stories by Bruce Coville and Lloyd Alexander—allowed us to scaffold student understanding. We could begin with easier, more transparent texts and then, as students grasped skills, move into more sophisticated texts with more complex themes. This transition within the fairy tale genre facilitated later application to a broader range of genres of narrative text.

As we mapped out our objectives for the study, it became evident that an inquiry into fairy tales would demand a great deal from these students. Our expectations were rigorous. We were asking students to think abstractly, read more thoughtfully, and write more deliberately. However, by pairing these rigorous demands with entertaining and accessible texts, not to mention a great teacher, we knew that success was possible.

Teaching the Unit—Reading Workshop

About a week before we planned to begin the actual study, Cheryl began introducing the stories. Each day, at the beginning and end of class, she would read aloud a retold fairy tale. She never mentioned that these were fairy tales; she didn't want students to get offended before we even got started. Instead she simply read.

Roald Dahl was an immediate hit. Students loved the violence and thought it was hysterical when their teacher uttered a swear word in class. Francesca Lia

Reading Workshop—Fairy Tale
Goals and Instructional Focus Progression

	Reading Comprehension Study	Accountable Talk Study
	Goal: Students will learn to analyze text for meaning, support their interpretations with text evidence, and evaluate the relevance of the author's message.	**Goal:** Students will learn to have meaningful Socratic seminar discussions that enhance student understanding of text.
Weeks 1–2	**Finding Meaning in Story** Students will use differences between traditional and retold tales to develop an interpretation of the author's message. • What is different about the retold tale? • Why do you think the author included those differences? • What message is the author communicating through his/her story? • "I think the author is saying _____" **Defending the Interpretation** Students will defend their understanding of the author's message using evidence from the text. • What evidence from the text supports your interpretation of the author's message? • Explain how the evidence supports the interpretation.	**Developing Appropriate Behaviors and Language for Discussions** Students will learn what is appropriate to say and do during a Socratic seminar discussion. • What is the purpose of a discussion? • How should participants interact during a discussion? • What language is appropriate to use when introducing ideas? responding to peers? disagreeing with peers?
Weeks 3–4	**Digging Deeper into the Themes and Messages of Story** Students will use specific text elements to develop their interpretations of a story. • How are characters and their actions portrayed? • What is the major conflict and how is it resolved? • Are symbols used? What is their significance? • Are aphorisms used? What are they? • Why did the author choose to use these elements in the manner he/she did? How do these elements work together to create meaning? **So What? Responding to the Author's Message** Students will reflect on and evaluate the meaning of text. • Do you agree with the author's message? Why? • Is the message relevant? Explain. • Who is the intended audience for this fairy tale? Do you think that the tale would have an impact on its intended audience? Explain.	**Using Evidence to Support a Discussion** Students will use evidence from the text and their own experiences to support their ideas. • What is the value of sharing evidence during a discussion? • What types of evidence are most effective? • What are appropriate ways to introduce evidence and connect it to the ideas being discussed?
Weeks 5–6	**Applying the Learning to Other Forms of Narrative Text** Students will apply strategies gained in their study of fairy tales to their reading of other forms of narrative text. • Do all narrative texts have meaning? • Which strategies are most appropriate to apply to other forms of narrative text? Why? • What additional strategies might be needed to infer meaning in other text types? **Evaluating Reading Progress—Self-Reflection and Teacher Evaluation**	**Concluding a Discussion** Students will learn appropriate ways to end a Socratic seminar discussion. • When is it appropriate to end a discussion? • Need everyone agree? Is some sort of resolution necessary? Why, or why not? **Evaluating the Discussion—Self-, Class, and Teacher Evaluation**

Block's eloquent and disturbing fairy tale adaptations held students spellbound. These stories didn't seem like fairy tales, and it wasn't until the third day that students realized that "Snow" was a version of "Snow White." By then, they were too much into fairy tales to be offended. They liked the stories and demanded that Cheryl read more. When I arrived with a basket full of fairy tale picture books and short story collections, most students were eager to dig in. For many it was something of a relief to be given permission to read texts that were fun to read and easily accessible.

To begin the study itself, Cheryl wanted to capitalize on students' engagement with the retold tales and build on their prior knowledge of the traditional stories. In the following lesson she teaches students to interpret the author's message by considering the differences between the traditional and the retold stories.

SAMPLE LESSON: ## Week 1—Reading Workshop

AREA OF STUDY:	**Reading comprehension**
FOCUS:	**Finding meaning in the story**
TEXTS:	*The Paper Bag Princess,* **by Robert Munsch;** *The True Story of the Three Little Pigs!* **by Jon Scieszka**
RESPONSE:	**Reading response journal entries in response to the prompt "I think the author is saying . . ."**

"What do you expect to find in a fairy tale?" Cheryl asked at the beginning of class. "What kinds of characters? events? settings?" These questions were easy. Students had been well steeped in traditional tales since childhood and were able to provide answers readily.

Traditional Fairy Tale Expectations
- Princesses are good, kind, beautiful.
- Happy endings. "They lived happily ever after."
- Prince rescues princess.
- Magical creatures: trolls, dragons, elves, wizards.
- Magic solves problems (or creates problems).
- Witches are bad.
- Animals can talk, act like humans.
- "Once upon a time . . ."
- People live in castles or woods.
- Make-believe lands.
- Teach a lesson.

The list could have gone on, but Cheryl stopped the students when she ran out of chart paper. Then she previewed her plans: "I'm going to share a fairy tale with you today that is a little untraditional. As I read, I want you to think about what is different about this story. How does it vary from these expectations? After the story is finished, we'll talk about the differences and think about why the changes were made."

She read aloud *The Paper Bag Princess,* by Robert Munsch. It begins as the traditional story of a princess in love with a prince whose romance is interrupted by a fire-breathing dragon. But, in this tale, it is the prince who is carried off by the dragon and the princess (wearing a paper bag because all her clothes had been burned up by the dragon's hot breath) who goes off to rescue him, armed only with wit and intelligence. Told in a very tongue-in-cheek manner, the story ends with the dragon defeated, the prince rescued, and the princess happily choosing a life of her own. She realizes that she is smart and independent and that the prince is a "bum." This funny little tale was a perfect introduction to the author's message. In it are many of the traditional elements of the fairy tale but just enough twists to make readers sit up, pay attention, and realize that the author has something to say.

The tale is a short one, and the reading moved along quickly. After closing the book, Cheryl returned to her original question, "What makes this story different from traditional tales?" Answers included, "The girl saved the boy." "The dragon was kind of goofy." "The prince is a jerk." "They don't get married." Cheryl's next question proved more difficult. "Why do you think the author chose to include these differences in his story?" Students stared blankly. Cheryl tried again. "You told me that usually it's the prince who rescues the princess. But in this story, the princess rescues the prince. Why do you think the author wrote it that way? What message do you think he wanted to communicate?" Lightbulbs went on; it was the word *message* that did it. *Meaning, theme,* and *interpretation* were too vague; *message* they understood. "Maybe he's saying that girls can be strong." "I think he's saying that a princess doesn't need a prince." "He could be saying that boys shouldn't think they are all that." Heads nodded, a few smiles broke through the traditional high school scowl, and hands started to creep up.

"Every storyteller tells his story in a way that communicates a message," Cheryl explained. "Part of our role as readers is to figure out what that message is. With fairy tales, especially retold tales, one way to find the message in text is to think about what is different, and why." She then issued the students a challenge: find the message of Jon Scieszka's *The True Story of the Three Little Pigs!* We passed out copies of the text, armed the students with Post-its to place on the pages wherever they found a notable difference, then allowed them time and space to read.

Twenty minutes later, everyone in the class had an interpretation about the author's message. Their interpretations varied tremendously but nearly all were appropriate for the text. In response to the prompt, "I think the author is saying. . . ." Alejandra commented, "I think what this author is saying is that you should be kind to your neighbors so that you can prevent problems. If the pigs had just given the wolf the sugar, they wouldn't have died." In her reading response journal, Amanda wrote, "I think the author is saying that you shouldn't judge someone until you have evidence to prove it." Even Alex, a student who rarely attempted to participate, responded, "I think the author is saying to listen to both sides of the story because some innocent person could be framed."

———◄○►———

"What happens when they interpret the message wrong?" Cheryl worried. My response: "Which interpretation is right and which is wrong? As long as they can defend their understanding and support it with evidence from the text, their interpretation is valid." This didn't really answer Cheryl's question, but it framed our approach to the dilemma in the classroom. We didn't want all students to think alike. Stories can be interpreted in different ways, and we wanted to encourage students to see the complexity of the themes that were explored. At the same time, we wanted students' interpretations of text to be rigorous and appropriate. So we began asking, "Why?" Challenging students to explain the reasoning behind their inferences forced them to look deeper at text and consider their interpretations more thoughtfully. It pressured them to recognize for themselves when their interpretations were off. We asked "Why?" during individual conferences and whole-class lessons, and frequently required students to defend their interpretations in their reading response journals in the following way:

- Author's message. "I think the author is saying . . ."
- Supporting evidence. Two or more pieces of evidence from the text
- Explanation. How does the evidence support your interpretation?

But Cheryl and I didn't want to be the only ones asking why. We wanted students to challenge each other as well. Discussing, comparing, and defending interpretations of text is an immensely powerful learning opportunity. It allows students to learn from their peers, encouraging them to be more thoughtful in their own analysis of text and introducing them to new considerations about the potential themes and messages in a story.

For this class, we decided that Socratic seminars would provide the best format for facilitating thoughtful peer discussions. This large-group format would allow students to hear a wide variety of perspectives and support the comprehension strategies that were being studied. And Cheryl prided herself on running great Socratic seminar discussions with her older students. Her juniors in AP English and her seniors in World Literature could hold sustained, in-depth discussions about complex pieces of literature. She had clear rules and expectations that guided the discussions, and was able to take herself out of the conversation entirely.

Ms. Hibbeln's Socratic Seminar Rules

1. Sit in a circle.
2. One person speaks and then calls on the next speaker.
3. Someone should always be talking.
4. Back up your thoughts with clues from the text.

A clear explanation of the rules, however, did little to support our tenth-graders' conversation. During their first foray into a Socratic seminar discussion, the talk fell flat. The topic was familiar: a great retold tale by Vivian Vande Velde that the class had read together and reflected on independently. We knew that students had plenty to say about the fairy tale and their interpretation of it, but somehow the discussion never gained any momentum. A student would volunteer to share his or her ideas, and then they'd all stare at each other for a moment until another student would share his or her own ideas. There was no back and forth in the discussion, no challenge, no energy. As one student bluntly put it, these discussions were boring.

Of course, we knew that these students were capable of more animated conversations; we had seen examples of such talk at lunchtime and between classes. But they needed help transferring the energy and response of a lunchtime social conversation to the world of the literature classroom. To assist, we decided to provide them with a model that would specifically teach the behaviors and language appropriate for a literature discussion.

SAMPLE LESSON: # Week 2—Reading Workshop

AREA OF STUDY:	**Accountable talk**
FOCUS:	**Developing appropriate behaviors and language for discussion**
TEXT:	**"Cinder Elephant," by Jane Yolen, from *A Wolf at the Door and Other Retold Fairy Tales,* edited by Ellen Datlow and Terri Windling**
RESPONSE:	**Student notes on observations; participation in Socratic seminar discussion**

Jane Yolen's "Cinder Elephant" is a poignantly funny tale starring a larger version of the princess. It explores themes of appearance and personal judgment, and presents a strong message about the superficiality of our culture's obsession with size. It was a story that students had previously read and enjoyed, and Cheryl and I decided that it would make a great subject for a model discussion. Cheryl gathered the students in chairs at the front of the room. She explained that the two of us would be having a mini-version of a Socratic seminar discussion. We would model the behaviors and language that they would later be expected to use in their own discussions. Their job: to observe and analyze. Cheryl passed out a two-column graphic organizer on which students were to record their observations. On the left, students were to record their observations of our behaviors; on the right, the words and phrases that we used to begin our comments.

Participating in a model discussion can be a challenge, especially with this crowd. On the one hand, there is a need to model the instructional focus clearly. On the other, it is essential that such a discussion sparkle with engagement and spontaneity, modeling the feel, not just the form, of an ideal Socratic seminar discussion. To prepare, Cheryl and I had met the day before to think through what behaviors and phrases we wanted students to note. We'd made a list, and each of us kept a copy in front of us for easy reference during the discussion. However, we were careful to hold back on sharing all the details that we wanted to discuss; we wanted the conversation in front of the students to feel authentic, not stilted.

We talked, the students listened. After about five minutes of modeling, we concluded and then shifted back into teacher mode in order to review the modeling with the students. What had they noticed about the conversation? Immediately, students observed that we talked to each other, that the conversation went back and forth, that we argued, and that although we were polite (sounding at times as though we were "on the news"), we still could be pretty harsh in defending our ideas. All agreed that this kind of discussion seemed far more interesting than their awkward attempts so far.

Cheryl then asked students to talk more specifically about the behaviors and language that we had used. Students had done a great job taking notes, and together the class was able to generate an extensive list of appropriate behaviors and language, a set of guidelines that would prove useful for students to apply to their own discussions:

Appropriate Behaviors for Socratic Seminars
- Be respectful.
- Make eye contact.
- Don't interrupt.
- Talk to the other person.
- Respond to what someone else has said.

Appropriate Language for Socratic Seminars
For Sharing Your Own Ideas
- "I think . . ."
- "I believe . . ."
- "I wonder . . ."
- "I feel that . . ."

- It's okay to disagree, but don't be mean about it.
- Use the text.
- It's okay to talk about personal examples if they relate to the conversation.
- Ask questions when you don't understand.
- Take time to think before you talk.
- Read the text before you start the discussion.
- Be willing to change your mind.
- Listen.

For Responding to the Ideas of Others
- "So, what you are saying is . . ."
- "I hear you saying . . ."
- "Oh, I see. So . . ."
- "I agree that . . ."

For Disagreeing with the Ideas of Others
- "I respect that, but . . ."
- "I understand what you are saying, but . . ."
- "However . . ."
- "I disagree because . . ."

The following day Cheryl gathered the students into the Socratic seminar circle and asked them to engage in a discussion about a new text. Although stilted at first, and certainly not always brilliant, students gradually began to use the language and behaviors that they had observed. There was an air of amusement about using the "newscaster" phrases, which the students often pronounced in a mock serious tone before going on to explain their ideas. But, for the first time, many of them had things to say during the discussion, and many even began to respond to one another. During the discussion following the Socratic seminar, students agreed that the conversation had been much better. And most said they liked using the phrases because, as one student explained, "It makes it easier to get started talking when you know what you want to say but you're not sure how to say it."

———◄○►———

By the end of the second week, students were very comfortable with the idea of finding messages in text. They had come to understand that literature explores themes and that the manner in which authors craft their stories around these themes often reveals a message. Students enjoyed the active role of being detectives searching for the message in the story. They looked forward to being able to share their ideas in Socratic seminar discussions.

However, as Cheryl and I listened to the discussions, reviewed reading response journals, and conferred with students individually, we were concerned about the quality of their work. Many of the messages that they interpreted remained superficial, and the supporting evidence that they provided was often marginal. This was especially true as we moved away from retold tales that were direct parodies of the traditional fairy tales. As the tales became more complex, students were unable to rely on simply comparing the traditional with the retold in order to develop an interpretation. They needed to analyze the text itself to see multiple themes and recognize multiple interpretations.

Cheryl and I both modeled our interpretations, talked about asking questions to dig deeper into the text, and demonstrated how to support ideas with evidence. But students struggled to apply our models to their own reading. They needed something more concrete. Cheryl stumbled upon a potential solution one day while reviewing her model thinking. As she reviewed her thought process, she realized that there were essentially four different types of text evidence that had led to her interpretation of the author's message. After some deliberation, we decided that an explicit examination of each of these types of evidence, one at a time, would help students improve their ability to interpret text. We called the different types of evidence "clues" and told students that, just as detectives were constantly searching for clues to solve a mystery, they needed to constantly search for clues to uncover meaning.

Finding the Author's Message in Text—Where to Look for Clues
- Characters and their actions
- Conflicts and their resolutions
- Symbols
- Aphorisms: words of wisdom from characters or the narrator

We began by looking at characters and their actions. Of course, students had been considering characters and their actions all along, but not necessarily with a conscious understanding of their purpose. Our goal was to make their examination more deliberate so that their interpretations of the author's portrayal of the characters would be more insightful.

SAMPLE LESSON: **Week 3—Reading Workshop**

AREA OF STUDY:	**Reading comprehension**
FOCUS:	**Digging deeper into the themes and messages of the story**
TEXT:	**"With His Head Tucked Underneath His Arm," by Bruce Coville, from** ***Oddly Enough***
RESPONSE:	**Highlighting and note taking in text; participation in Socratic seminar discussion**

"Characters, their actions, and the consequences of those actions . . . thinking about these pieces of the text are one of the ways we can work to interpret the author's message," Cheryl began. "Today we are going to look at an original tale by Bruce Coville, 'With His Head Tucked Underneath His Arm.' The main character in this tale is named Brion. As we read, I want you to pay particular attention to Brion. Think about how the author portrays him. Are we supposed to like him or not? Notice his actions. What does he do? And pay attention to the consequences of those actions. Do good or bad things result? As we read, look for those three things: how the character is portrayed, his actions, and the consequences of those actions. We'll use your observations a bit later to develop an interpretation of the author's message."

Cheryl then began to read "With His Head Tucked Underneath His Arm." This tale follows the story of Brion, a young pacifist who is killed by a medieval king for his refusal to serve in the king's army. After having his head chopped off by the executioner, Brion's ghost haunts the king and the kingdom in an effort to end the perpetual wars of the fictional continent of Losfar. Written with wonderfully descriptive language, lots of great action, and enough twists and turns to keep the students guessing, Coville's tale is both engaging and rich in meaning.

With her students following along in their own copies of the text, Cheryl read aloud through approximately one-third of the story—right up to when Brion's head is sliced from his body and rolls into the waiting basket. She then paused and referred to her original list of three things to notice. "So what do you think? How are we supposed to feel about Brion?" she wondered aloud. "I think we're supposed to admire him," one student began, "because he uses really positive terms to describe him, like when he says 'he was not the sort to live a lie,' and 'he hated even more the idea of killing some stranger in a war he did not believe in.'" Other students readily agreed, pointing out other positive attributes and descriptions that Coville had accorded to Brion.

"So, we can agree that Coville wants us to admire Brion," Cheryl summarized. "Now, what are Brion's actions in this story?" Since they had been introduced to the expectations before the reading began, students were able to quickly identify the major actions that Brion had taken in this section of the story: preventing a woman from being unfairly beaten, standing up to a soldier, and then telling the king of his convictions. "And what are the consequences of those actions?" Cheryl pressed. Students responded that Brion was jailed and then executed.

Now came the moment of truth. "So, we have a young man that we are supposed to admire who stands up for what he believes in and, as a result, is jailed and then executed. What message do you think the author might be building with this story so far?" Cheryl's question hung in the air for a moment. "Maybe," Mario began, "he's trying to tell us that you should just keep your mouth shut because what you believe could get you killed. Brion stood up for what he believed in, and it didn't change nothin'. All it did was get him killed, and if he'd just stayed quiet, then he would've survived." Several students chimed in with their agreement before Jasmine stepped in to disagree: "I think that it's more about showing that sometimes it's worth standing up for what you believe in. Yeah, Brion died, but he didn't have to kill anyone else and the woman that he helped, lived. So even though he had to sacrifice his own life, he still went to his death knowing that he did the right thing." Cheryl allowed the debate to continue like this for several minutes, always encouraging students to back up their interpretations with evidence from the story that directly related to the character, his actions, and the consequences of those actions.

"Okay." Cheryl refocused students' attention. "You've done a great job of looking at Brion, his actions, and the consequences of his actions to interpret Coville's message so far. But the story is not over. Now you are going to continue reading on your own. As you do, I want you to continue to notice Brion, his actions, and the consequences of his actions. Take notes in the margins, underline important parts of the text, and then work toward using those elements to develop your own interpretation of the text."

The students moved back to their chairs and couches to continue reading. The story had grabbed them, and many were eager to continue working on their own. As Cheryl and I conferred with individual students, we were impressed that most were able to apply the strategies that we had discussed together. They were continuing to take notes and underline in the text as they noticed Brion's actions, and most were developing thoughtful understandings of the author's message and recognizing multiple meanings in the story.

By the time they moved back together to discuss the story, Cheryl and I knew we were in for a rich Socratic seminar. And the students did not disappoint. They brought an impressive range of interpretations of the text to the discussion, and all were able to support their understanding of the author's message by pointing to explicit examples of characters' actions and the consequences of those actions. Students discussed the importance of power, the futility of war, and the honor of standing up for your convictions. Most pointed out Brion's actions to support their interpretations, but several used the character of the king, his actions, and the consequences of those actions to support their interpretations. "I think that the author is saying that no matter how powerful you are that you still have to respect other people," one student commented. "The king in this story is obviously really important and has a lot of control, but he is really mean and disrespectful to everyone. He has Brion killed just because Brion disagrees with him. Then Brion comes back and starts haunting him. If the king had been more respectful, then he never would've had those problems."

———◄o►———

Examining various types of evidence in isolation proved to be a great help in getting students to see layers of meaning. Over the next week and a half, we reinforced students' ability to interpret meaning in tales by examining characters and their actions, and then we moved on to consider conflicts and their resolutions, symbols, and aphorisms. As we studied each, Cheryl and I modeled our own use of evidence to interpret authors' messages, students practiced using a common text and then discussed their findings in Socratic seminars, and students worked to apply their learning to their independent reading. We also returned to previously read texts to reconsider them through a different lens: "Were there symbols used in "With His Head Tucked Underneath His Arm"? Do the symbols support your earlier interpretation of the author's message? If not, how might your interpretation change?" "How does analyzing the conflict resolution in this story change your understanding of its message?" These were interesting questions that led to great discussions about the themes explored in fairy tales. As students considered texts through multiple lenses, they came away with an understanding that the messages were more nuanced than they had originally suspected. They began to question the text more perceptively, to reread, and to listen to their peers more thoughtfully during Socratic seminars.

Cheryl and I knew that they had become more sophisticated readers when the class revolted at the idea of aphorisms or "words of wisdom." Three weeks earlier they would have been thrilled if we had told them that the words of the narrator or a character can represent the essence of the author's message; now they were merely frustrated. "How can a few lines summarize the whole message?" they complained. "There's more to it than that." "What's the point of reading the story if they're just going to tell us the meaning? That's boring." "It's not any fun to use words of wisdom. I like looking for clues better and figuring out the message on my own. I think that the message is better that way."

To complement students' more sophisticated interpretive skills, we gradually led them into more sophisticated texts. The macabre and funny works of Roald Dahl and Jon Scieszka were replaced over time by tales by Lia Francesca Block, Lloyd Alexander, and Bruce Coville. The works of these authors are subtler and have room for multiple interpretations. They are certainly tales of wonder, but they follow the older, darker models of fairy tales—less singsong, more complex in their presentation, more three-dimensional in their characterization. This movement was intentional. It responded to student progress in thinking skills, and it ensured that the strategies of interpretation that students were developing could be applied to a wide range of narrative texts, not simply formulaic versions of children's fairy tales.

If we wanted students to really retain and use their newly developed interpretive strategies, we would have to make them matter. We needed to explicitly teach students to see the connections between the messages of a fairy tale and the reality of the here and now. This is the "so what?" of interpreting the author's message. Many students, especially struggling readers, have an attitude about literature analysis that sounds something like this: "So the author communicated a message, experimented with a theme, or grappled with an idea—why should I care?" As teachers, it is our job to help students make the connection between the fantasy realm of story and the reality, or potential reality, of the real world. "How does this message connect to specific current or historic events? to experiences in your own life? Is the message relevant? Why, or why not? Do you agree or disagree with the message? Why?"

SAMPLE LESSON:	## Week 4—Reading Workshop

AREA OF STUDY:	**Reading comprehension**
FOCUS:	**Responding to the author's message**
TEXTS:	**"Snow," by Francesca Lia Block, from** *The Rose and the Beast*
RESPONSE:	**Reading response journal entries**

As Cheryl had predicted, "Snow" was a powerful story for her tenth-graders. It prompted lots of great insights and debate about the themes and messages in the text. Listening to student discussion about the tale, we knew that it was time to push them to respond to the author's message, to connect it to their own reality and evaluate it in light of the real world. Although this was a natural step, and some students had independently begun evaluating the messages that they found, we had resisted introducing the concept to the class. We knew that if we pushed the idea of response and evaluation too early, students would automatically move to the evaluation piece before really digging into the text to consider the multiple levels of meaning. However, now that students were able to use the text to develop, question, and pursue deeper inferences, it was time to connect that text back to the real world.

Cheryl began class by thinking aloud. She stood near the chart that had been developed the day before, showing the variety of messages students had found in "Snow." She ran her hand over the chart and began to talk with the kids. "You know, 'Snow' really caught my attention. There was something about the story itself and the depth of the discussion that you all had yesterday that kept me thinking even after I left school. I especially kept thinking about the message that Maria shared. She said, 'I think the author is saying that negative, abusive love can be really powerful, and it takes a strong person to resist it or break away from it.' At first I found that message, and that aspect of the fairy tale, really disturbing. I wanted the tale to just be about the good love of the brothers. But the more I thought about it, the more I realized that Maria was right. In this tale, the gardener's love was really bad and really powerful; he almost got Snow. And then I started wondering . . . Do I agree with that message? Does it relate to the real world? Does it connect to my experience?"

Cheryl paused and sat down by the overhead projector. "Those were the questions that were going around in my head as I drove home. And those are the questions that should be going around in all of our heads when we come across a powerful story with a powerful message. So when I got home, I took out my journal and wrote a response. And I'd like to share that with you now." Cheryl placed on the overhead a transparency that showed her own journal entry. In it, she described her knowledge of women in abusive relationships—the reluctance of many to leave and the frequency with which they returned to their abusers. Cheryl shared some of the details of her own relationships, details that both supported and contradicted Maria's inference. It was an open, honest response that directly connected to the messages found in "Snow."

She read the entry aloud with the class. Then she turned it over to them. "What do you think? Do you agree that the message holds true in the real world? Can you relate to it?" It took students a few minutes, but gradually they, too, began to share real-world examples connected to the idea that "negative, abusive love can be really powerful." Some examples were general and superficial; other connections were heartbreaking; all tied the fairy tale story back to reality.

After students had had a chance to share, Cheryl called for a break in the discussion. She praised the students for their responses and explained that they were doing exactly what great readers of stories do. They were connecting the themes and messages in the text to the real world, evaluating them, relating them to their own experiences, and using them to reveal truths. Then she asked students to take out their journals and reflect on their own. Referring to the chart filled with messages students had found in "Snow," Cheryl told students to take any message and respond to it. She posted a chart with the questions she had shared aloud earlier: "Do I agree with that message?" "Does it relate to the real world?" "Does it connect to my experience?" She encouraged students to use these questions to help them focus their responses. Finally, she told students to be as specific as possible; the more direct the connection, the more powerful the impact of the message.

We were asking students to think in a new direction, and it was a challenge. Several sat staring into space with a blank page in front of them. Cheryl and I walked around the room and conferred. We asked them privately the same questions Cheryl had listed for the class, reviewed the student discussion, and went back over Cheryl's model response. Although none of the information was new, talking to students one-on-one somehow prompted them to be able to make a connection that encouraged a more sophisticated understanding of the text and their own lives. The result: thoughtful, insightful responses to a challenging tale— for example, the following one:

Response to "Snow," by Francesca Lia Block
Linda N., Grade 10
I think the author is saying that there are many different kinds of love and that you have to be careful to think about the reasons why people show love to you. In "Snow," many people love Snow, but some love her for selfless reasons and some love her for selfish reasons. The brothers love her because they just do. They want her to be happy and will do anything that it takes to make her happy even if that means letting her go away, something that would make them sad. The gardener loves her for really selfish reasons; he wants to own her. He is always thinking of what's best for him, not what's best for her. If Snow had gone with him, she would probably have been really unhappy, but since she decided to stay with the brothers, she'll probably be happy for the rest of her life.

I think that this message is really important in the real world. I mean, there are lots of different people who say that they love you and want the best for you, but really, they just want the best for themselves. One connection that I have is to gangs. The people in a gang say that they want the best for you, they say that you are family. But if they really wanted the best for you, then they wouldn't want you to join the gang at all. But they have to get you to join because they need more members to protect themselves. They are like the gardener that way, they always are looking out for themselves. And also, if a gang member is killed, then the other members of the gang are sad, but they get over it; it can kinda be a source of pride. But the parents of that person are devastated. Their lives will never be the same. Parents are more like the brothers in the story. They are willing to sacrifice and change their lives for their children. I know a lot of people who are thinking about joining a gang, and I think this story really applies to them. They need to think about whose love has their best interest—the selfish love of the gang members who want them to come join, or the selfless love of their parents who are pressuring them not to.

The final weeks of the study were dominated by Socratic seminar discussions and independent reading conferences. Both were designed to take the knowledge and skills that students had gained during the fairy tale study, and support their application to a wider range of narrative texts. Conferences focused on students' independent reading books, the majority of which fell into the category of realistic fiction. Sitting down one-on-one with students, we thought together about the messages that these texts conveyed. We considered the characterization of protagonists, the symbolism of places and objects, and the manner in which conflicts were resolved. Students consistently amazed themselves (and us) during these conferences. They would explain the story, think through the evidence, provide an insightful interpretation, and then, with an expression of surprise on their faces, remark, "I never thought about that before. Wow!"

Socratic seminar discussions were similarly designed to support students' strategy transfer. Cheryl broadened the range of texts that she gave the class. She introduced fantasy, allegorical, and realistic fiction short stories. She challenged students to use the same strategies for finding meaning in these texts that they had with the fairy tale texts. Subsequent discussions, although not always breathtaking, revealed just how far students had come. They eagerly debated authors' messages, challenged one another's interpretations, and sought out additional evidence to support their opinions. They discussed the relevance of the ideas in the text and compared multiple texts against one another. When asked if this was more difficult now that the stories they were discussing were no longer fairy tales, students were thoughtful but firm in their opinion. "Fairy tales were helpful for getting us to think about messages and find ways to see them," explained Raygie, speaking for the group, "but now that we know how to interpret stories, we can do it with anything." An overstatement, to be sure, but one that indicated significant growth.

Teaching the Unit—Writing Workshop

When it was first suggested to Cheryl's students that they would be writing a fairy tale of their own, they were less than impressed with the idea. But after they had been immersed in Scieszka, Dahl, and Stanley's raucous versions of tales during reading workshop, enthusiasm grew. Students liked the way that the babyish characteristics of traditional tales fell away to be replaced by gruesome endings, funny mix-ups, and slightly racy dialogue. They also liked the idea that retelling a story meant that a foundation was already provided. Somehow it didn't feel as intimidating to change characters as it did to build them from scratch. By the time we were ready to begin writing workshop in earnest (a date that roughly corresponded to the middle of the second week in the reading workshop study), students were fairly eager to begin building their own tales.

Thrilled as we were with the students' enthusiasm, Cheryl and I knew that we needed to rein it in a bit. We didn't want them racing full steam ahead into the drafting process (or as one student suggested, just changing the names of the people and places in the story). This study was about more than simply rewriting a single tale. The goal was for students to learn how, as authors, they could manipulate the elements of story in order to communicate meaning. In order for this goal to be achieved, we needed to make the planning process more deliberate.

Writing Workshop—Fairy Tale
Goals and Instructional Focus Progression

	Text Structure Study	Writing Process Study
	Goal: Students will learn to manipulate the structures of narrative text to communicate meaning through story.	**Goal:** Students will develop the ability to plan and write narrative text deliberately.
Weeks 1–2	**Defining a Fairy Tale and a Retold Tale** Students will develop a definition of a fairy tale. • What are examples of fairy tales? nonexamples? • What elements must a fairy tale have? not have? Why? • What is the purpose of a fairy tale? • How are retold tales different in their purpose and characteristics from traditional tales? **Analyzing the Elements of Story** Students will recognize and analyze the characters, setting, plot, and meaning of a traditional fairy tale text. • Who are the characters? What is the setting? the plot? the conflict? • How do these text elements work together to create meaning? • What is the impact when one or more element is changed?	**Planning—Manipulating the Elements of Story** Students will manipulate the elements of a traditional story (characters, setting, plot, conflict) in order to plan a new tale. • How do you want to change the descriptions of the characters? • Where do you want to set the tale? • When do you want to start the story? • What is the conflict and how will it be resolved? • How do all of these changes work together to build a message? Is this a message that you support? Why, or why not? If not, how can it be changed?
Weeks 3–4	**Crafting the Story** Students will analyze and learn to use action, dialogue, interior monologue, and exposition in the telling of a story. • What is action? dialogue? interior monologue? exposition? What is the purpose of each? • How do authors use these elements to tell a story? • Which are most effective? Why? **Communicating the Message** Students will analyze and learn to use techniques that effectively communicate meaning in text. • How do authors leave clues in their texts? • Look for and analyze the effectiveness of techniques such as event patterns, rhyme, repetition of language, the use of symbols, expression of characters' hopes or fears. • How does the use of these techniques support the communication of meaning?	**Drafting—Telling the Tale** Students will use their fairy tale plans to guide the drafting of an original story. • Organize your proposed fairy tale adaptations into a storyboard. • Draft the tale using appropriate language, tone, and craft techniques. **Making Changes and Additions** Students will appropriately incorporate new content or craft ideas into the draft. • Which techniques are most appropriate to incorporate into your story? Why? • How will the use of these techniques support your purpose? • Where and how can these techniques best be integrated into your particular story?
Weeks 5–6	**Engaging the Audience** Students will analyze and learn to use appropriate techniques to engage an audience. • Which texts do you find most engaging? Why? • How do authors use leads to capture the attention of their audience? Which leads are most effective? Why? • How do authors use plot twists, surprise endings, and/or a unique tone or point of view to hold the attention of their audience? Which of these techniques are most effective? Why? • How does the use of these techniques support the communication of meaning?	**Looking at the Story as a Reader** Students will reread and analyze their own work, and that of their peers. • Put yourself in your audience's shoes. What can you infer about meaning? • What evidence from the text do you have to support your inferences? • What suggestions do you have to make the story and/or message stronger? **Evaluating the Writing** • Establish a set of evaluation criteria • Measure your final published piece against established criteria • Reflect on learning

Week 1—Writing Workshop

AREA OF STUDY:	**Writing process**
FOCUS:	**Manipulating the elements of the story**
TEXT:	**"Rapunzel"**
RESPONSE:	**Story planning using graphic organizer**

"Okay," Cheryl began. "You've seen what Roald Dahl and Jon Scieszka can do with a fairy tale. Now it is time to work on your own. I know that some of you have some great ideas, but before we start writing, we need to do some planning. You need to be sure that the changes you want to make will work together to create a message that you like. Let me show you what I mean by explaining a little bit of my process." On the previous day, each member of the class, Cheryl included, had selected a traditional tale, read it through carefully, and broken that tale down into its elements. They recorded their analysis on a graphic organizer that included space for characters, setting, plot, conflict, and message. On this day and subsequent days, students would use these organizers to experiment with changing various elements of the story to see what the effect of such changes would be. Cheryl's plan was to model that process using the fairy tale "Rapunzel."

Aloud, Cheryl reviewed her breakdown of "Rapunzel" with the class, then paused and reflected for a moment: "You know, I've never understood why the witch in this story is so mean. I wonder what would happen if I changed her into a nice character." She placed a clean version of yesterday's graphic organizer on the overhead and rewrote the characters' names. However, this time, in the descriptions, the witch became "sweet, protective, wants the best for Rapunzel." "Now," Cheryl thought aloud, "if the witch is actually nice, why has she locked Rapunzel into the tower?" She paused again. The kids began to make suggestions: "Because Rapunzel was a bad girl and had to be punished." "Because she was protecting her from her parents." "She wasn't really locked in, she just felt like it because the witch was overprotective." Cheryl listened and then took one of the kids' suggestions. "I think I'm going to go with the idea that she was locked in because the witch was trying to protect her from a charming but selfish young man. So next to the prince's name, I'll write down that he was charming, selfish, and trouble." Cheryl wrote as she spoke, underlining *trouble* twice.

With these elements in place, the story began to take shape. Cheryl wrote out a plot (see Figure 6.1) in which Rapunzel's parents turned to the witch for help to protect their beautiful but foolish girl from the charming, older prince. The witch, supporting the parents' desire to see Rapunzel become a strong and independent woman, locks her in the tower and feeds her a steady diet of great literature and music.

Figure 6.1 Cheryl Hibbeln's Plan for Retelling "Rapunzel"

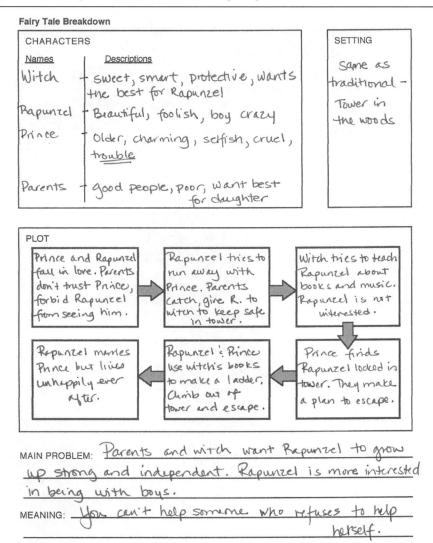

Fairy Tale Breakdown

CHARACTERS

Names	Descriptions
Witch	Sweet, smart, protective, wants the best for Rapunzel
Rapunzel	Beautiful, foolish, boy crazy
Prince	Older, charming, selfish, cruel, trouble
Parents	good people, poor, want best for daughter

SETTING

Same as traditional — Tower in the woods

PLOT

| Prince and Rapunzel fall in love. Parents don't trust Prince, forbid Rapunzel from seeing him. | Rapunzel tries to run away with Prince. Parents catch, give R. to witch to keep safe in tower. | Witch tries to teach Rapunzel about books and music. Rapunzel is not interested. |
| Rapunzel marries Prince but lives unhappily ever after. | Rapunzel & Prince use witch's books to make a ladder. Climb out of tower and escape. | Prince finds Rapunzel locked in tower. They make a plan to escape. |

MAIN PROBLEM: Parents and witch want Rapunzel to grow up strong and independent. Rapunzel is more interested in being with boys.

MEANING: You can't help someone who refuses to help herself.

As she wrote, Cheryl would occasionally go back and fix something if it wasn't working. She questioned and thought aloud how about how the pieces all fit together. As she neared the end of the plot, Cheryl considered some of the possibilities with which she could end the story. She decided to let Rapunzel follow the original story line—climbing down her hair and riding off into the sunset with the prince. However, this time around, riding off with the prince was not the usual happy ending. Because the witch was nice and the prince a cad, this was no longer a "happily ever after" victory, it was a disappointment. This new version of the story, Cheryl decided, sent the message that if a person is determined to do something, even if it is not in their best interest, it can be impossible to stop them.

Cheryl looked up at the students. Satisfied with her own story, it was now time to set them to work on theirs. She reminded students of where to start: "Choose one character that you want to change. Then ask yourself how that will change the story, the other characters, the plot, and the meaning. Remember, you are just playing with the story today; nothing is set in stone, so feel free to be creative." Then she sent them off to work. A few hesitated, but most were able to jump right in. Having a graphic organizer to work from was a huge help. Having used it the day before to break down the original story, students were familiar with the format. And the fact that they could simply write down notes about the story itself, rather than having to write things out in complete sentences, allowed these usually reluctant writers the opportunity to truly experiment. By the time they came back together at the end of class, a few were quite literally bouncing with enthusiasm about how they intended to change their story. We suddenly had an evil Jack, a fat Cinderella, and a gang-running Little Red Riding Hood on our hands. For better or for worse, they were off and running with their stories.

———◄◦►———

Over the next few days, we encouraged the students to continue to manipulate their stories. With Cheryl's guidance they experimented with changing the starting point, the ending point, the conflict, and the setting. We had worried that students would be reluctant to consider further changes; many of these kids liked to stick with the first idea that came into their heads. However, the organizer was easy enough to use, and their experience with it the first time around had been pleasant enough, so most were willing to try two or three different adaptations of their story.

For each potential story they plotted, students were asked to consider the message it conveyed. Did the elements of their story work together to communicate a message? What was it? Was this a message that they liked and wanted to write about? If not, how could they change things? Responding to these questions was a challenge for many; they'd never before planned a story this way. Some found themselves stuck on how to end the story to communicate the message they wanted. Others had an ending that communicated their message, but it didn't necessarily fit with other parts of the story. To solve these dilemmas, Cheryl and I spent a lot of time conferring with students individually. We discussed alternative plans, proposed possible solutions, and thought through potential problems. Although time-consuming, this work was worth the effort. By the time students began to draft their stories, each had a clear vision of the elements of the story and how they wanted them to fit together to communicate a message.

A clear vision and a clear story are two different things. Their early writing was voluminous but not particularly interesting. The stories were full of "and then she told . . . ," "so he decided . . . ," "but they said . . ." statements that told what happened but made it all sound like a long-winded, third-hand gossip story. Any attempt at message was totally lost in the hard-to-follow narrative. When I arrived for an observation at the end of the second week, I was greeted by a frustrated Cheryl. She handed me typed transparencies of a couple of students' tales that were representative of this problem. "Here, I knew enough to pull together a couple of stories to use as models, but I don't know where to go from here. Can you please figure something out?"

SAMPLE LESSON:	## Week 2—Writing Workshop

AREA OF STUDY:	**Text structure**
FOCUS:	**Adding dialogue**
TEXT:	**"Cinder Elephant," by Jane Yolen, from *A Wolf at the Door and Other Retold Fairy Tales*, edited by Ellen Datlow and Terri Windling**
RESPONSE:	**Class participation in text analysis and revision; individual revision of original stories**

On the overhead, I placed two (hastily written) versions of the same scene. In the first, Jane Yolen's "Cinder Elephant" sparkled with energy and life. In the second, the same scene was flat. I had rewritten the piece removing all the dialogue and replacing it with the same "she told," "he decided," "they said" statements that peppered the students' work. The rest of the language in the scene was left the same, but with the dialogue taken out, the whole piece came across as lifeless. The students had read the text earlier in reading workshop, so they understood the context of the scene.

Students were able to see immediately that the difference between the two scenes was in the use of dialogue. Now it was time to drive the point home. I put a copy of part of Jasmine's story on the overhead. Together, we read part way through. "What do you think?" I asked. Students knew that they needed to be polite, and the first few comments were halting attempts at compliments. But finally Dontay said what they were all thinking: "It's kind of like the boring Cinder Elephant story. I mean, I don't want to be rude, and I know mine's not any better, but it's kinda bad. I guess it could use some dialogue."

We read back through Jasmine's text, looking for places where it would be appropriate to add dialogue. Fortunately, it wasn't difficult to find potential sites. Each time we came across an interaction between characters there was an opportunity for dialogue. As we read, we looked for key words such as *told, agreed, decided, said.* I circled these words on the overhead and bracketed sentences that could be replaced with dialogue. Such visual clues would be helpful when students went to look at their own stories.

For Jasmine's one page of text, we found four possible locations for adding dialogue. Not wanting to swing the pendulum too far in the other direction and overwhelm the scene with dialogue, I suggested we choose the two places where dialogue would be the most interesting and revealing. The students narrowed the selection, and together we brainstormed a few lines of dialogue for each place. When we were finished, we reread the scene. Much better. It was more interesting and made more sense.

I reviewed the process, Cheryl passed back their notebooks, and they got to work. All were able to find a few places to add dialogue to their own stories, and the results ranged from humorous to dramatic. A few students were reluctant to return to their stories and tamper with the writing they had first laid down, but most saw value in making the changes and were willing to give it a try. My favorite moment came as students were leaving for the day. Darius, a very active student who was rarely on task, strolled across the classroom while acting out the dialogue he'd just written, voice intonations and all. At the door he turned and said, "Now, that's dialogue, Ms. L. Ain't it cool!"

———◇———

Over the next few days, Cheryl continued to work with the students to make their stories come alive. They added interior monologue, stronger actions, and vivid verbs. Most lessons followed the pattern just described: first an example using a well-written, previously read published text, followed by a modeled revision using student work. We found that this combination worked well. By first providing a strong example, at times contrasted with a weakened version of the same story, students understood the purpose behind the lesson. By then modeling the process of incorporating dialogue, vivid verbs, or stronger actions into a sample piece of student work, students were provided with guidance for how to get from where they were to where the example demonstrated they needed to be.

By the middle of the third week, stories were much more lively. But as Cheryl and I reviewed their latest round of drafts, we realized that they were still missing something. The messages that had seemed so clear in their planning failed to be communicated in their written stories. For a few, the messages could be found in the ending . . . sort of. Others had cheated a bit and written down the message as a moral at the end of the narrative. But for most, the intended meaning was absent entirely. We initially wondered if students had simply changed their minds about what they were communicating, but conferences quickly revealed that no, they were sticking to their original messages, and in most cases, they believed that the message was obvious.

Cheryl and I decided that we needed to more deliberately teach our budding writers to leave clues in the story. As readers, they were becoming increasingly confident as they worked to find clues about the text's message. They needed to follow the opposite process as writers, leaving clues that stood out as a big red flags to their audience.

| SAMPLE LESSON: | ## Week 3—Writing Workshop |

AREA OF STUDY:	**Text structure**
FOCUS:	**Communicating the message; patterns of three**
TEXT:	**"The Three Little Pigs"**
RESPONSE:	**Class participation in text analysis and revision; individual revision of original stories**

Fairy tales love patterns—patterns of three especially. "The Three Little Pigs," "The Three Billy Goats Gruff," "Goldilocks and the Three Bears"—in each case something happens three times, with the first two times following the same pattern and the third time the pattern's changing to emphasize the message. A house of straw is too weak and can easily be blown down; a house of sticks is too weak and can easily be blown down; a house of bricks is strong and cannot be blown down. The message: better to spend the time and prepare so that you are ready for adversity. These patterns work well because readers become accustomed to the repetition of an event ("he huffed and he puffed and he blew . . ."), and when the expected result changes, the audience knows to sit up and pay attention. "The Three Little Pigs" would be far less meaningful and far more boring if there were only one pig: "Okay, so the wolf blew at the brick house and it didn't fall down. Well, duh, it was made of bricks. So, what's your point?"

Cheryl used this example to introduce the concept of building patterns. By contrasting the original story, "The Three Little Pigs," with its abbreviated version, "The One Little Pig That Built His House of Bricks," students quickly understood the value of patterns in communicating a message. (Cheryl read both of these stories aloud using the same picture book. The abbreviated version was literally abbreviated; she started two-thirds of the way through and simply added "Once upon a time . . ." to the tale before introducing the third pig.) To ensure that they recognized how clear a pattern needs to be, Cheryl charted the progression with the students, noting repeated character actions and key words and phrases.

Patterns of Three: Repetition in "The Three Little Pigs"
- 3 pigs leave home. "The first little pig . . ." "The second little pig . . ." "The third little pig . . ."

- 3 new houses built. One straw, one sticks, one bricks
- 3 visits from the wolf
- "Little pig, little pig. Let me come in." (x 3)
- "Not by the hair of my chinny, chin, chin." (x 3)
- "Then I'll huff and I'll puff and I'll blow your house in." (x 3)
- 3 huff-and-puff attempts. Two successful, one failure
- 3 escapes from the big bad wolf. Two by running away, one by having a safe house

Wanting students to have a wide range of models of the use of patterning techniques, Cheryl gave the class ten minutes to find additional examples of patterns of three. Students combed through their folders and revisited picture books, and came up with quite an impressive collection. In "Cinderella," her foot is the third one onto which the glass slipper is fitted. In "Rumpelstiltskin," he gives the princess three chances to guess his name or lose her daughter. In "The Smith, The Harpist, and the Weaver," a tale by Lloyd Alexander, the Lord of Death visits three tradesmen and offers them magical tools in exchange for the tools that they have long used and trusted. As students shared, Cheryl charted, heads nodded, and understanding grew.

Now came the challenge. "Look into the tale that you are telling and see if you can find opportunities to build patterns," Cheryl instructed. "The pattern doesn't need to have been in the original. It doesn't need to dominate the whole story, it can just be a small part. Find a way to use repetition to build toward your final events so that it makes your message clear. Show why the pig needed to build a house of bricks, so to speak. Remember to make your pattern really obvious by repeating words and phrases and characters' actions exactly. We'll be around to help you."

Students returned to their own stories with some hesitation. The concept made a lot of sense within the stories they had read, but figuring out patterns for their own tales took a great deal of creativity and insight. Some were able to find places for patterns on their own. A few already had included a pattern and just needed to make it more obvious. Many needed individual help. Fortunately, the models that students had found earlier provided lots of different possibilities for how to incorporate patterns. Because of this, Cheryl was able to link her suggestions for students' stories directly to a familiar example, making incorporation of the suggestion more approachable. In their final publications, not every student made use of a pattern of three; it wasn't appropriate for all tales. But for those tales that did use patterns, this literary device proved remarkably helpful, allowing students to communicate their intended message much more successfully.

————◦————

A nice parallel developed at this point between reading and writing workshop. In reading workshop the class was taking a closer look at finding clues in the story. In writing workshop, we emphasized leaving clues. We returned to the stories they had previously read, this time "thinking like writers." Students analyzed how authors had used various literary devices to build meaning. They then returned to their own stories to see which devices would work best for communicating their own meaning. Among the possibilities considered: refrains in narration and dialogue, foreshadowing events by stating a character's hopes or fears, and the use of meaningful symbols.

As students worked on revising their stories and incorporating new techniques, Cheryl found it valuable to set occasional deadlines. By now, most student work was no longer in notebooks, although notebooks were still kept close for trying out an idea that they weren't yet ready to add to the story itself. Drafts were written on the computer or on lined paper and scribbled on, crossed out, and quite literally cut and pasted as students made changes to their work. About once each week, students were required to put all their additions, deletions, and revisions together into a new draft, which Cheryl then collected. This process helped students to clarify their thinking and allowed Cheryl and me to take a more clinical look at the work so that we could better assess needs.

Looking through the second round of drafts, we noted many improvements in structure and technique, but grammar remained a problem. "I can't stand it any longer," Cheryl said. "We've got to do something about their verbs." Their verbs were indeed a mess. And they had been for some time. But we had held off addressing the problem, knowing that a focus on grammar is more effective when the content of students' writing is largely in place.

SAMPLE LESSON: ## Week 4—Writing Workshop

AREA OF STUDY:	**Conventions of the English language**
FOCUS:	**Consistency in verb tense**
TEXT:	**An altered version of Block's "Snow"**
RESPONSE:	**Class participation in grammar analysis and revision; individual revision of original stories**

As Cheryl and I began to think about how to teach verbs, we realized what a daunting task we had ahead of us. The English language has so many different verb conjugations in so many different tenses that it is impossible to simply present a hard-and-fast rule for students to follow. Of course, the very nature of its complexity is why the students were having trouble with grammar in the first place. In an effort to find a focus, we reread students' stories looking for patterns in their errors, consulted grammar texts, and asked a sampling of students questions about verbs. Our research turned up a wide range of misunderstandings but a couple of nearly universal difficulties: maintaining consistency in tense throughout a story, and correctly conjugating verbs when more than one verb is used in a sentence. These would be the two issues that Cheryl would address with the whole class.

Cheryl pulled a couple of paragraphs from a recently read tale ("Snow") to corrupt. She replaced the correct grammar in the original story with errors that were representative of students' common problems. The underlined words in the following passage were intentionally changed for teaching purposes. The words were not underlined in text provided to students.

> Bear answered the door. Like all the brothers he <u>has</u> a fine, handsome face, burnished skin, huge brown eyes that regarded everyone as if they <u>are</u> the beloved. He was slightly heavier than the others and his hair <u>is</u> soft, thick, close cropped. He shook the gardener's hand and welcomed him inside, politely avoiding the bundle in the gardener's arms until the gardener said, I don't know where to take her.
>
> Bear brought him into the kitchen where Fox, Tiger, and Buck were <u>ate</u> their lunch of vegetable stew and rice, baked apples and blueberry gingerbread. They <u>ask</u> the gardener to join them. When Bear told them why he <u>is</u> there, they allowed themselves <u>turned</u> their benevolent gazes to the child in his arms. She stared back at them and the gardeners heard an unmistakable burbling coo <u>came</u> from her mouth.

Before sharing this corrupted version of "Snow" with students, Cheryl explained the focus. "Today we are looking at verbs. Because your stories are written in 'Once upon a time' time, the whole story should be in past tense. Many of you are in past tense part of the time and present tense part of the time. Now, I know that you know the difference between past and present"—she did a verbal check with a few examples—"but I also know that within a story, it's not as simple as just putting an *-ed* at the end of all your verbs. Some of you have tried that, and it's not pretty. So we're going to look at a sample piece of text with some verb errors and see if we can figure out how to be consistent about getting our stories into past tense."

Cheryl placed a transparency of the sample text on the overhead and passed out copies to students as well. By asking students to edit along with her, Cheryl was not only ensuring their attention but also giving them the tactile experience of editing grammar, and creating with them a reference guide that would be handy when they were ready to look at the verbs in their own texts.

Cheryl read the whole text through once to allow the students to hear potential errors. Then the class went back over the text one sentence at a time. For each sentence, Cheryl would ask, "What is the verb? Is it in past tense? Do we need to change it? Why, or why not?" Most students could find errors, but articulating the "why" was a challenge. "Why does the text need to say 'he *had* a fine, handsome face'?" Cheryl would challenge. "Yes, *had* is past and *has* is present, but telling me that isn't enough. Why does it have to be in the past?" Haltingly, students came to understand that their verb tenses depended on their stories, on who was doing what, when. "He *had* a fine, handsome face" because the observation about his face took place in the past. "Fox, Tiger, and Buck *were eating* their lunch" because that is what those three characters were actively doing at that moment; *were* already makes it clear that the moment was in the past.

After they'd been through the paragraph and corrected the verbs, the class agreed on a few rules:

- All the action and description in the story should take place in the past.
- If a verb is working by itself, it should be in the past tense. *Example:* Little Red Riding Hood *walked* into the forest.
- If two or more verbs are working together, the first verb should be in the past tense. *Examples:* The Three Little Pigs *were building* their houses. Cinderella *wanted to go* to the ball.

They also agreed that, for now, they wouldn't worry about verb tense in dialogue or conditional verbs (verbs that involve *should* or *would*).

With these rules in mind, Cheryl sent them off to their own stories, asking them to follow a process similar to the one the class had worked on for "Snow." She encouraged students to work with a peer, knowing that talking about the verbs they were using would help to clarify understanding. The work was not easy, and many needed considerable help. But several students later admitted that this was the first time since elementary school that a grammar lesson had actually made sense.

———◄○►———

By the beginning of the fifth week of writing workshop, students were tired of getting feedback from Cheryl and me. They were working on draft number three (more drafts than most had ever written) and were fairly content with their work. Most believed their stories were interesting and their messages clear. The ideas that their teachers kept providing in written feedback or oral conferences felt like unnecessary nit-picking.

Many stories were good. All had come a long way. But few really had the interest and clarity of message that their authors believed they did. Knowing that students were beginning to tune out her teacherly advice, Cheryl decided to have them give each other some formal feedback on their stories. In reading workshop students had become experts at finding messages in stories and supporting their findings with text evidence. Why not let them use their expertise to find the strengths and weaknesses in each other's tales?

SAMPLE LESSON: # Week 5—Writing Workshop

AREA OF STUDY:	**Writing process**
FOCUS:	**Looking at the story as a reader; peer review**
RESPONSE:	**Written response to peers**

Cheryl set up strict guidelines: constructive criticism of the text only, no putting an author down; give specific suggestions; and use a separate piece of paper to give feedback; don't write on the author's work. She structured a feedback format—

Part 1: I think the author is saying . . .
Part 2: Evidence
Part 3: Suggestions

She reminded students that they would be held responsible for their work as peer editors. Then she handed out the latest drafts randomly. The students' job: read and critique the work of their peers.

As they worked, the classroom was quieter than I had ever heard it during writing workshop. Each member of the class knew how much time and effort had gone into the drafts, and each took his or her role as a reviewer very seriously. Looking over shoulders, Cheryl and I saw good use of evidence and great suggestions. We also observed a lot of students struggling to find the author's message and then explaining their difficulty in writing. Interestingly, many of these peer editors had the same difficulties and made the same suggestions that Cheryl and I had. This made us smile because it showed how much the students had learned. Even if they were struggling to see and address the shortcomings in their own stories, students had developed enough understanding of author's craft to see and address shortcomings in the stories of others, tales they were less invested in and thus able to evaluate more critically. Here's one student's response:

Critique of Kris A.'s "The Three Little Wolves"
Crystal S., Grade 10
1. I think the author is saying that you shouldn't always want more than what you have, and that if you do, you can end up with nothing.

2. Evidence: In this story the pig is hungry and trying to eat the little wolves. He always has the food right in front of him, but each time the wolf tells him that there is something better, and he goes off in search of it. This happens three times. Each time he ends up even hungrier because he didn't just eat the pig. The last time the pig gets himself killed.

3. Suggestions: I think that you should take out the stuff about the different kinds of houses. It's cute, but it doesn't really help your meaning. When the pig is talking with the wolves, you should have him repeat the exact same things each time, or maybe just a little different. This will make it clearer that it's a pattern. You should move the part about the stomach rumbling to the end. Instead of having him break a flowerpot to wake up the alligators, have his stomach rumble. That way it makes it seem like it is even more his fault that he got killed. It's a really good story. I like it.

After about twenty minutes, Cheryl rotated the papers to another reviewer. And later to a third. At the end of the hour, each author received back their own story along with three sets of feedback. Many were dismayed; some were offended. The dismay and offense were caused not by comments that were cruel but by confusion. Most authors thought that their stories were so clear, yet many of the reviewers didn't understand the message or found little evidence to support it.

Not wanting the students to leave frustrated, Cheryl called the kids back together and reminded them of how far they had come. She expressed her confidence in students' ability to further improve their stories and emphasized that the suggestions were all about making a few thoughtful changes, not about rewriting everything. She used specific student examples and demonstrated how by changing a bit here and a part there, the story could be strengthened. By the time they left, the combination of frank peer feedback and an encouraging teacher pep talk had had its impact: students realized that they needed to take another hard look at their tales and, more important, they were willing to do it.

◄◦►

During the editing process, students' enthusiasm for their stories went in cycles. After a big success or a particularly helpful lesson, students were energized about continuing the work. But, at other times, they felt frustrated, mired in a sea of suggestions that seemed never-ending. However, with a final deadline in sight, the last week of work was highly productive. Cheryl and I sat with students and reviewed their drafts in relation to the class-developed fairy tale writing rubric. This, along with the peer feedback, helped students recognize the strengths and weaknesses in their work. Charts and student notes about prior lessons provided guidance for how to address weaknesses and build on strengths. And, of course, students had the opportunity to ask for help from their teacher and their peers. Suddenly, the buzz of talk in the classroom ran at a higher pitch, with students more eager for help and constructive criticism. I found myself accosted the moment I entered the classroom door with requests for writing conferences. Cheryl and I were delighted by this renewed enthusiasm. It represented real ownership and pride in their work, and a strong desire to succeed.

Evaluating Student Progress . . .

By the time the study drew to a close, the pride that students felt in themselves and their work was unmistakable. Students had begun asking to take work home. Peers who were not traditionally friends sought out one another for help. Students began coming in between classes to share new story ideas and inferences about their reading. And every student turned in a story . . . a story that had been revised more than once and was typed! For this group, that alone was a huge accomplishment.

The students knew they had been challenged and were justifiably proud of themselves for having worked hard to meet that challenge. Their exit conferences and written reflections revealed that they were well aware of the areas in which they had grown, and more important, also recognized the areas on which they needed to continue to work. Mainstream junior English classes would still be a shock for the majority of these students, but this study (paired with the analysis study that followed; see Chapter 7) provided a strong foundation in the skills that they would need to keep up next year.

. . . in Reading Workshop

Perhaps the biggest change that we observed in students' reading was a change in attitude. At the beginning of the study, fairy tales were simply entertaining. By the end, students recognized that the stories often had a larger purpose. They approached their reading with a more analytical mind-set, looking to find clues that would lead them to uncover the meaning of the text. And, for the most part, they were successful in their search. All students were able to infer meaning in text. The sophistication of their interpretations varied, but most recognized that texts had multiple meanings, and they were able to insightfully discuss the merits of different interpretations using evidence from the text. Most were able to thoughtfully respond to the messages they found in text and evaluate their relevance in the real world. Participation in Socratic seminars had grown. No longer were just a few students participating; most were now active contributors to these discussions, sharing their own ideas and challenging the ideas of others. Within the realm of fairy tales, the study was very much a success.

For other forms of narrative fiction, the transfer of interpretive skills from fairy tales to more sophisticated texts took time. Even after the fairy tale study was officially finished, Cheryl spent considerable time supporting students' application of the strategies to other types of narrative text. Many reading conferences and quite a few class discussions were devoted to thinking through possible interpretations of realistic and historical fiction stories. Slowly but surely the transfer occurred. Admittedly, these students were nowhere near ready to analyze *The Great Gatsby*, but they were making progress in that direction. Most could think abstractly about plots and characters in their independent reading texts, a few could recognize the use of symbols, and all knew that stories contained meaning.

Here are some student reflections on how studying fairy tales helped them become better readers:

> When I read now, I think about the story on two different levels. There's the story with the characters and the action, and there's the story with the message. So the characters are talking and doing things in the story, but they are also doing those things to build an idea. When I read, part of my brain is just enjoying the story, but part of my brain is thinking about why the author is choosing to make the story the way it is.
> —*Angelina C.*

> Before, when I read, I wouldn't always really pay attention. I would read the words, but I'd be off in my own dream. But now, I don't do that as much because I know that there's more to the story than just a story. Usually the story is telling you something important that you can learn from. So now I look for clues about that message when I'm reading. It makes the story a lot more interesting.
> —*Alex S.*

> It has helped me to become a better thinker. Now I know that I have to think while I read and really let the author get into my head. If I do that, then I can understand what they are saying and it helps me to think about the story and about life, too.
> —*Darius J.*

. . . *in Writing Workshop*

Students produced a wonderful range of original fairy tales. Characterizations ranged from simple to complex, settings from traditional to modern, and messages from sweet to amusing to frighteningly serious. The tales were written with a clear vision. Each student knew what he or she wanted to communicate and had become confident in manipulating elements of the story to fit the ideas and the story line. Each had worked to integrate appropriate writing techniques, adding dialogue, vivid verbs, and patterns of three while still maintaining individual voice and style. The results were strong. Students had created truly unique tales that revealed a great deal about the author's ideas and personality.

However, weaknesses remained. The greatest weakness was simply that of polish. These were not students who had grown up as readers, and consequently they struggled to shape their language in a manner that could really tell their stories. In addition, students had difficulty taking themselves out of the story and looking at it from a reader's perspective, and consequently some things were not clearly explained and the clues that they embedded within the story to point toward their meaning were not always obvious. These were craft difficulties that would be overcome with additional practice in reading and writing narrative text.

Here are samples of student-written fairy tales.

The Three Little Wolves
Kris A., Grade 10

Once upon a time there were three little wolves who lived near a wood. In that wood lived a ferocious pig who was always hungry. One warm summer day the pig came to the edge of the wood looking for food.

He came on the first little wolf tending his garden. *Mouthwatering, juicy tender meat, barbecue sauce,* the pig thought to himself. *I am so hungry.* He crept over to the wolf's house. As soon as the wolf saw him he ran inside, trembling.

"Little wolf, little wolf, come out and play," shouted the pig.

"I'll never come out, go away!" responded the wolf.

"Then I'll push and I'll shove and I'll make you pay." The pig started to force the house down.

Realizing that he was trapped, the wolf made a deal. "Don't eat me, pig!" he begged. "I am skinny and hairy. I wouldn't taste good. Go eat my brother instead." He shoved a picture of his fat brother toward the pig and pointed him in the right direction.

That looks more yummy! snorted the pig, licking his snout. He went away to look for the second wolf.

He came on the second wolf playing in the mud. *Mouthwatering, juicy tender meat, barbecue sauce,* thought the pig to himself. *I am so hungry.* He crept over to the wolf's house. As soon as the wolf saw him he ran inside, trembling.

"Little wolf, little wolf, come out and play," shouted the pig.

"I'll never come out, go away!" responded the wolf.

"Then I'll push and I'll shove and I'll make you pay." The pig started to force the house down.

Realizing that he was trapped, the wolf made a deal. "Don't eat me, pig!" he begged. "I am dirty and smelly. I wouldn't taste good. Go eat my brother instead." He shoved a picture of his clean brother toward the pig and pointed him in the right direction.

That looks even more yummy! snorted the pig, licking his snout. He went away to look for the third wolf.

He came on the third wolf sitting in the sun. *Mouthwatering, juicy tender meat, barbecue sauce,* thought the pig to himself. *I am so hungry.* By now the pig's stomach was grumbling so loudly that the wolf heard him before he even came close. The third little wolf ran inside, trembling.

"Little wolf, little wolf, come out and play," shouted the pig.

"I'll never come out, go away!" responded the wolf.

"Then I'll push and I'll shove and I'll make you pay." The pig started to force the house down.

Realizing that he was trapped, the wolf made a deal. "Don't eat me, pig!" he begged. "I am sick with cancer. My insides are all diseased and I wouldn't taste good. But my neighbor is healthy and clean and fat. Go eat him instead."

By now the pig was tired of all this running around. But the wolf's description of the neighbor sounded irresistible. So he went next door.

This is going to be the yummiest ever! he thought as he approached the house. He opened the door and tiptoed inside. *Man, it's dark in here. Who lives in this house?* When he turned on the lights, he was shocked to find an alligator family sleeping. He turned to run. But just at that moment his stomach growled, "Greolooara . . ." The greedy sound woke the alligators. And that was the last that was ever heard from the pig.

A Promise Is a Promise
Amanda J., Grade 10

Once upon a time there was a girl named Red. Red lived with her mom and her stepdad at the edge of a forest. At least she used to live with her stepdad. He had mysteriously vanished two weeks earlier.

One day Red's mother called to her and asked her to take some things to her grandmother's house. "But don't go through the woods," her mother warned. "There are fierce creatures in there."

Red just shrugged. Her mother never used to worry about the woods, but ever since her stepdad disappeared, her mom seemed to be paranoid about her going in there.

"Promise me," her mom commanded.

"Okay, I promise," Red called as she left.

Red started out along the road, but soon grew tired and decided to take the shortcut through the woods. "Mom will never find out," she said to herself. "And nothing will happen. It's not like some new scary creature just moved in here two weeks ago."

As she walked along, Red heard noises coming from the bushes close to her. Then she saw a pair of green eyes staring at her. "Oh snip!" she yelled and started to run.

The wolf crawled out in front of her. "Please don't run. My ear really hurts. I saw you walking in the woods and I am wondering if you could help me," said the wolf in a painful voice.

When Red looked at the wolf she was shocked. This wolf wasn't fierce like her mother had said, it was pitiful. He looked like he was starving and a piece of his ear was missing. Red saw that he was in a great deal of pain and decided to help him.

"What happened to you?" Red asked.

"Two weeks ago I was just minding my own business when a man and woman came into the woods. They were yelling at each other and the next thing I knew there was a gunshot and the man fell down. Anyway, I started to run. The woman chased me. She fired the gun and a bullet went straight through my ear," the wolf explained.

As Red listened to the wolf's story, the hair on the back of her neck stood up. The wolf was injured two weeks ago. Her stepdad disappeared two weeks ago. Her mom started being scared of the forest two weeks ago. "Could the wolf's story be about my mom and stepdad?" Red wondered.

Red wanted to know more. In order to keep the wolf talking, she volunteered to help. Red ripped off a piece of her sweater and began to bandage the wolf's ear. As she worked, she questioned him further.

"So what did this woman look like?" Red asked, trying to prove to herself that it wasn't her mother.

"The woman was tall, skinny, had brown eyes, and long, dirty blond hair."

Red's arms got goose bumps. The way the wolf described the woman it sounded exactly like her mother.

"And how do you know all these details?" Red asked, hoping the wolf had made a mistake.

"She caught up to me, after I was shot. She put a rope around my neck. She dragged me back to where the man's body was. She made me eat the body right down to the bones. It was quite tasty . . . well, in a way," the wolf admitted, licking his lips. "Anyway, she made me promise that I wouldn't tell anyone. She said that if I did, she would kill me. . . . So now you have to promise me that you won't tell. Because I don't want to be killed."

Red continued on to her grandmother's house. All the way there and all the way back she tried to convince herself that this wasn't her mom. It couldn't be. She tried to just put it out of her mind.

As soon as Red walked in the door of her house she stopped in her tracks. She saw the wolf's skin on the wall with the bandage still attached to his ear.

Her mom was waiting for her, the skinning knife still in her hand.

"Mom . . . ," Red said in shock. "What did you do?"

Her mom just smiled. "You promised me you wouldn't go into the woods today."

Suggested Texts

A huge range of fairy tale texts is available, ranging from the very traditional picture books to novel-length retold tales with adult themes. Our favorite retold tales are listed here (be sure to check the adult-level texts for appropriateness of theme before using them in the classroom with younger students). Traditional tales are very easy to find; visit your local library or rummage through your own child's room. Be sure to make the more traditional texts available to students as well, especially as they begin planning their own writing; many have only a partial understanding of childhood tales.

Note that the following list, and the tales used during our study, are very Western. This focus was intentional, for two reasons:

- Familiarity. Students had grown up with stories like "Rumpelstiltskin," "Cinderella," "Hansel and Gretel," and so on. In reading workshop, knowledge of these traditional tales helped students easily recognize changes made in retold versions of the tales. This recognition, in turn, helped to facilitate students' ability to infer meaning. In writing workshop, students were able to build their new stories on the foundation of familiar tales. This allowed them to focus more directly on the manipulation possibilities and consequences.
- Availability. A wide range of Western fairy tales and adaptations is available. The variety ensured that we could keep our reluctant readers readily engaged over the course of a six-week study. It also enabled us to move from less sophisticated to more sophisticated texts as students progressed in

their ability to infer meaning. And, finally, because so many modern manipulations of Western tales exist, students had great models on which to draw when they began their own fairy tale writing.

For our purposes, and the needs of this particular class, it was appropriate to narrow the scope of tales that were used. However, this emphasis is in no way meant to imply that tales from other traditions must be excluded. Amazing wonder tales from around the world have been used very successfully in similar studies. Stories from Africa, Asia, Eastern Europe, the Middle East, the Caribbean, Oceania, and Native American cultures have enormous possibilities for classroom use. It can be very powerful, for example, to compare Cinderella stories from around the world (there are dozens of variations). Teaching students to infer societal values based on folk traditions is both a powerful reading exercise and a great way to engage students in learning about other cultures. If appropriate for your purpose and the needs and abilities of your students, I would very much encourage the use of multicultural tales in the classroom.

Fairy Tales
Picture Books
Robert Munsch, *The Paper Bag Princess*
Jon Scieszka, *The True Story of the Three Little Pigs!*; *The Stinky Cheese Man and Other Fairly Stupid Tales*
Diane Stanley, *Rumpelstiltskin's Daughter*

Grades 6–10 (Young Adult)
Lloyd Alexander, *The Foundling and Other Tales of Prydain*
Francesca Lia Block, *The Rose and the Beast: Fairy Tales Retold* (mature themes)
William J. Brooke, *A Telling of the Tales; Untold Tales*
Bruce Coville, *Oddly Enough; Odder Than Ever*
Roald Dahl, *Revolting Rhymes*
Ellen Datlow and Terri Windling, eds., *A Wolf at the Door and Other Retold Fairy Tales*
Gail Carson Levine, *Ella Enchanted; The Wish*
Donna Jo Napoli, *Jimmy, the Pickpocket of the Palace; The Magic Circle; The Prince of the Pond; Zel*
Vivian Vande Velde, *The Rumpelstiltskin Problem; Curses, Inc., and Other Stories*

Grades 10+ (Adult)

Ellen Datlow and Terri Windling, eds., *Black Thorn, White Rose; Ruby Slippers, Golden Tears; Snow White, Blood Red*

James F. Garner, *Politically Incorrect Bedtime Stories: Modern Tales for Our Life and Times*

Denise Little, ed., *Twice Upon a Time*

Jane Yolen, *Sister Emily's Lightship and Other Stories*

Jack Zipes, ed., *Spells of Enchantment: The Wondrous Fairy Tales of Western Culture*

CHAPTER 7

Response to Literature

"Introduction to Raymond Carver's "Cathedral"

Tobias Wolff

A hot night, summer of 1982. I was lying on the couch with a story of Ray's that had recently come out in the Atlantic. *I'd had it around for several days but hadn't yet read it because I tend to avoid stories by my contemporaries when I'm hard at work on something of my own, as I was then. Tolstoy, that's the ticket. Hemingway. Flaubert. Someone monumental, someone impossible to imitate or envy. No complications. When you get to the end you think, Man, that Tolstoy sure could write!—and go on about your business.*

But a new story of Ray's always exerted a tidal pull on me. I was bound to succumb; it was just a matter of time, and the time had arrived. The story was "Cathedral." I began it with the excitement you feel when granting yourself a deferred pleasure, but before long I began to feel this pleasure give way to discomfort and even resistance, for reasons I will describe later. I was fighting the story. But after a few pages it disarmed me and I surrendered to it, and as I read on I felt myself drawn up by it. I felt as if I were levitating there above the couch. I was weightless, filled with a sense of profound, inexplicable joy. Blessed, and conscious of it, I understood that I was in the presence of a masterpiece.

No doubt Ray knew what he had wrought. He never bragged, but humble as he was in his dealings with other people, he did not pretend humility about his work. He had a pretty good idea what he was doing, and what he'd done. Still, a story like this demands a response. You might know you've written something extraordinary, but you can't help wondering if other people know it too. That's the point, after all, unless you're keeping a diary. Anyway, it gave me great satisfaction to track him down—he was on the road somewhere—and tell him how his story had affected me. And I feel the same kind of pleasure now, introducing "Cathedral" in this volume. It is good to be able to say, This is good.

But I did not jump to that conclusion. At first, as I've mentioned, I found myself resisting the story. It's hard to say now exactly what my problem was then, but it had to do with the tone. It seemed, in its terse, brittle factuality, to verge on self-parody: "His wife had died. So he was visiting the dead wife's relatives in Connecticut. He called my wife from his in-laws'. Arrangements were made." That affectless voice has its source, naturally, in the character of the narrator, a hard, grudging man whose idea of a joke is to ask his blind guest, Robert, which side of the train he sat on. He seems incapable of generosity, understanding, love, or pity. He doesn't even have a name. There seems to be nothing to him. Ray had an amused contempt for the term "minimalism" as a way of describing his work, but after the first few pages of "Cathedral" I started to wonder if he hadn't written a truly minimal story.

And then everything changes. There is no one moment you can point to and say, There's the hinge. It comes on you by almost imperceptible degrees, a gathering apprehension of the fear that drives the narrator's harshness and cruel humor. He's a frightened man, trapped in terrible, self-enforced solitude and unable to imagine a way out of it. Robert's blindness and the recent death of his wife form a mirror image of the narrator's fear of dependency and loss. No wonder, as he says, "A blind man in my house was not something I looked forward to."

He reveals his humanity almost in spite of himself. It may seem a stunted, ineducable sort of humanity, but wonder enough that it's there at all. And then something else happens. The narrator begins to enjoy Robert's company. He even allows himself to say so. And in the course of a night spent "watching" a special on cathedrals—that's right, he's got Robert planted in front of the tube—the two men come together to build a cathedral of their own, a space of perfect fellowship and freedom, wherein each is granted a miracle of sight by taking on the vision of the other. The effect is complex and mysterious, laying bare our hunger for human connection and the unexpected possibilities inherent in that connection. It is a triumphant ending, yet achieved without any falsification of voice or character. The apparently minimal terms of the story have become the foundations of a soaring act of artistry and hope.

————◇————

Now, *this* is a response to literature. Wolff's description of Carver's story is both personal and profound. It reveals the immediacy of a reader, sharing frustrations, distractions, and ultimately, an intense respect for "Cathedral." Reading this introduction is akin to sitting down to a good chat with a fellow literature lover. It is approachable and familiar; I read it with interest, and shared it eagerly. There is something of a sense of peering behind the curtain to see the wizards of contemporary literature here—it invites the reader to be part of the club. At the same time, this introduction beautifully illuminates Carver's story. Wolff's discussion of the characters, themes, and conflicts in "Cathedral" is clear and insightful. It enabled me to reread "Cathedral" with an entirely new level of appreciation. Previously, I had grown impatient with the story, skimmed through to the end and set it aside without much thought. With Wolff's guidance I was able to understand Carver's characters better, to see their underlying humanity, and to recognize the universality of their experience. Certainly, Carver's story stands on its own. But having Wolff's introduction alongside allows the reader to pursue an independent understanding that mirrors Wolff's own—one that is both personal and profound.

Thinking Through the Genre

Wolff's essay is a far cry from the literature analysis essays that I, like the majority of American secondary students, was required to churn out in school. Those essays were formulaic, cold, and clinical. They had none of the passion, humor, or enlightenment that fills Wolff's piece. Why the difference? Obviously, Tobias Wolff is a far more accomplished writer than I was as a teenager. But there is a more fundamental difference: we were given different instructions. The editors who put together the book for which Wolff was writing asked authors to "introduce a story in English or English translation that left them breathless, held them in awe, or otherwise enthralled them when they first read it. We offered them a wide latitude in these introductions: teacherly comments, reminiscences of that first encounter, anything that would provide an intriguing entrance into the story for the uninitiated" (Hansen and Shepard 1994). Wolff was allowed to choose a text and respond to it in a manner that he deemed appropriate. My instructions, on the other hand, were to write a five-paragraph theme essay about a text (and often a thesis) that the teacher deemed appropriate.

Sound familiar? It ought to. The five-paragraph theme essay has dominated secondary English classrooms in the United States for nearly a century. This fixture has become paramount, often crowding out other opportunities for creative and reflective response (Newkirk 1989). Bomer (1995) bemoans this dominance, writing, "What we teach students in limiting them to the exposition of literature is that though their first impressions may be subjective, ultimately they must squelch their response in favor of genres of writing that aspire to more objectivity. . . . By creating an environment that values essayistic modes of response, we, to some extent, force reductionist, scientistic ways of thinking."

Students deserve more. They need to know that a response to literature is more than just a requirement set out in the state standards. They need to integrate response into the fabric of their readerly lives, thinking of it not as an end-of-the-book, teacher-imposed assignment but as a necessary part of understanding and creating text. The occasional formal, public response should grow out of constant informal, private interactions—responses to text in which readers question the text, connect to its meaning, develop inferences about its characters, and synthesize earlier understandings with the new ideas that the text presents.

To nurture this understanding in students, it is helpful to think of responses to literature in three categories: reflective, creative, and analytical. All three should be taught and valued in the classroom. Although unique, they often work together, building upon one another as students grapple with their understanding of literature. However, not every type of response is appropriate for every student to use with every text.

Reflective Response

Reflective responses are what the reading workshop lessons in the other chapters of this book are all about. Mini-lessons, peer discussions, margin notes, reading response journal prompts, and end-of-class sharing are all intended to encourage reflection. They push students deeper into the text, encouraging them to interact meaningfully with the literature and promoting "thoughtful literacy" (Allington 2001). Katherine Paterson compares this constant reflection to the making of a pearl in an oyster. In her analogy, the details of the book are like grains of sand, and it is through the act of reflecting that the literature becomes a pearl. She writes, "The reading of a book takes time. . . . I read, I talk, I look, I listen, I hear, I fear, I love, I weep, and somehow all of my life gets wrapped around the grain."

Reflective responses need to be valued, both in the classroom and in the grade book. Students need to be allowed the time, space, and opportunity to wrap their lives around literature. Their efforts need to be encouraged and rewarded. Students should receive credit for the understandings they develop and display during discussions, independent reflections, and reading conferences. Such reflection is not simply a means to an end, it is an end in itself. Being able to consistently and thoughtfully reflect on text is one of the most important measures of a literate individual.

Creative Response

Professional writers not only reflect on text. They use texts to inspire their own writing. A line of a poem, the actions of a character in a story, a quotation in a journal article, an argument in an editorial may be the inspiration that will lead to a great piece of original text. Writers are acutely aware of the use of language and craft employed in other texts and may borrow a great idea to imitate in their own work. Or they may choose to draft a poem, story, or nonfiction article in direct opposition to an image, idea, or craft element that rubs them the wrong way, engaging in a creative dialogue through their own writing. When they read, writers are highly sensitized to all the nuances of the piece, and from these nuances they generate ideas for their own work. Bomer (1995) compares this highly engaged awareness of reading to his own attempts at carpentry:

> I am a very bad carpenter, but occasionally, when the house needs a new set of bookshelves, say, I build something. When I am thus engaged, I have eyes for carpentry; I notice every joint of every cabinet I see, constantly telling myself, Oh, sure, I could do that, or Maybe if I had the right tools, or just, Wow. That's what it's like for authors to read. Responses analogous to mine about carpentry go into their notebook, and from the accumulation of such noticings, art grows.

To encourage students to think and respond like writers, they need to be provided with great pieces of literature to read, time to reflect, and models that teach habits of collection and creation. Students need to be taught to keep a writer's notebook in which they consistently record great lines of literature, craft notes, observations about the world around them, and reflections about their readings and experiences (see Bomer 1995 and Fletcher 1996 for ideas on the development of a writer's notebook and its uses within the classroom). They need to be taught to plumb their notebooks for ideas and inspirations. And they need to be given time throughout the year to develop their creative responses. Although there are many standards to address and many tests to prepare for, the year should not become so packed with units of study and curriculum that we remove the opportunity for students to think and respond creatively to literature.

Analytical Response

Analytical responses, like creative responses to literature, should grow naturally out of reflective responses. And, like creative responses, they should not be required for every piece of literature that students read. Adult readers will develop an analytical response only when they are particularly compelled by something in the text, when they feel they must correct a wrong or want to share a unique understanding with others. In this manner, a more clinical, analytical response builds on the more informal, personal response. For example, I do not write an analytical response to every book that I read, but I may be inspired to write a response if I am struck by the characters in a book and want to share my understanding of those characters with others through a book review or journal article. Or I may write a letter to the editor if I am particularly offended by an article or editorial in the paper. In these cases, my passion for writing a more formal response extends the informal response from my initial reading. It is a way of taking my personal reflections, crystallizing them into an analysis, and then writing a review, essay, or letter that may be shared publicly.

Students must be engaged in a similar process. They need to have some control over the texts and ideas to which they choose to respond. This means that students should not be required to respond with a formal analysis to every text that they read or every genre that they study. They need to have an authentic purpose for writing an analysis, beyond the typical "you need to be able to do this for state tests . . . middle school . . . high school . . . college" response that we have all used but that simply indicates we don't really have a good reason for making them write something that they don't want to write and we don't really want to read. Students need to develop their analysis from their initial reflective response, using the raw reflection to bring energy and life to the analytical piece. They need to use effective vehicles through which to deliver their analysis. Essays are desirable at times, but not always. Letters to the editor, reviews, even public speeches can be useful forms of analytical response to which students should have access. And although they need to practice their ability to respond analytically, such writing should not be overused. Studying and writing analytical responses two or three times during the year, in conjunction with appropriate units of study of a particular genre, author, or text, is effective.

Of course, the form and purpose of various types of analytical response must be taught before students are truly able to utilize such responses effectively. And it is that effort to which the remainder of this chapter is dedicated. Two of the teachers who taught units of study described in earlier chapters in this text followed those units with a study of an analytical response. Donna Bates, whose work with short stories is profiled in Chapter 5, taught her students to write reviews. Cheryl Hibbeln, whose study of fairy tales is described in Chapter 6, followed this work with a study of analytical essays. Examples from both of these classrooms are used to demonstrate the possibilities of how to appropriately teach analytical responses in the language arts classroom.

Planning the Study

Even before Donna, Cheryl, and I began planning for our literature units of study, we knew that we wanted an analytical response component to follow. Both Donna's sixth-graders and Cheryl's tenth-graders would be subject to end-of-the-year statewide assessments that required written literature analyses. Both sets of students would need to be able to write formal literature analyses during their future years of middle school, high school, and beyond. And both sets of students were sorely lacking in their ability to write such papers. Their previous experiences with "English essays" had followed the traditional format in which teachers provide the majority of the outline and ideas. This left students with little knowledge of the genre that they were able to apply independently.

Fortunately, the earlier studies in both these classrooms had prepared students well to tackle the analytical response genre. By studying reading and writing of the literature first, without concern for formal analysis, students were able to develop an understanding of and appreciation for literature that would provide the substance for a later written analysis. In Donna's classroom, for example, the students had spent a great deal of time thinking through the perspectives of the characters in the short stories they had read. They had developed an appreciation for the experiences of the characters, the history of their lives, the conflicts they encountered, and the interactions they had as well as for their own reactions. Students had reflected in their reading response journals and in discussion groups about what they had learned from characters, what they valued about the story, and what had been the lasting impression that the text provided. All of this work provided a rich beginning for an analytical response.

In addition, by engaging in the writing process of the short story genre, students gained valuable insights into the structure and style of short stories. They had been trained to appreciate texts as readers and analyze texts as writers. Both of these approaches would prove valuable when they began the process of formally reviewing the literature. While their readers' lens taught them to appreciate the individuality of the characters and the value of the conflict, their writers' lens allowed them to see the craft behind these elements. This duality of vision led Donna and me to choose the review as the mode of the analytical response genre most appropriate to follow a study of short stories. Writing reviews requires writers to express an appreciation (or lack thereof) for the literature—the level of engagement the story permits, the believability of the characters, the credibility of the plot, and so on. At the same time, writers of reviews must support their opinions of the story by analyzing the author's language, structure, and craft. The process of constructing a strong analytical review of a short story seemed an appropriate coda to a genre study of short stories.

On the other hand, Cheryl's students were well prepared to write essays in response to their study of fairy tales. The main thrust of their reading and writing workshops had been looking at how meaning is woven into text. In reading workshop they had sought to find meaning, interpret evidence, and respond to the messages in text. In writing workshop they had worked to use the actions and personalities of their modified fairy tale characters, new plot twists, patterns in the action, and variations in the language to communicate a unique message through their fairy tale. This focus on message, both in its crafting and its interpretation, laid a strong foundation for writing analytical essays. The very nature of this mode of the analytical response genre is defensive—take a stand and support it. Cheryl's students had been taking stands about the messages found in fairy tales throughout the previous study. They were encouraged to take a stand during their Socratic seminar discussions and in their reading response journals. They had been defending their interpretations of the tales by finding appropriate textual evidence and explaining its relevance. And they had taken a stand in their own writing by selecting a message and then crafting a story to support that message.

As I worked with Cheryl, and later with Donna, to plan for the analytical response units that would follow their literature units of study, it readily became clear that although there are differences in the particulars between reviews and essays, many of our major goals for the studies were the same. In both cases, we wanted students' analytical writing to grow out of their regular reflections. We wanted their writing to demonstrate a thoughtful and unique understanding of text. We wanted students to understand that the most powerful reviews and essays are ones in which they write as readers, sharing their personal understanding and experience. We wanted students to develop a strong voice to use in their writing. And of course, we wanted them to follow appropriate analytical conventions in structure, especially supporting their opinions and interpretations with text evidence.

An additional goal was set, for the teachers: not to take over students' work with our own agendas. For English teachers who have been well trained in the practice of writing the five-paragraph theme essay it can be very difficult to let students choose their own texts, find their own thesis, develop their own arguments, and explain their own evidence. There is a constant temptation to "just let me tell you what to write and how to write it." Although we knew that such teacher overreaching fails to produce strong analytical writers (even though it may produce a one-time batch of strong analytical essays), it was very difficult to let students struggle to find their own way. More than with any other genre, we had to constantly remind ourselves throughout these studies that this was the students' work and that they needed to be the ones making the decisions.

Teaching the Unit

Exploring the Analytical Response Genre (Week 1)

Donna's class began with a review of Jell-O. This sounds rather strange, given that ultimately we wanted students to write engaging, insightful responses to literature, but in reality it was the perfect starting point. Donna's and Cheryl's students all

Workshop—Response to Literature
Goals and Instructional Focus Progression

	Text Structure Study	Writing Process Study
	Goal: Students will learn to recognize and use the structures, styles, and techniques of analytical text in order to convey their unique understanding of a piece of literature in an appropriate format.	**Goal:** Students will learn when and how to develop an appropriate analytical response out of their reflective responses to literature.

Exploring the Analytical Response Genre

	Text Structure Study	Writing Process Study
Weeks 1–2	**Understanding the Genre** Students will construct a clear definition of an analytical response. • What is the purpose of this text? • What are the essential elements of the text? What is the purpose of each of these elements? • What are the characteristics unique to this particular analytical form (review, analytical essay, letter to the editor, etc.)? What characteristics might this form share with other types of analytical response?	**Experimenting Within the Genre** Students will "try out" an analytical response using a familiar subject (e.g., food review, sports analysis). • Establish appropriate criteria and analyze subject. • Establish a purpose for writing a response to the subject. • Write a response that incorporates your experience with the product and your knowledge of the genre. • Reflect. Does work meet the expectations of the genre? Does it reflect your own experience? Why, or why not?

Applying the Genre to Literature

	Text Structure Study	Writing Process Study
Weeks 3–4	**Applying the Genre to Literature** Students will tailor their understanding of analytical response to apply to literature. • How is an analytical response about literature different from an analytical response about other types of subjects? the same? • What are the essential elements of an analytical response to literature? • How are these elements organized? What is the purpose of each section of the response?	**Choosing a Subject and Establishing a Purpose** Students will review response journals, literature collection folders, etc. to select a text to use as the subject of their response. • Is this a text that you really cared about (positively or negatively)? • Is this a text that has enough substance and evidence to support a formal analytical response? • What is your purpose for writing about this particular text?

Crafting the Response

	Text Structure Study	Writing Process Study
Weeks 5–6	**Using Evidence Effectively** Students will analyze texts to gain an understanding of the effective use of supporting evidence. • What is the purpose of using evidence? • What types of evidence are possible? text evidence? anecdotal evidence? other? • Which evidence is most effective? Why? • How do authors connect their evidence to their purpose? **Crafting a Strong Introduction and Conclusion** Students will recognize and use introductions and conclusions that are clear, to the point, and engaging to their audience. • What is the purpose of an introduction and/or conclusion in an analytical response? • What introductions and/or conclusions are most effective? Why?	**Organizing Evidence** Students will gather and organize their evidence in a manner that best supports their purpose. • What evidence is available? • Which evidence best supports your purpose? • How can evidence be most effectively organized to support your purpose? **Writing with Voice** Students will draft responses using a strong voice appropriate to the subject and structure. • What tone do you want to set in your writing? Why? • How can that tone be effectively integrated throughout the text? **Revision, Publication, and Evaluation** • Establish a set of evaluation criteria • Measure final piece against established criteria • Reflect on learning

recalled previous experiences with literature analysis, and nearly all remembered these experiences with dread. We wanted to approach this study differently. We didn't want their responses to literature to have the same old dry, boring, distant feel; we wanted enthusiasm, energy, and authentic response, all of which could be found in the Jell-O review. To begin, we immersed students in reading the type of responses that we later wanted them to write. Donna's class read reviews of restaurants, video games, TV shows, movies, and food. Cheryl's class read analyses of sports teams, handwriting, musicians, and Oscar dresses. These subjects drew students in, while the style and structure of the writing provided wonderful models. Taking away the literature component for the moment allowed students to thoughtfully read and analyze the genre of analytical response itself, focusing solely on a single cognitive task rather than simultaneously struggling to integrate their understanding of literature. It is much easier to read, understand, and analyze a review of a new brand of potato chips than it is to read, understand, and analyze a review of a text by Langston Hughes.

A description of Donna's Jell-O lesson follows. In it she carefully balances a need to immerse students in the genre of analytical response with a need to push students toward analysis themselves. She allows students plenty of time to read and enjoy sample reviews as readers but also insists that they consider the texts as potential writers. The balance achieved here is somewhat different from that in the other genre studies in this book. Here, there is no reading workshop component that is separate from the writing workshop component. Few people sit down to read reviews or analytical essays regularly. When they do pick them up, it is with a purpose: to help them decide whether to buy or attend something; to understand the current problems with a favorite sports team; or to know how to interpret and use census data. Although we certainly could have included a reading workshop component that focused solely on reading analytical responses, we decided against this option. Not only did it feel somewhat less than authentic (given that we ourselves infrequently read such material), but it also would have been impractical—there just aren't enough good samples of the genre available. Instead we sought to achieve the balance between reading as readers and analyzing as writers within each individual workshop session.

SAMPLE LESSON: ## Workshop on Reviews

AREA OF STUDY:	**Text analysis**
FOCUS:	**Understanding the genre; determining its purpose**
TEXT:	**"Jell-O," by Casey D., from *Teen Ink*; various other texts**
RESPONSE:	**Three-column chart for identifying the title, response, and purpose of various reviews; class definition of the purpose of a review**

On the overhead Donna placed a transparency of a student-written review for Sparkling Grape Jell-O:

> There are two loves in my life. One is my dog Sammie. The other is Sparkling Grape Jell-O. I can't begin to tell you how wonderful it is, but I'll try to describe what makes it so special.
>
> The first time I tried Sparkling Grape Jell-O, I was sick with strep throat and had to stay home from school. My mom went to the store and brought back a pint of Ben and Jerry's and two packets of Jell-O, one cherry, which is boring, and Sparkling Grape. Normally I hate Jell-O, but my mom made the Sparkling Grape with carbonated water. Several hours later, she put a bowl in front of me. Cautiously, I took a tiny spoonful and the amazing taste of Concord grapes with an explosion of bubbles went down my throat. From then on I was hooked. Now, I eat Sparkling Grape Jell-O as often as possible. I still haven't gotten tired of that cool, tingly feeling every time I put a spoonful in my mouth.
>
> I guarantee a great meal if you add Sparkling Grape Jell-O to your menu. It is refreshing, exciting and delicious!

The tone is light, the description fresh, and the overall effect very personal. Donna had specifically chosen this review because its personal nature would appeal to students and set an appropriate tone for the study.

The class read through the review together. "What do you think?" asked Donna. Student responses ranged from the simple and straightforward "Cool!" to the more thoughtful "I like how he compares the Sparkling Grape Jell-O to the normal cherry Jell-O, because I know I don't really like regular Jell-O, and if he hadn't told me that this stuff was different, then I probably wouldn't have paid much attention to the review" to the cynical "I wonder if he is being paid by the Jell-O company. I mean, he is so positive he ought to at least get free Jell-O or something" to the predictable "He seems kinda dorky." Donna allowed the conversation to flow for quite a while, first encouraging general comment, then ensuring that all students had a chance to share their reactions by asking them to "turn to a partner and talk."

Only after students had reacted as readers did Donna begin to develop a more analytical focus. "Today we are beginning to think about reviews," she explained. "As you've probably figured out by now, the text that we just read about Jell-O is a review. Eventually we will move toward thinking and writing literature reviews. But for now we are just going to think about reviews in general. In a few minutes, you'll have a chance to look at a variety of different reviews for different products. But before we do that, I want you to think for just a minute. What do you suppose is the purpose of a review? Look back over this review. Why do you think the author wrote it?"

Responses varied. Our cynical student commented, "He wants to sell more Jell-O so that they'll keep making it and he'll still be able to get it." Others decided, "He wants to share what he loves with others." "He wants to explain his obsession with Jell-O." and "He really likes the stuff and wants to convince others to try it, too." All students were keenly aware that Casey was writing for an audience. And all were very much aware that he was sharing his own opinion about a product. They weren't all expressing themselves in those words yet, but understanding was growing.

Donna released the students to go back to their tables and read the samples that were waiting for them there. We had pulled reviews of everything from rap albums to movies to colleges to high chairs. A few professionally written book reviews were thrown in, along with a few student-written reviews from previous years. A variety of sources was also represented, with samples from the *New York Times Book Review* as well as the local paper, *Teen Ink,* and popular magazines. We didn't expect that students would (or could) read all these different texts, but we wanted them to have a flavor of the possibilities. Donna encouraged the students to choose a review, read it, talk about it with a friend, and respond to it. Then she instructed students to consider its purpose. To support this process, she had students fold a blank sheet of notebook paper into three columns. In the first column they were simply to record the title of the review; the second column was for their response; the third was for their thoughts on the review's purpose.

Students were allowed plenty of time to immerse themselves in reading the reviews. There was no minimum set for the number of reviews to which they needed to respond, nor were there any particular reviews that they were forced to read. We wanted them to live in the genre, and we knew that in order to do this, they needed time, space, and choice.

Once all students had had a chance to read and consider reviews on their own, Donna began to encourage students to come to a common understanding. She instructed them to review their notes, compare ideas with others, and work together to develop a common definition of the purpose of a review. The result: "The purpose of a review is to share your reactions, connections, questions, opinions, and judgments about a product or service with others so that they can choose whether or not to purchase it or participate themselves." A bit long-winded, to be sure, and it would need to be tailored more narrowly when it came time for literature reviews. However, students were off to a strong start, with plenty of examples of reviews and a strong understanding of the purpose for the genre.

In the days that followed, students delved more deeply into analyzing the reviews. They developed a list of essential components, assessed the style of writing, and thought through what made the best reviews stand out over the others. Then it was their turn to experiment within the genre. Again, we chose to wait on the literature piece. We wanted to give students the time and space to live within the genre for a while before asking them to integrate their understanding of short stories. So, in came the chips. We brought in three different varieties of chips: Doritos, Wahoos, and generic tortilla chips, and we had a little tasting party. Working with peers at their tables, students developed a list of criteria to consider: crunchiness, flavor, aftertaste, messiness, spiciness, and so on. Then, for each variety of chips that they tried, students made notes about their reactions.

On subsequent days students crafted their own chip reviews. They were free to choose any of the varieties as long as it was good or bad enough to make them want to share their reactions and recommendations with others. The reviews didn't need to be long, but they did need to include the essential elements of a review: name of product, description of product, recommendation, rating, and details about their response to the product. The results ranged from amusing to downright hysterical. Many students really put themselves into these reviews, writing with a sincerity that actually did capture the "art" of chip eating. Before collecting students' efforts, Donna and I decided to extend the exercise by encouraging a bit of reflection. The following lesson was designed to create a bridge from writing about chips to writing about literature by asking students to identify the characteristics of their own work that were already strong and those that needed to be improved.

SAMPLE LESSON: ## Workshop on Reviews

AREA OF STUDY:	**Writing process**
FOCUS:	**Experimenting with the genre; assessing work in order to recognize the characteristics of a helpful review**
RESPONSE:	**Reviews of reviews**

Students sat at their desks, each with his or her chip review. They'd spent the previous night drafting and polishing, and now it was time to turn in the reviews, or so they thought. After a brief discussion of the process—"How was this activity? What was difficult? What was easy?" "What did you learn from writing the review?"—students were instructed to be sure their names were on their reviews and to get out a blank piece of paper. "Each time we write, we learn," Donna reminded the students. "We learn while we are writing, and we also learn by looking back at our writing to consider how it could be improved the next time around. You probably won't write many chip reviews, but you will write reviews of other things, including literature, at various times in your life. So, before you hand in your papers, I want you to look them over and analyze them so that we have an improved appreciation for the characteristics of a great review."

Donna informed students that they would be looking at the reviews of other students at their table. They folded their papers into four rectangles, and along the top wrote the following prompts: Author's name? What was helpful about the review? What was not so helpful? What could be done to improve the review? With that, Donna instructed the students to pass their reviews clockwise, to read, and then to respond (appropriately) to the prompts about the review. Time was limited, and students got right to work. Some read the review all the way through before making comments; others wrote notes as they read. Donna's introduction had prepared students to be thoughtful in their criticism, emphasizing that this was not a competition but rather an opportunity to learn together. Students responded accordingly, writing well-considered notes with an eye toward the future. They rotated through four different reviews, allowing between five and seven minutes for each. The last review they read was their own. We wanted students to look critically at their own work once they had had a chance to examine other possibilities.

Once the reviewing was done, we asked students to turn to a peer and compare notes. What characteristics had they repeatedly placed in the "helpful" category? What things had they found "not so helpful"? What were the most important things that could be done to improve reviews to make them more helpful? To discourage students from comparing negative criticisms about particular reviews and instead to think more abstractly about the general characteristics of good reviews, we instructed students to work with a peer at another table who had examined a different set of reviews.

A highly animated conversation ensued. Students had had practice analyzing texts from the perspective of a writer throughout the short story writing workshop, and now they put all their critical lenses to work. When we called them together a short while later, we were amazed at the thoughtful, detailed lists of "helpful" and "not so helpful" characteristics that they had found:

Reviewing Our Reviews

Helpful Characteristics	*Not So Helpful Characteristics*
Stand-out adjectives	General adjectives: good, bad
Author has strong, clear voice	Author has no voice
Description of product	No description of product
Lots of details	Few details
Evidence to support opinions	No evidence to support opinions

Many different criteria	Only one or two criteria
Explanation of *who* would/would not like product	No explanation of *who* would/would not like the product
Explanation of why the product is/is not recommended	Ambiguous recommendation; doesn't explain why product is/is not recommended
If rating system is used, it is explained	Although rating system is used, it is not explained
Uses punctuation to make a point!	

Perhaps more amazing were students' ideas about how to improve reviews. While some suggestions were a bit pedestrian ("Reviewers need to add more details to explain what they are saying"), others were remarkably astute and revealed a perception beyond what we had anticipated: "Reviews that show the author's reaction are a lot more interesting to read. Reviewers should put themselves in their writing because it's not really the chip that is interesting, it's their reaction to the chip that makes you decide whether or not you want to buy it."

It was with mixed feelings that students handed in their own chip reviews. After this lesson, some were reluctant to turn in something that they now knew how to improve. If they insisted, Donna allowed them to work on it more, but in general, we discouraged significant revisions. The goal of the lesson was not to learn how to improve this particular review but to learn how to improve reviews in general. We didn't want to spend precious class time revising a piece that was intended as a learning tool rather than as a final product. It was time to begin to apply their knowledge of analytical writing to literature.

————◄○►————

Applying the Analytical Response Genre to Literature (Week 2)

During the second week, in both classrooms, we turned our attention back to literature. It was time to consider how to integrate what students now knew about the genre of analytical response with the knowledge they had gained from the preceding study of literature. We began this transition by exploring sample reviews and analytical essays about literature in Donna and Cheryl's classrooms, respectively. This part of the study was much easier for Donna than for Cheryl. Book reviews are relatively easy to locate, and although we had to search a bit in order to find reviews that maintained the fresh, personal style we wanted students to emulate, we were eventually able to obtain some great samples. On the other hand, high-quality analytical essays about literature that were at an appropriate reading level for our struggling tenth-grade students were essentially nonexistent. Despite several trips to the bookstore and multiple searches on the Internet, we came up empty-handed. So, Cheryl and I wrote examples ourselves. We attempted to emulate Tobias Wolff's style, developing essays that were both personal and, we hoped, somewhat profound, but we crafted the text using a structure and topic that was appropriate for our students. Our writings, along with a few samples of great essays from Cheryl's older students, became the models for the class.

We also wrote alongside the students. As they progressed through the steps of review, reflection, outlining, drafting, editing, and publishing, so did we. The following lesson is one example of that process. In it, Cheryl models the process of reviewing her reading response journal in order to select a fairy tale about which to write. Although nervous about the prospect, she had agreed that students should be allowed to choose the fairy tales that they would analyze in their essays. She knew that this would likely mean more work as a teacher (after all, it is a lot easier when all the students are writing an essay about the same topic and we can just give them the appropriate thesis, supporting arguments, and so on). However, Cheryl also knew that allowing students to choose their own tales would go a long way toward ensuring that each student had a unique purpose for writing about their fairy tale and would be able to bring a fresh perspective and unique voice to the text.

SAMPLE LESSON: ## Workshop on Essays

AREA OF STUDY:	**Writing process**
FOCUS:	**Choosing a subject and establishing a purpose**
RESPONSE:	**Selection of texts and written explanation of choices**

Cheryl sat in front of the students, clutching her reading response journal. The night before, she had gone through her own review process, marking various pages with Post-it notes, highlighting sections, and writing additional comments in the journal itself. Even from the outside, it was clear that she was using her journal as a tool in her writing process. Once students were quiet and settled, she began to share.

"For the past week or so, we've been talking about writing analytical essays. And in the past few days we've narrowed our focus a bit more to thinking about writing analytical essays about literature. You've done a good job identifying what an analytical essay will look like and its purpose, and you wrote some good essays analyzing sports teams, school dress code policies, and music groups. Now it's time to think about which piece of literature you would like to write about. You can choose any of the fairy tales that we read together or ones that you read on your own. You can choose a traditional tale or a retold tale. It is up to you. But . . . [Darius groans. "You knew there would be a 'but,' didn't you, Darius?"] . . . it needs to be a tale that is appropriate for writing an essay about."

Students' faces were expressionless. It was unclear whether they were unhappy or just confused. Cheryl continued: "When I was thinking about what would be appropriate for my own essay, I went back to the descriptions you had developed of analytical essays. As I reviewed them, two things became clear: a good essay has to be about a story I really care about, and have an idea that I can support with lots of evidence." She paused and posted a chart on which she'd written these two criteria. "So, with these considerations in mind," she concluded, "I went back to my reading response journal and my fairy tale folder and started to review the stories that we had read."

Cheryl began to leaf through her notebook, displaying various pages on which she'd written notes. As she reviewed, she spoke to the students about why various stories would or would not make good subjects, from her point of view, for an essay. Among the reasons for rejecting a story: "This one just didn't grab me." "I liked this one, but it just seemed too obvious; I'm not sure there's enough there to write a whole essay about." "I'm still confused about this story." Other stories, she indicated, were possibilities: "I liked this story, and even though I'm still a little confused by the ending, it might be interesting to explore it further in an essay." "This was an engaging story, but I really disagreed with the message in the text. It could be fun to write an essay explaining the message and telling why I think it's wrong."

Finally, Cheryl arrived at the story that she wanted to use. "Okay, this is the one. There were some others that were possibilities, but 'With His Head Tucked Underneath His Arm' is absolutely the right story for me to write an essay about. To begin with, I loved the story and I totally believe in its message. Second, there's lots of evidence that I've already written down in my notebook that supports my understanding of the message; I've got quotes, examples, and even a pattern of three. Finally, this was a story that there was some disagreement about during our Socratic seminar discussion. Different people understood the message in different ways, and some people disagreed with the message. After the discussion I remember feeling a bit frustrated because not everyone agreed with me. So now I have the opportunity to more formally put forward my understanding through an essay, and I can get more people to agree with me. This is the story for me."

Cheryl closed her notebook, satisfied with her own process. Now it was time to turn it over to the students. But before releasing them, she asked them to describe what they had just observed. Students noted her use of the reading response journal and the fact that she had written all over it. They noted her use of the two main criteria she had originally set forth, and they asked her to add a third criterion to the list: "a point of view that I want to convince others of." They reiterated some of her reasons for considering and rejecting stories. And they observed that she had reviewed many stories before choosing one, that she hadn't just picked the first possibility. Before releasing the students, Cheryl added, "Just because 'With His Head Tucked Underneath His Arm' is the right story for me doesn't necessarily mean that it is the right story for you. You need to find a story that meets these three criteria for yourself."

With that, she sent them off to review their own reading response journals and fairy tale folders. Most students diligently returned to their journals and began rereading, snickering at some of the things they had written and shaking their heads in disbelief at others. We provided them with Post-it notes and highlighters, and many made use of these tools to mark potential stories, highlight useful ideas or evidence, and make notes on the page about how they might craft their journal response into an essay. A few students struggled and needed additional support. Cheryl quickly formed an impromptu small group of struggling students to review journals together. They didn't really need to be told what to do but found it helpful to hear the criteria repeated aloud and to listen in on the thoughts of their peers.

Once students had settled on a story, Cheryl asked them to write down on a notecard their name, title of the selected story, and rationale for choosing it. The act of writing their choices down helped students solidify their thinking, and the notecards provided great information to support Cheryl's planning for future lessons. By the end of the period, nearly everyone had found a story about which, they believed, they could write a solid analytical essay. Much to Cheryl's relief, the fact that they got to choose the subject for their essays built enthusiasm for the essay writing itself. Dorcella summed up the feelings of many when she commented, "This was okay. Before, the teacher has always picked the story and told us what we were supposed to write about. I've always hated English essays. But this was actually kinda interesting."

———◄o►———

Once students had selected a story, we made sure that they spent a few days exploring the story more thoroughly: rereading, making notes in the margins, reflecting in their journal, talking with peers. This time for reflection and immersion in the literature made it possible for each student to approach the analytical writing with a fresh and deeper understanding of both the literature and their own responses.

Crafting the Response (Weeks 3 and 4)

Before the drafting could begin, structural analysis was needed. Students needed a clear, organized scaffold on which to construct their analytical responses. Using a model (which, in both Donna and Cheryl's classrooms, were ones we had drafted ourselves), the class thought through the purpose behind each paragraph of the text, creating together an outline form that could be applied to students' own reviews and essays. (For an example of how this might be done, see the sample lesson in Chapter 4, Week 3—Writing Workshop.)

It was at this point that the most significant differences showed themselves between the writing of a review and the writing of an essay. In Donna's class, the students found that the essential structural elements of a review are introduction, summary of the text, description of the pros and cons of the text, and recommendation. Cheryl's students had earlier decided that the purpose of an analytical essay was "to communicate your understanding of and response to a piece of literature to others who were also familiar with the story, and to defend your position." This definition was similar to the review definition but with a different focus on argument and audience. Thus, the essential structural elements of the two modes of the analytical response genre differed. Cheryl's students decided that their essays needed an introduction explaining the message you see in the text (your thesis statement), evidence defending your understanding of that message, a personal response to the message, and a conclusion.

Students in both classes noted the importance of personal response and powerful evidence in analytical writing. And as they began outlining and drafting their work (using an outline and the reflections about the literature that they had previously collected), they strove to include both of these elements. However, students can at times think they are being more effective at explaining their position, using evidence, or showing their response than they actually are. As Cheryl and I reviewed her students' initial efforts at drafting, we realized that there were big gaps in several areas, but one of the biggest was in using evidence. In the following lesson, Cheryl demonstrates the importance of using strong evidence to prove a point.

SAMPLE LESSON: ## Workshop on Essays

AREA OF STUDY:	**Text structure**
FOCUS:	**Using evidence effectively**
TEXT:	**Ms. Hibbeln's analytical essay for "With His Head Tucked Underneath His Arm"**
RESPONSE:	**Independent search for additional evidence**

On the overhead was a now familiar section from Cheryl's essay. It described her understanding of the message of "With His Head Tucked Underneath His Arm" and supported that understanding with evidence. Students had participated in its organization and observed as Cheryl drafted it. But today they would be analyzing it more clinically. "I've been reading some of your essays," Cheryl explained, "and I am a bit concerned. You have great ideas and great understandings of the fairy tales you've chosen, but you're not always supporting those ideas with evidence. Remember, you want to convince others of your point of view [she referred to students' own earlier conclusions], so you really need to prove your point. What may seem obvious to you will not necessarily be obvious to your readers. You've got to support your ideas with plenty of evidence."

She moved to the overhead projector. "Today we're going to look back at one of the sections of my essay. As we analyze this section, I want you to consider three things: What types of evidence are used? Does the evidence support the main idea in this section? and Has the thesis been proved? Remember, I'm trying to prove that the author's message is, 'We should stand up for what's right even in the face of danger.' You have to decide if I've succeeded."

Reading through the text together, the first thing that the students noted was the variety of evidence. Cheryl had used quotations from the story, examples of character actions, and a pattern of events to illustrate her point. Students were then asked to decide whether each of those pieces supported the main idea. The answer—yes. (One student commented, "Of course they support your main idea; we designed them that way, remember?") And finally, students considered whether Ms. Hibbeln had succeeded in proving her thesis. Again, the answer was yes.

By now, students were a bit restless. They had seen this text before and were familiar with the elements that had been used to prove the thesis. But Cheryl's methodical process had a point. "What would happen," she wondered aloud, "if we removed one of these pieces of evidence? Which piece do you think is the least important?" After listening to a few students' suggestions, Cheryl made an executive decision and covered the information about the pattern of three with a thin strip of masking tape. Then she reread the now abbreviated text and again posed her main question: "Have I proved my thesis?" In general, despite the removal of some evidence, students still felt that she had proved her point, although perhaps not as forcefully.

Cheryl repeated the process, this time covering over one of the quotations with tape. "Have I proved my thesis?" she asked again. This cycle—covering pieces of evidence with tape, rereading the shortened text, and rethinking its persuasive power—was repeated until nearly all the evidence was concealed. All that remained unobstructed on the overhead was the thesis statement and one short sentence that referred to a single character's actions. By now, students were adamant that Cheryl's point was no longer proved. "You just don't have enough evidence anymore, Ms. Hibbeln," Dontay explained. "Now it's just your idea and it's like we're just supposed to trust you or something. That don't work."

He was absolutely right, it didn't work. And now was the time to drive the point home. Cheryl had typed up several examples of students' work. Emphasizing that these samples were representative of nearly everyone's work, Cheryl put the typed samples on the overhead. As the class reviewed them, Cheryl repeatedly asked the same questions that she had asked of her own work: What types of evidence are used? Does the evidence support the main idea? and, the kicker, Has the thesis been proved? Almost all the students acknowledged that although the evidence in these examples was good, it just wasn't enough to prove the thesis.

Seeing the defeated looks on her students' faces, Cheryl switched off the projector and launched into a pep talk: "Okay, so now we know that we need to go back and look for more evidence to support our ideas. This is a challenge, but it is not insurmountable. You know how to find this evidence. Quotes, character actions, patterns of three—these are all things that we looked for before during reading workshop in our fairy tale study. The evidence is there, and you know it is there. You used it before to draw your conclusions about the messages in text. You just need to go back and look more carefully at the text. Reread the stories, look back through your journal entries, compare notes with a partner. Don't worry about integrating the evidence into your essay today; we'll rewrite later. For now, just work on finding the evidence."

It was with mixed feelings that we watched students slump back to their desks to begin work. On the one hand, these kids were already at risk, and Cheryl and I hated doing anything that would dampen their fragile sense of self-esteem. But, at the same time, we knew that we wouldn't be doing them any favors in the long run if we lavished praise on work that lacked rigor. This day was a hard one. It required lots of individual pep talks and writing conferences, suggestions about where students might find potential evidence, and cheerleading when they located the perfect quote or example. But it paid off in the long run when students were able to know that they had really proved their point, not just to themselves, but to anyone who read their work.

<o>

Gradually, with a lot of support and opportunities to review their texts, students strengthened their use of evidence. They learned to vary the type of evidence that they used, and they learned how to weave the evidence into the fabric of the essay. (For ideas on how to teach this, see Chapter 4, Week 4—Writing Workshop.)

Unfortunately, as students worked on the more technical aspects of analytical responses, we found that they were losing the voices with which they had begun. This was true in both Cheryl and Donna's classrooms. Despite the fact that all students had started with an idea or response that excited them, this excitement was not coming across in their written work. Yet we knew, and the students knew, that unless a sense of immediate, personal response is interjected into the analysis, the text doesn't work. In the following lesson, Donna seeks to demonstrate how students could integrate their own responses and emotions into the texts they had already written.

SAMPLE LESSON: ## Workshop on Review

AREA OF STUDY: **Writing process**
FOCUS: **Writing with voice**
RESPONSE: **Editing reviews in order to use a stronger voice**

> One of the most important things about "Thank You M'am" is Ms. Johnson. She says important and unexpected things. For example, once she admits to Roger that she did things in the past that she is ashamed of. She is a good character.

Donna posted a chart paper with this portion of a review of Langston Hughes's story at the front of the room. It wasn't from any particular student, but it might as well have been. It looked exactly like many of their review paragraphs—flat, boring, filled with details, but lacking in voice.

"Does this persuade you to want to read this story?" Donna asked. "One of the things you told me, way back when we were beginning to look at reviews, was how important it was for the author to have a strong, clear voice, for the reviewer to share his or her own experiences with, and reactions to, the thing being reviewed. Remember the Jell-O review? That made us want to eat Sparkling Grape Jell-O because it was fun and exciting; it vividly described the author's experience. We need to put that same excitement back into your short story reviews. I know you know what I'm talking about because back when we started this project, each of you could tell me why you really felt passionate about reviewing the story that you chose. Now you need to find your voice.

"Let's work together to give this sample review a voice," Donna continued. "To begin, we need to decide what kind of voice we want. Should this be a sarcastic review? appreciative? irreverent? impressed? awestruck? What do you think?" Together the class (after some debate about what those words meant) decided that most of them really liked and respected the character of Ms. Johnson and that an appreciative tone would be appropriate. Once this groundwork was laid, Donna moved into the text itself. "Let's look at the first sentence. 'One of the most important things about "Thank You M'am" is Ms. Johnson.' How can we present that idea with a more appreciative tone? How can we restate it to make it more personal, more about our reaction to the text?" Donna solicited a variety of ideas and then synthesized them into a single sentence, which she wrote on the overhead: "One of the things I valued most about 'Thank You M'am' was the strong presence of Ms. Johnson." A few simple changes, but, as Donna pointed out to her students, these changes clearly put the responsibility for the opinions on the writer and provided an immediate sense of the writer's admiration for Ms. Johnson.

Donna emphasized these same goals when looking at subsequent sentences of the original review: "Why does it matter that she admits that she has done things in the past? How does that affect your opinion of Ms. Johnson? Why does that make you appreciate her?" Again students submitted opinions and Donna distilled the ideas down into:

> She comes alive on the page thanks to rich dialogue that is filled with unexpected revelations. At one point she reveals that she, too, has a past that contains experiences she is ashamed of. This was not something I would expect an adult to admit to a teen, especially one who had attempted to rob her. But the fact that she does admit it is what makes Ms. Johnson so intriguing. She is not the stereotypical older woman—she has a backbone, a sense of humor, compassion, and a wealth of experience that is hinted at, but never fully revealed. As a reader, I found myself trusting Ms. Johnson, wanting to know her better and wanting to learn from her. Throughout the text I could hear her voice guiding me through the story, teaching me patience and understanding.

A much more meaningful paragraph. "Now what do you think?" Donna asked the class. "Does this paragraph persuade you to want to read the story?" Students unanimously agreed that the new paragraph was much more inviting.

Before excusing students to go work on their own, Donna wrote out on chart paper her expectations.

Put Your Voice into Your Review
1. Find the tone appropriate for your response to your story.
2. Put yourself into the review—use "I."
3. Show your reactions. Say how you felt directly, and use adjectives to describe elements of the story that show how you felt.
4. Explain why the evidence that you chose to include is important to you.

Then, with an encouragement to "be creative," a suggestion to start by reviewing original entries in their reading response journals for their "first reaction," and a reminder to "keep your notes, don't throw anything away," Donna dismissed her students.

Some got right to work. They had known what they wanted to say and loved having the freedom to say it. Others felt trapped by what they had already written: "How can I add into this? It all fits together the way it is." In these cases, Donna suggested that they try rewriting one paragraph from scratch: "Read what you've got. Think about your reaction to that piece of the text and the reasons behind that reaction. Then turn the page and write it again. Don't worry about fitting it all together for right now; just write off the top of your head." This didn't work for everyone, but for many it did. They were able to create something that integrated their original ideas with a fresh and unique voice. For those who continued to struggle, Donna and I sat one-on-one reading and revising sections of their work. At first, we simply asked students the same kinds of questions that Donna had posed during her shared writing: What do you think about this? Why is this important? How does this change your opinion? Then, using student responses, we would help students to reconstruct their paragraph, actually writing sentences built on their dictation. Gradually we would shift the writing burden to the student, and eventually, after reviewing their process individually, we would leave the student to carry on independently.

Slowly but surely the voices came through. And as they worked, students continued to refer to a unique source of inspiration—the Jell-O review. The inviting, personal tone of that review was so powerful that even though it had been weeks since we had first read it, and even though it was about a product vastly different from short stories, students continued to find it a great model. It was an easy and accessible reference point. During revisions, the original question "Does this review persuade you to want to read this story?" warped into "Is my review as personal and persuasive as the Jell-O review?" A funny question, certainly, but one that inspired many students to improve their work by more thoroughly integrating voice into the text.

◄○►

During the final week of the study, Donna and Cheryl both worked to smooth out some of the technical aspects ("Do we underline or italicize the title?" "How do we insert the quotes?"), strengthen introductions and embolden conclusions, and incorporate some of the more enjoyable aspects of analytical writing, such as titles, rating systems, and bylines. Following the model that she had used earlier with their chip reviews, Donna encouraged students to share their reviews with peers, who in turn provided feedback. Cheryl's students also read each other's work with an eye toward figuring out whether arguments were proved. And, of course, multiple writing conferences were held to strengthen both student writing ("This evidence doesn't quite work. Can we look for another example?") and their confidence ("Yes, you can and should include your reaction here! You can do it!")

Evaluating Student Work

Cheryl called me at home after she had collected her students' essays. "I don't know," she commented. "There are some good things here, but I'm just not sure they are as solid as they could have been if I'd taught them the traditional way. Yeah, their reactions and responses are good, and the ideas are strong. It's really clear that there's an individual person writing each one of the essays; they're unique, and I like that. But I know that their evidence could still be stronger, their arguments clearer, and their conclusions more forceful. Maybe I should have told them more what to do. What do you think, did we do the right thing?"

Cheryl got part of her answer the following day. As we reviewed the study with the students, they were able to point out what they did and did not do well with their essays. They were able to explain their process and make suggestions for how they could apply this study to future analytical work. And it was clear from their comments, both written and oral, that they took ownership of their work in a way that no scripted, whole-class essay would have made possible. "I got to write what I thought," wrote one student. "I liked that because now my ideas are right there. I've proved them, and now other people can read them and understand the story better."

Students in Donna's class voiced similar reactions. But the real indicator of the success of the studies would come during later weeks when students were better pre-pared to respond to literature in a manner that was both rigorous and personal.

Here are samples of the analytical responses that students created.

Analysis of *The True Story of the Three Little Pigs!* by Jon Scieszka
Darius J., Grade 10

We've all heard the story of the three little pigs. The big bad wolf comes to eat them up. He knocks on each door and threatens to "huff and puff and blow the house down." Poor little, innocent pigs, right? Not so fast, says Jon Scieszka. In his twisted version of the tale it is the pigs who are bad and the wolf who is poor and innocent. This is a funny tale with an important mes-sage—that people have to be careful about passing judgment.

Alexander T. Wolf intends to be a good neighbor, not a killer. He is just an unfortunate victim of circumstance. After deciding to make a cake for his "dear old granny," Al realizes that he needs more sugar. So he goes to his neighbor (who happens to be a pig) to borrow some. He does not have bad intentions toward his neighbor, but the pig's reaction to the wolf's being there causes a bad chain of events. The pig is unwilling to respond to Al's knocking because he is unwilling to help a wolf. Alexander decides that nobody is home and starts to go. But then, since he has a terrible cold, he sneezes and "the whole darn straw house fell down. And right in the middle of the pile of straw was the First Little Pig—dead as a doornail." Alexander didn't intend to kill the pig. It was his cold that did it. A cold that was made worse by the First Little Pig's refusing to let Al in.

The prejudice that the first pig showed toward the wolf runs in the family. The Second Little Pig also refused to let him in and so did the Third Little Pig. He shouted, "Get out of here, Wolf. Don't bother me again. . . . And your old granny can go sit on a pin!" This causes the wolf to become very angry. To defend his grandmother's honor, the wolf tries to break down the pig's door to beat him up. Now remember, the only thing that the wolf wanted was to borrow a cup of sugar to make a cake. It was the pigs who started trouble with their insults and their prejudice.

Of course, just at that moment the police arrive. "Big Bad Wolf" the morning papers announce. Al ends up locked in jail and the media sells lots of papers claiming that he is a murderer. But, "Nobody knows the real story, because nobody has ever heard my side of the story."

Everyone believes that wolves are always the villains of the story, because that is how fairy tales always show them. The pigs, the police, and the media all judge the wolf unfairly. They stereotype Al because of his looks. The pigs refuse to open their doors. The police lock him up even though he didn't commit a crime. The media destroy his reputation by making assumptions and changing the story until they get something that will make top headlines.

This kind of judgment happens in real life, too. Every day people are judged unfairly because of their looks, their age, or the color of their skin. It hurts them and it hurts the people who do the judgment. In Scieszka's story Al suffered, but so did the two pigs who died and the remaining brother who was left alone. Also, the taxpayers who had to pay for him to be in jail suffered. Scieszka's message is important for all readers to hear. People need to know that prejudice hurts everyone and that they should be very careful before making judgments.

Review of "An Education" by Marie G. Lee
Marissa A., Grade 6

Helen looks through a closet for wrapping paper. She is looking ahead to a celebration for her high school graduation. Instead she finds a secret from her family's past. A book with Korean writing on it reopens questions about her heritage.

This is how "An Education," a story by Marie G. Lee, begins. It is a great story that explores issues of racism and family honor. Helen's father doesn't want to teach her about the past. He would prefer that Helen think of herself as an American, so he tries to keep their Korean heritage hidden. Helen tries to do what her father tells her, but she always has questions about where she comes from and why some of the other kids make fun of her. Then, at graduation one of the other students whispers the word *chink* as Helen walks across the stage to get her diploma. Helen's father sees her embarrassment and confusion and finally realizes that the family can't ignore its past. That night he starts to teach Helen about Korea, starting with the book she found in the closet.

Reading the story, I got pulled in by the realistic characters and situations. The dialogue and language are easy to read, and it is mixed with a vivid tone that puts you right there in the room. I could feel Helen's shock and horror as I read, and I was embarrassed along with her. The first few sentences are a bit slow. But it quickly becomes so interesting that you don't want to stop reading.

One of the things that I valued the most about "An Education" was the way that Helen dealt with all the messy situations in the story. People called her names and her father made her feel like being Korean was awful. Those situations must have been very frustrating. Helen must have felt very alone, like she didn't fit into either her parents' world or her school world. If I had been in that situation, I would probably have gotten very angry or just started crying. Helen didn't do that, she just stayed calm and handled everything very simply. She knows that her dad loves her so she trusts him instead of getting angry with him. She decides that the graduation ceremony is too important to her friends and family, so she doesn't make a scene. As a reader, I could see how all of this was tearing her up inside, but I really admired the strength she showed on the outside.

I would absolutely recommend this text. It is interesting, surprising, and full of different emotions. It teaches the reader a lot about the difficulties of being a second-generation immigrant to this country. Helen, the main character, is vivid with emotions and very believable. This is a great short story.

Suggested Texts

As mentioned earlier, finding good sources for reviews and essay samples can be a challenge. A few of the sources we used are listed here, but even these will need to be carefully examined to ensure that the style and content are appropriate for students. In addition, check the local newspaper (the Saturday edition often has a

"Family" section that offers reviews by and for young people) and popular magazines, especially when looking for reviews or essays about things other than literature. Another possibility—call a local liberal arts college or university and ask for
sample admissions essays. Many schools require students to include some sort of
response to literature or the arts as part of their application.

Often, the best resources are ones that you generate yourself. Try writing
your own essay or review using a style, structure, and subject appropriate for the
expectations you have of students. And don't forget to save copies of student work.
Analytical pieces from current and former students can make great models as well
as prove powerful motivators.

Responses to Literature
Grades 3–10
Write Time for Kids. Tel.: 800-662-4321; <http://www.teachercreated.com/
writetime/>. Materials drawn from magazines like *Time for Kids* are
published in kits for appropriate grade levels (grades 2–8). Each kit
includes a "persuasive" section with at least one or two book reviews.

Teen Ink. Tel.: 617-964-6800; <http://TeenInk.com/>. Monthly publication
written by and for teenagers. This is probably my favorite source of
analytical material to use in the classroom because it feels so authentic.
Reviews cover books, movies, music, colleges, and other things. A few
strong analytical essays are also published here—look at both the "nonfiction" and "college essays" sections.

Grades 10+ (Adult)
Charles McGrath, ed., *Books of the Century: A Hundred Years of Authors,
Ideas, and Literature.* The best of the *New York Times* book reviews, of
well-known and lesser-known works, from the past century as well as
a few essays.

New York Times Book Review. <http://nytimes.com/pages/books>. This
grandparent of all book review sections is strong in content and style.

Evaluating Student Work

This appendix includes several sample evaluation rubrics and guidelines that were used in the studies profiled in the genre-based chapters of this book. As with the studies themselves, these rubrics are intended to provide ideas, not mandate evaluation standards. There is no one right way to make a rubric, as the variety of the rubrics shown here will attest. The methods and standards that are used in individual classrooms should derive directly from the original expectations of the study for that genre in that classroom. Readers should adapt, rearrange, revise, or rework these rubrics as appropriate for their classrooms.

Guidelines for Developing and Using Evaluation Rubrics in the Classroom

Develop Rubrics in Collaboration with Students

In each study, teachers spent time with the students developing the rubrics that would be used for evaluation. Teachers kept a running list of the lessons that were taught and the strategies that were studied. These lists provided many of the criteria that were incorporated into the rubrics. Published texts or models of proficient reading behaviors and responses were analyzed by the classes to provide benchmarks of mastery. Work from former students was also analyzed to benchmark various levels of proficiency.

Use Rubrics During the Study for Student Self-Evaluation and Progress Assessment

Once rubrics were developed and benchmarks established, students were encouraged to assess their own work using the rubrics. Reviewing their writing or responses to literature with specific standards in mind helped students to recognize both strengths and weaknesses and to improve their work, where appropriate, during the study itself.

Evaluate Reading and Writing Separately

Both reading and writing need to be evaluated; each should be evaluated on its own. Although reading and writing within a genre go hand in hand, student achievement in one does not automatically indicate ability in another.

Suggestions follow for evaluating reading and writing.

Reading Evaluation   Teachers in the studies used one or more of the following methods to evaluate student reading:

- *Review of reading response journals.* Students were asked to select reading response journal entries that they believed demonstrated achievement of specific evaluation criteria. These entries were then evaluated by both teacher and students against the rubric.
- *Individual exit conferences.* With journals or specific readings in hand as evidence, students sat down with teachers to discuss specific readings and their individual progress.
- *Final reading tests.* Using a previously unseen reading, students were asked to read, demonstrate the use of appropriate strategies, and respond to questions appropriate to the genre. Student work was then evaluated against the reading rubric.

Writing Evaluation   The primary method for evaluating student writing was to read and assess the final written product within the genre study. Additionally, teachers conferred with the students individually and considered their self-evaluations when determining final rubric placement.

Award Grades for Both Achievement and Effort

In addition to making a final evaluation of academic achievement, teachers regularly evaluated students' effort. Students were held accountable for turning in drafts, participating in classroom discussions, and reading and responding to common classroom texts and independently selected texts. Regular reading conferences, review of reading response journals and writer's notebooks, classroom observation, and occasional taping of classroom discussions were used to ensure that students regularly participated and put effort into the work of the study.

Writing Rubric Memoir

Criteria	4	3	2	1
Event Selection	Event seems very significant to the author's life.	Event seems kind of significant to the author's life.	Event does not seem significant to the author's life.	Author does not seem to be aware of significance of the event.
Structure	Memoir is clearly focused on a single memorable moment. All additional text events directly support the significance of the memorable moment.	Memoir is mostly focused on a memorable moment. Some of the additional text events support the significance of the memorable moment.	Memoir has a central event. Other events are included that have some relevance to the central event but do not necessarily show its significance.	Memoir includes multiple events that are disconnected and do not reveal significance.
Style and Technique	Author consistently reveals the significance of the events through engaging details, compelling language, and a balance of action, thoughts, and dialogue.	Author sometimes reveals the significance of the events through details, compelling language, and a balance of action, thoughts, and dialogue.	Author tells the significance of events through direct statements.	No effort is made to reveal the significance of the events to the reader.
Mechanics and Presentation	No mistakes in spelling, grammar, or punctuation; neat and clean.	A few minor mistakes that do not interfere with the reader's ability to comprehend the text; neat.	Many minor mistakes. Mechanics and presentation make text somewhat difficult to read.	Many or careless mistakes and sloppy presentation make text very difficult to read.

Comments: **Score:**

Thinking Through Genre: Units of Study in Reading and Writing Workshops 4–12 by Heather Lattimer. Copyright © 2003. Stenhouse Publishers.

Writing Rubric for Feature Article

Criteria	Point Score (4, 3, 2, or 1)

The text is informative.   _____

Information is new or presented in a fresh way.

There is an appropriate amount of information.

Information comes from a variety of sources appropriate to topic.

The text is well organized.   _____

Information is organized around a "big idea."

Organizing structure is appropriate to topic and "big idea."

Subtitles, topic sentences, evidence tags, and so on, are effectively used.

The text is engaging.   _____

Stories, examples, and quotations are interesting to the reader.

Language is carefully crafted to pull reader into text.

The features—   _____

Support the information and the "big idea."

Engage reader's attention and pull reader into text.

The overall work is—   _____

Neat: text is legible, layout is clear, organization supports text.

Mechanically correct: all or nearly all spelling and grammar are correct.

Comments: **Total:** _____

Reading Rubric for Editorial

Criteria	Point Score (3, 2, or 1)

Successful editorial readers will be able to—

Ask and respond to the essential editorial questions.   _____

Explain author's argument in their own words.   _____

Ask thoughtful questions of the text.   _____

Ask thoughtful questions about the issue.   _____

Assess the merits of the editorial and explain their assessment
using evidence from the text.   _____

Assess their position on the issue using evidence from the
editorial as well as their questions and their own background
knowledge.   _____

Explain how the editorial and their interactions with the text
altered their positions on the issue.   _____

Comments: **Total:** _____

Reading Rubric for Fairy Tale

Criteria	3	2	1
Recognizing author's message	Student consistently recognizes multiple layers of themes or messages in a wide range of fairy tale texts: simple picture books to complex young adult tales.	Student regularly recognizes one or more themes or messages in most fairy tale texts.	Student occasionally recognizes a single theme or message in simple fairy tale texts.
Defending understanding of author's message with evidence	Student can consistently defend own understanding of themes or messages in the text using a range of text evidence, including analysis of characters, conflicts, symbols, and aphorisms.	Student can regularly defend own understanding of themes or messages in the text using specific text evidence.	Student can occasionally defend own understanding of theme or message in the text using general descriptions of text evidence.
Responding to author's message	Student can consistently and thoughtfully respond to author's message with insightful connections to own experience, other texts, and real-world situations.	Student can regularly and thoughtfully respond to author's message with connections to own experience and real-world situations.	Student can occasionally respond to author's message with connections to own experience.
Applying the strategies to other genres	Student shows strong evidence of being able to apply strategies learned in fairy tales to narrative texts in other genres.	Student shows evidence of learning to apply strategies learned in fairy tales to narrative texts in other genres.	Student is not yet able to effectively apply strategies learned in fairy tales to narrative texts in other genres.

Comments: **Score:**

Thinking Through Genre: Units of Study in Reading and Writing Workshops 4–12 by Heather Lattimer. Copyright © 2003. Stenhouse Publishers.

Works Cited in the Foreword

Bakhtin, M. M. 1986. *Speech Genres and Other Late Essays,* trans. V. W. McGee. Austin, TX: University of Texas Press.

Christie, F. 1989. *Language Education.* Oxford, UK: Oxford University Press.

Cope, B., and M. Kalantzis. 1993. *The Powers of Literacy: A Genre Approach to Teaching Writing.* Pittsburgh: University of Pittsburgh Press.

Edelsky, C. 1992. *With Literacy and Justice for All.* London: Falmer Press.

Rosenblatt, L. M. 1978. *The Reader, the Text, the Poem: The Transactional Theory of the Literary Work.* Carbondale, IL: Southern Illinois University Press.

Works Cited in the Text

Allen, Janet. 1995. *It's Never Too Late: Leading Adolescents to Lifelong Literacy.* Portsmouth, NH: Heinemann.

Allen, Janet, and Kyle Gonzalez. 1998. *There's Room for Me Here: Literacy Workshop in the Middle School.* Portland, ME: Stenhouse.

Allington, Richard. 2001. *What Really Matters for Struggling Readers: Designing Research-Based Programs.* White Plains, NY: Addison-Wesley.

Atkin, S. Beth. 1993. *Voices from the Fields.* Boston: Little, Brown.

Atwell, Nancie. 1998. *In the Middle: New Understandings About Writing, Reading, and Learning.* 2d ed. Portsmouth, NH: Heinemann.

Babbitt, Natalie. 1997. *Tuck Everlasting.* New York: Farrar, Straus and Giroux.

Baddeley, Gavin. 2001. *Goth Chic: A Connoisseur's Guide to Dark Culture.* Medford, NJ: Plexus Publishing.

Block, Francesca Lia. 2001. "Snow." In *The Rose and the Beast: Fairy Tales Retold.* New York: HarperCollins.

Bomer, Randy. 1995. *Time for Meaning: Crafting Literate Lives in Middle and High School.* Portsmouth, NH: Heinemann.

Bomer, Randy, and Katherine Bomer. 2001. *For a Better World: Reading and Writing for Social Action.* Portsmouth, NH: Heinemann.

"Book Banning" by Zack H. 2002. *Teen Ink* (Opinion), January. <http://TeenInk.com/Opinion/>.

"Brand-Name Schools." 2000. *In Write Time for Kids—Level 5.* Westminster, CA: Teacher Created Materials. <http://www.teachercreated.com/writetime/>.

Burgess, Melvin. 2001. *Billy Elliot.* New York: Scholastic.

Calkins, Lucy. 1994. *The Art of Teaching Writing.* Portsmouth, NH: Heinemann.

———. 2001. *The Art of Teaching Reading.* New York: Longman.

Calkins, Lucy, with Kate Montgomery and Donna Santman. 1998. *A Teacher's Guide to Standardized Reading Tests: Knowledge Is Power.* Portsmouth, NH: Heinemann.

Carver, Raymond. 1994. "Cathedral." In *You've Got to Read This: Contemporary American Writers Introduce Stories That Held Them in Awe,* ed. Ron Hansen and Jim Shepard. New York: HarperCollins.

Coville, Bruce. 1994. "With His Head Tucked Underneath His Arm." In *Oddly Enough.* New York: Pocket Books.

Datlow, Ellen, and Terri Windling, eds. 1993. *Black Thorn, White Rose.* New York: Avon Books.

Dickens, Charles. 1981. *A Tale of Two Cities.* New York: Bantam Doubleday Dell.

Dillard, Annie. 1987. *An American Childhood.* New York: HarperCollins.

Eden, Abigail, and Iyad Fattom. 2001. "Is Racial Profiling Justified?" *New York Times Upfront* 134 (8), November 12.

Fitzgerald, F. Scott. 1925. *The Great Gatsby.* New York: Charles Scribner's Sons.

Fletcher, Ralph. 1993. *What a Writer Needs.* Portsmouth, NH: Heinemann.

———. 1996. *A Writer's Notebook: Unlocking the Writer Within You.* New York: Avon Books.

Fletcher, Ralph, and JoAnn Portalupi. 1998. *Craft Lessons: Teaching Writing K–8.* Portland, ME: Stenhouse.

Flynn, Nick, and Shirley McPhillips. 2000. *A Note Slipped Under the Door: Teaching from Poems We Love.* Portland, ME: Stenhouse.

Gantos, Jack. 1998. *Joey Pigza Swallowed the Key.* New York: HarperTrophy.

"Going the Distance." 1997. *On the Go Zone.* Needham Heights, MA: Silver Burdett Ginn.

Grannick, Carol Coven. 2001. "The Inside Ballerina." *Cricket Magazine* 29 (3): 45–49.

Graves, Donald. 1983. *Writing: Teachers and Children at Work.* Portsmouth, NH: Heinemann.

Green, Kevin, and Nick Brown. 2002. "Should Students Do the Grading?" *New York Times Upfront* 134 (13), April 8.

Gutmann, Amy. 1987. *Democratic Education.* Princeton: Princeton University Press.

Hamilton, Kendall, and Patricia King. 1997. "Playgrounds of the Future." *Newsweek,* May 12.

Hansen, Jane. 1987. *When Writers Read.* Portsmouth, NH: Heinemann.

Hansen, Ron, and Jim Shepard, eds. 1994. *You've Got to Read This: Contemporary American Writers Introduce Stories That Held Them in Awe.* New York: HarperCollins.

Hanson-Harding, Alexandra. 2002. "Monster Pets." *Junior Scholastic* 104 (May 6): 8–9.

Harvey, Stephanie. 1998. *Nonfiction Matters: Reading, Writing, and Research in Grades 3–8.* Portland, ME: Stenhouse.

Harvey, Stephanie, and Anne Goudvis. 2000. *Strategies That Work: Teaching Comprehension to Enhance Understanding.* Portland, ME: Stenhouse.

Howe, James. 2001. "Everything Will Be Okay." In *When I Was Your Age,* Vol. One, ed. Amy Ehrlich. Cambridge, MA: Candlewick Press.

Hughes, Langston. 1986. "Thank You M'am." In *Sudden Fiction: American Short-Short Stories,* ed. Robert Shapard and James Thomas. Salt Lake City, UT: Gibbs Smith.

Hummel, Charles. 1999. *Tyranny of the Urgent.* Downers Grove, IL: Intervarsity Press.

Hunter, Bill. 2000. "It's Time to Pay the Price." *Write Time for Kids—Level 5.* Westminster, CA: Teacher Created Materials. <http://www.teachercreated.com/writetime/>.

"Jell-O" by Casey D. 2000. *Teen Ink* (Reviews), September. <http://TeenInk.com/Past/2000/September/Reviews/Jello.html>.

Jimenez, Francisco. 1999. *The Circuit: Stories from the Life of a Migrant Child.* Boston: Houghton Mifflin.

Kay, Julia, and Rocio Nieves. 2002. "Should Teens Be Tried as Adults?" *New York Times Upfront* 134 (8), January 21.

Keene, Ellin Oliver, and Susan Zimmerman. 1997. *Mosaic of Thought: Teaching Comprehension in a Reader's Workshop.* Portsmouth, NH: Heinemann.

Kidder, Tracy. 1999. *House.* Boston: Houghton Mifflin.

Kline, Christina Baker, ed. 1997. *Child of Mine: Original Essays on Becoming a Mother.* New York: Dell.

Krakauer, Jon. 1993. "Death of an Innocent: How Christopher McCandless Lost His Way in the Wilds." *Outside Magazine,* January.

Kurth, Peter. 1990. *American Cassandra: The Life of Dorothy Thompson.* Boston: Little, Brown.

Lamott, Anne. 1994. *Operating Instructions: A Journal of My Son's First Year.* New York: Fawcett.

Lee, Marie G. 1996. "An Education." In *But That's Another Story,* ed. Sandy Asher. New York: Walker.

"Lighter Loads? Silly Bill Targets Student Backpacks." 2002. *San Diego Union Tribune,* April 27, op-ed page.

Munsch, Robert. 1980. *The Paperbag Princess.* New York: Annick Press.

Murray, Donald. 1982. *Learning by Teaching: Selected Articles on Writing and Teaching.* Portsmouth, NH: Boynton/Cook-Heinemann.

Myers, Walter Dean. 2001. *Bad Boy: A Memoir.* New York: HarperCollins.

Newkirk, Thomas. 1989. *More Than Stories: The Range of Children's Writing.* Portsmouth, NH: Heinemann.

"No Helmet, No Skating?" 1996. *Junior Scholastic,* February 23.

Oates, Joyce Carol. 2001. "To Invigorate Literary Mind, Start Moving Literary Feet." In *Writers on Writing: Collected Essays from the New York Times,* John Darnton. New York: Henry Holt.

Paterson, Katherine. 1981. *Gates of Excellence: On Reading and Writing Books for Children.* New York: Elsevier/Nelson.

Portalupi, JoAnn, and Ralph Fletcher. 2001. *Nonfiction Craft Lessons: Teaching Information Writing K–8.* Portland, ME: Stenhouse.

Porter, Alicia. 1997. "A Study of Gothic Sub-Culture: An Inside Look for Outsiders." <http://gothics.org/subculture/>.

Quindlen, Anna. 1994. *Thinking Out Loud: On the Personal, the Political, the Public, and the Private.* New York: Fawcett Columbine.

———. 1998. *How Reading Changed My Life.* New York: Ballantine.

———. 2002. "In a Peaceful Frame of Mind." *Newsweek,* February 4.

Romano, Tom. 2000. *Blending Genre, Altering Style: Writing Multigenre Papers.* Portsmouth, NH: Boynton/Cook-Heinemann.

Rylant, Cynthia. 1985. "Slower Than the Rest." In *Every Living Thing.* New York: Aladdin Paperbacks.

Sachar, Louis. 1998. *Holes.* New York: Dell Yearling.

Salinger, J. D. 1964. *The Catcher in the Rye.* Boston: Little, Brown.

Scieszka, Jon. 1989. *The True Story of the Three Little Pigs!* New York: Puffin Books.

Smith, Steph. 2001. "Dancing with Pride." *Scholastic News* 70 (Nov. 12): 4–5.

Soto, Gary. 1993. "The Mechanical Mind." In *Local News: A Collection of Stories.* New York: Scholastic.

Stanley, Diane. 2002. *Rumpelstiltskin's Daughter.* New York: HarperTrophy.

Sullivan, Robert. 2001. "Paid to Play Games." *Time for Kids* 6 (March 30): 4–5.

Uchida, Yoshiko. 1995. *The Invisible Thread.* New York: Beech Tree Books.

Upadhyay, Ritu. 2002. "Sudan's Lost Boys Find a Home." *Time for Kids* 7 (Feb. 22): 4–5.

Vilbig, Peter. 2002. "Expanded Drug Tests in Schools?" *New York Times Upfront* 134 (14), May 6.

Walker, Alice. 1973. "The Flowers." In *In Love & Trouble: Stories of Black Women.* New York: Harcourt.

Wiggins, Grant. 1998. *Understanding by Design.* Alexandria, VA: Association for Supervision and Curriculum Development.

Wolff, Tobias. 1994. Introduction to "Cathedral." In *You've Got to Read This: Contemporary American Writers Introduce Stories That Held Them in Awe,* ed. Ron Hansen and Jim Shepard. New York: HarperCollins.

Yep, Laurence. 2001. "The Great Rat Hunt." In *When I Was Your Age,* Vol. One, ed. Amy Ehrlich. Cambridge, MA: Candlewick Press.

Yolen, Jane. 1990. *The Devil's Arithmetic.* New York: Penguin Books.

———. 2001. "Cinder Elephant." In *A Wolf at the Door and Other Retold Fairy Tales,* ed. Ellen Datlow and Terri Windling. New York: Aladdin Paperbacks.

Zinsser, William. 1998. *On Writing Well: The Classic Guide to Writing Nonfiction.* New York: HarperPerennial.

Zipes, Jack, ed. 1991. *Spells of Enchantment: The Wondrous Fairy Tales of Western Culture.* New York: Penguin Books.